THE MIGRANT TEXT

The Migrant Text

Making and Marketing
a Global French Literature

SUBHA XAVIER

McGill-Queen's University Press
Montreal & Kingston · London · Chicago

© McGill-Queen's University Press 2016

ISBN 978-0-7735-4759-9 (cloth)
ISBN 978-0-7735-4760-5 (paper)
ISBN 978-0-7735-9936-9 (ePDF)
ISBN 978-0-7735-9937-6 (ePUB)

Legal deposit second quarter 2016
Bibliothèque nationale du Québec

Printed in Canada on acid-free paper that is 100% ancient forest free (100% post-consumer recycled), processed chlorine free

This book has been published with the help of a grant from the Canadian Federation for the Humanities and Social Sciences, through the Awards to Scholarly Publications Program, using funds provided by the Social Sciences and Humanities Research Council of Canada.

McGill-Queen's University Press acknowledges the support of the Canada Council for the Arts for our publishing program. We also acknowledge the financial support of the Government of Canada through the Canada Book Fund for our publishing activities.

Library and Archives Canada Cataloguing in Publication

Xavier, Subha, 1975–, author
    The migrant text : making and marketing a global French literature /
Subha Xavier.

Includes bibliographical references and index.
Issued in print and electronic formats.
ISBN 978-0-7735-4759-9 (hardback). – ISBN 978-0-7735-4760-5 (paperback). –
ISBN 978-0-7735-9936-9 (ePDF). – ISBN 978-0-7735-9937-6 (ePUB)

    1. Canadian fiction (French) – Québec (Province) – Minority authors –
History and criticism. 2. French fiction – Minority authors – History and
criticism. 3. Immigrants' writings, Canadian (French) – Québec (Province)
– History and criticism. 4. Immigrants' writings, French – History and
criticism. I. Title.

PS8199.5.Q8X39 2016   C843'.6099206912   C2016-900936-X
                                                       C2016-900937-8

This book was set by True to Type in 10.5/13 Sabon

For my mother Chandranee, my father Francis,
my brothers Navajeev and Dinesh

Contents

Figures

Acknowledgments

This book has been on a long journey, from its inception as a dissertation project to my first articles and the various iterations it took along the way before becoming *The Migrant Text*. Over the course of its writing, I migrated from Madison to Miami and then to Atlanta, with frequent trips to Paris and Montreal. I am deeply indebted to the many teachers, scholars, friends, and family members who guided and supported me along the way.

Initial research for this book was funded by a Vilas Travel Grant and a dissertation fellowship at the University of Wisconsin-Madison. Subsequent trips to Paris and Montreal to conduct interviews and access marketing data were made possible thanks to generous funding from an Orovitz award and several General Research awards at the University of Miami. Funding and support from Emory University helped steer this book toward completion. My editor at MQUP, Kyla Madden, provided invaluable input throughout, with patience, diligence, and remarkable precision. The three anonymous reviewers improved the quality and rigour of this book immensely through their careful, expert readings. A part of chapter 1 appeared in the January 2010 issue of *Contemporary French and Francophone Studies: Sites* and portions of chapter 5 appeared in the Spring 2005 issue of the *International Journal of Canadian Studies* and in the January 2010 issue of *Trans*. I would like to acknowledge Routledge Taylor and Francis, the *IJCS*, and *Trans* for permission to rework, translate, and reprint some material here.

At the University of Wisconsin-Madison, I was privileged to work with a brilliant and insightful group of teachers and scholars. Aliko Songolo ushered this project into existence with his infinite patience, wisdom, and kindness. Deborah Jenson, who continues to inspire me as a woman and a scholar, taught me the value of intellectual exchange and helped hone the dissertation into the beginnings of *The Migrant Text*. I am grateful for careful readings and feedback by professors Nancy Kaiser, Venkat Mani, Thomas Armbrecht, and the late Steven Winspur. From all of you I learned the valuable art of reading.

I found support in a terrific cohort of friends who sustained me through my graduate career. Thank you to Marcy Farrell and Quince Gaynor who accompanied me on my first and most memorable research trip to Montreal. Les Haygood, Gretchen Suechting O'Dell, Mouhamedoul Niang, Trésor Yoassi, Linda Brindeau, Maria Slocum, Sage Goellner, Tom Yoshikami, Molly Michels, Bob Ash, thank you for the beautiful gift of your friendship. Christian Flaugh, I cherish your continued support as a colleague and friend.

I was fortunate to work with truly inspiring colleagues at the University of Miami who saw this book through many of its early stages. Gema Pérez-Sànchez, thank you for your generosity as a mentor and friend. You are a model of brilliance and compassion. George Yudice, you went above and beyond to help in times of need and provided helpful criticism at various stages of this project. Thank you Ralph Heyndels, David Ellison, and Marc Brudzinski for your insightful feedback. To my friends Chrissy Arce, Carlos Fernandez, Tracy Devine-Guzman, Christina Civantos, Sameet Kumar, Jane Connolly, Suzanne Braswell, Heather Allen, Joel Nickels, Carrie Sieh, Brenna Munro, Margarita Zisselsberger, Markus Zisselsberger, Shweta Oza, and Moktaria Burgess, thank you for many great meals, laughter, consolation, and encouragement.

At Emory University, in the final stages of the project, Valérie Loichot was a constant source of support, encouragement, and inspiration. Elissa Marder, Geoffrey Bennington, Claire Nouvet, Dalia Judovitz, Vincent Bruyère, Abdul JanMohamed, Deepika Bahri, Clifton Crais, Nathan Suhr-Sytsma, Susan Gagliardi, and Ana Teixeira, thank you for stimulating conversations and intellectual exchanges.

Many scholars who I was honoured to meet along the way transformed the manuscript through their incisive critiques. My thanks go to Rebecca Walkowitz, Vinay Dharwadker, Tejumola Olaniyan, Christopher Miller, Simon Harel, Charles Forsdick, Lydie Moudileno, Jean-Marc Moura, Alec Hargreaves, Mireille Rosello, Mary-Jean Green, Ursula Mathis-Moser, Jacques Chévrier, and Papa Samba Diop. For sowing the seeds of *The Migrant Text*, unbeknown to us all, I would like to recognize my very first professors of French literature at the University of Toronto, Janet Paterson, the late Fred Case, Julie LeBlanc, and Brian T. Fitch.

I am grateful for graduate students – present or future colleagues – Lennie Coleman, Dana Chirila, David Borman, Muchiri Ng'ang'a, Hicham Mazouz, Robyn Banton, Bronwyn Averett, Blair Watson, and

Marion Tricoire. All of your research and questions challenged and sharpened my own. I am especially thankful to Marion Tricoire for her tireless work finding English translations and editing parts of the manuscript. Special thanks to Yazan Kamaluldin for his help with the index.

Several writers graciously accepted to speak to me about the creative and marketing processes of their novels, shedding light on their work in unforeseen ways. For this, I recognize the generosity and candour of Mehdi Charef, Naïm Kattan, Dany Laferrière, Ying Chen, and Calixthe Beyala. I was humbled to be in your physical presence after having lived with your words for so long.

To Jim Michael and Sarah Michael, who supported me through the highs and lows of this project, I am blessed to be a part of your family. Katie Michael, Eleanor Michael, and Sonya Barbezat, thank you for the gift of sisterhood in which I drew great strength. Joey Meyer and Keith Sklar, I am grateful for your wit and kindness through it all. Nate Meyer, Calvin Meyer, and Nora Sklar, the very thought of you was enough to brighten the gloomiest of my workdays.

I send deep gratitude to my beloved aunts and uncles in Colombo, Panadura, and Moratuwa who accompanied me on this journey from afar: the late Augusta Weerasuriya, Shelton and Jayanthie Amarasuriya, Godwin and Manora Weerasuriya, Lloyd and Sarojini Weerasuriya, Raja and Elfie Weerasuriya, Consey Weerasuriya, B.J. Vincent, and Baron de Livera.

To my mother, Chandranee Xavier, who dropped everything at a moment's notice to travel to Miami or Atlanta and help with childcare and home-life when I needed to travel or write, I am thankful from the bottom of my heart. This book would not have been possible without your faith and love. To my father, Francis Xavier, for your unfailing enthusiasm and the courage which was the wellspring for this book, I am grateful. To my brother Navajeev Xavier, for your wisdom, constant support, and inspiration, and to my brother Dinesh Xavier, for your loyalty, unwavering optimism, and outpouring of love, thank you. This book is very much about our shared journey.

To Charlie Michael, who translated my words, read and reread them, edited and re-edited them, this book is as much yours as it is mine. Thank you for your dedication to *The Migrant Text* and for sharing in its many migrations. Most of all, I am intensely grateful for your love, devotion, and companionship. You are always my toughest advocate and my finest critic. To Jeevan James, whose depth and curiosity moved me to higher places at the lowest of times, and Avishan Joseph, whose smile and energy grounded me as this book prepared to take flight, thank you with all that I am.

THE MIGRANT TEXT

Major, Minor, Migrant

Novels about immigration have proliferated in the French-speaking world and beyond for many decades now, owing to mass migrations and the generations of immigrant voices they have produced in Europe and the Americas. Though immigration may be nothing new to countries like France or Canada, the 1970s marked a sudden increase in global flows of people and saw the beginning of a steady stream of immigrant literary production that has grown exponentially with every passing decade. What is particularly unique to the waves of immigration to Western hub cities in the late twentieth and early twenty-first centuries is the sheer diversity of people and the cross-cultural bonds that are forged through various forms of immigrant cultural production.

The literary output by and about immigrants in French-speaking countries is today as notable as that which is produced in the English and Spanish-speaking worlds. Moreover, this literature is increasingly translated into English and a host of other languages shortly after initial publication in French, thus expanding its global reach and significance for readers, students, and scholars of literature in any language. People from all over the world, from Morocco to China, Iraq to Haiti, and Algeria to Cameroon, are writing in French and publishing in France and Quebec. When writers of Chinese, Iraqi, or Algerian origin – fluent in their native tongues and at least one other language other than French – choose to write in French, it is difficult not to wonder why, since they have so many other major languages at their disposal. Even the function of French as a major language today is put into question more and more, when English seems to be overtaking other Western languages through its preponderance.[1]

Every one of the authors in this study came to the French language out of a certain kind of necessity; it was the language of their newfound home, the host country to which they emigrated from their respective homelands. Yet their decisions to write in French were carefully thought out, even in the case of writers who are not sufficiently fluent in their heritage languages to write in them.[2] To pick up the pen in the language of the former colonizer or slave owner – as is the case for many of the writers we will analyze in the following chapters – is not without its political and cultural burdens. Appropriating a language, making it one's own to tell a different story, however, is not without its freedom and – as we shall see – its rewards.

Literary theorists who write about immigration often refer to it as "minor literature," drawing on Gilles Deleuze and Felix Guattari's use of Franz Kafka's concept.[3] For Deleuze and Guattari, literature must satisfy three criteria in order to be considered "minor." First, the language must be affected strongly by what the authors call "deterritorialization." This might seem not too far astray from our main concern here, as most all of the case studies in the pages to come evince a certain rapport with a French colonial heritage. But the Kafka example used by Deleuze and Guattari goes further still, since their concept of deterritorialization implies an impossible language: "L'impossibilité de ne pas écrire, impossibilité d'écrire en allemand, impossibilité d'écrire autrement" (1975, 29)].[4] [The impossibility of not writing, the impossibility of writing German, the impossibility of writing otherwise (1986, 16).] Scholars Pascale Casanova and Lise Gauvin, however, point out an erroneous reading of Kafka by Deleuze and Guattari who ignore the fourth impossibility that Kafka mentions in his Letter to Max Brod. Kafka's fourth impossibility is that of writing itself: "Die Unmöglichkeit zu Schreiben (denn die Verzweiflung war ja nicht etwas durch Schreiben zu Beruhigendes, war ein Feind des Lebens und Schreiben ...) also war es eine von allen Seiten unmögliche Literatur" (1989, 360). [The impossibility of writing (since the despair could not be assuaged by writing, was hostile to both life and writing ...) Thus what resulted was a literature impossible in all aspects (1977, 289).] Casanova thus notes that for Kafka, writing in German as a Jew from Prague was nothing short of a tragedy, "une aporie littéraire insoluble" (1997, 244) [an unsolvable literary aporia], rather than anything he recommended as a condition for minor literature as Deleuze and Guattari claim.[5] Gauvin points out that what Deleuze and Guattari call "minor literature" is a transformation of Kafka's "kleine literatur" [small literature] through the biography of the writer (2003, 28–9).[6] Gauvin accordingly questions the term's use, as renamed by Deleuze and Guattari, when applied to Francophone literature from outside the hexagone, as does Casanova, who argues that writers from the periphery had to choose between writing in their "small" national languages or "betraying" this belonging to assimilate into larger literary movements (1999, 243). Critic François Paré also devised a similar concept of "petite littérature" to describe the defining characteristics of a poetics of "exiguity" that are shared by all writers who create from the margins of a Eurocentric model of literature (1994).

The present study circumvents the distinction – whether legitimate or not – between major and minor literature, small and large literary movements, centre and periphery, though it certainly draws inspiration from the works mentioned above. Our writers do not dissociate themselves from the language(s) of the country where they live and write, Canada or France. The French language is in fact rife with possibilities – often nonexistent or unattainable in other languages, especially native ones. If indeed there is deterritorialization, as Deleuze and Guattari would have it, it is apparent only through what is missing from the text. In other words, the linguistic impossibility most often experienced and channelled by successful writers is precisely the one that involves *not* mentioning, articulating, or even expressing thought patterns in the mother tongue. Moreover, the relationship to this marginalized language, be it completely absent or feebly present, is also the dynamism that drives the text.

To return for a moment to the Deleuze-Guattari framework, it seems insufficient to fit the plurality of migrant texts into the second characteristic proposed by these authors – that of the *homme-politique* or the *homme-machine*. This is not a literary form that bypasses individuality, whether on the level of enunciation or of collective agency, as Deleuze and Guattari suggest it should. Here, political engagement is often subordinated to the drive for book sales and to attract a French or French-Canadian readership. Individuality is therefore not jettisoned in the migrant text – rather it is embraced in a literature that is sold via its strong autobiographical tendency. This individualism, many times isolated by critics, goes against the Kafka project, which – as articulated by Deleuze and Guattari anyway – purveys a necessary Oedipal fantasy in order for "minor literature" to find its place in a political program. This Marxist dimension of the word "minor" thus implies a revolutionary potential that migration alone can bring to the table. Yet it is exactly to the contrary that the authors of migrant texts must often work, fixing themselves at the centre of the capitalist project, which after all is the source of immigration itself – for better and for worse.

This book proposes an alternative literary reading of migration, working its way out from a large body of theoretical writing on migration born of the social sciences and literary criticism. Critical works on migration in literary studies do not sufficiently acknowledge the rich body of research that the social sciences have brought to bear on the subject and one of the aims of this book is to put these two larger disciplines back into conversation with one another by considering the socio-cultural, economic, and political impetus of migrant texts. Drawing on the socio-critical model of literary analysis, the present study seeks to reinforce the relationship between the literature of migration and its antecedents in the social sciences. For the purposes of restricting our field of analysis, we will use Robin Cohen's definitional features of diaspora (2008, 16) to distinguish migration from the scope of its sister field, diaspora studies, although the intersections between the two are numerous.[7] In the paragraphs that follow, we will very succinctly trace some of the leading ideas that have shaped our understanding of migration studies today and which have culminated in turn in the search for a poetics of migration over the last three decades.

MIGRATION STUDIES: A BRIEF INTERDISCIPLINARY REVIEW

The study of migration as a discipline has been largely confined until very recently to the social sciences, with human geography and economics leading the charge.[8] Immanuel Wallerstein's World System Theory (1974) as reappropriated for migration studies through the writing of sociologists like Saskia Sassen (1988, 1991), James Fawcett (1989), and Joaquín Arango et al. (1998) recast international migration as a function of globalization and the dynamics of market creation therein. They emphasize the importance of transnational networks and institutions as well as the cumulative causation (Massey 1990) whereby international immigration sustains and propagates itself within host countries. Sassen (1991), for instance, points to the magnetism of global cities in attracting immigrants and creating migrant networks that further spur movement toward the host country as a nexus of new economic, cultural, and political capital. Sassen's work is then crucial to a nuanced understanding of the place of cultural production by immigrants. Race and ethnicity play a critical role in the work of these sociologists who are acutely aware of the societal inequalities that result from the presence of immigrant populations, but the cultural impact of immigration was perhaps first addressed among sociologists in the writing of Roland Robertson on globalization (1992). Robertson's world culture theory stems from his idea of globalization as "a compression of the world and the intensification of consciousness of the world as a whole" (1992, 8). This global consciousness, fostered, among other things, by the increased movement of people across national boundaries, spurs a reflexive response to the new sense of sharing one world. Robertson's work emphasizes how an awareness of global interdependence gives rise to a new world culture. Robertson's later writing begins a complex dance between globalization and the socially constructed localities that comprise it (1997), something we also see in the writing of sociologist Manuel Castells (1996, 1997, 1998, Castells et al., 1999) and the global versus local debate that ensued. Migrants are in many ways the purveyors of this interdependent reality and the reason why sociological models have failed to come up with any one coherent theory of migration. Since migration goes beyond the explanatory power of socio-economics by the sheer diversity of motivating factors and migratory experience, the field as a whole has lent itself to increasing interdisciplinarity.[9]

International migration has also become an important area of theorization among political scientists because population growth is today directly linked to immigration in most Western societies. Immigration policy is now at the forefront of these countries' national political agendas, with special emphasis on border control, regulation, integration, and citizenship. The theoretical approaches that are often mobilized to navigate the turbulent waters of immigration policy include Marxism, realism, liberalism, the "national identity" approach, domestic politics, and institutionalism (Meyers 2000). National identity has been an especially widespread regulatory tool in the immigration policies of both countries that are the focus of this study (France and Canada) as A.R. Zolberg's early research suggests (1978). This continues to holds true today, as France even launched a public debate on national identity in 2009 followed by substantial reforms in 2013, while the national identity question in Quebec can be directly linked to its immigration policy beginning in the 1970s, continuing through its "Énoncé de politique en matière d'immigration et d'intégration" introduced in 1990 on a pluri-annual basis, and right up to its proposed public consultation over the next set of reforms for the 2012–2015 period. Other theoretical approaches have equally elucidated the dynamics of policy creation in France and Canada, where partisan and domestic politics in France (de Wenden 1994; Thränhardt 1995) and institutionalism in Canada (Whitaker 1987; Abella 1988) have respectively shaped immigration measures for almost a century.

In the field of anthropology, scholars like Arjun Appadurai and James Clifford have made substantial contributions to the study of migration through concepts such as *ethnoscapes* (Appadurai 1990) and *routes* (Clifford 1997), which suggest the opening of new ways of understanding and theorizing increased flows of people across nation-states in the global age. Both scholars dismiss the heavy burden placed on localization and rootedness, favouring the prevalence of contact zones and meeting points where migrant sensibilities – and the artistic production that ensues – come to fruition. The typical sites of anthropological enquiry have hence shifted over the last few decades to include the deterritorialized realities of the global age and the disjunctive economy and culture that results from the embattled relationship between states and nations as well as the movement of people, capital, technology, media, and ideas across political boundaries of every kind. Nadje Al-Ali and Khalid Koser (2002) – whose edited collection brings together work by social scientists in various fields – emphasize a transnational communities approach to diaspora studies, signaling how the very definition of "home" has changed for international migrants as transnational practices redefine and create new spaces for connection. Al-Ali and Koser challenge the traditional dichotomy between an originating national space and singular ethno-national migrant communities through essays that uncover the processes whereby place and identity are socially constructed.

Just as writing on globalization inevitably tackles the issue of immigration as a vital feature of the global age, so another body of theory around the concept of cosmopolitanism has taken on the ethical dimensions of migration in its relation to nationalism and questions of race and ethnicity. Appadurai signals the dawn of a transnational age where an emergent cosmopolitan culture comes into conflict with national cultural forms (Appadurai and Breckenridge 1988). Pheng Cheah on the other hand disagrees, arguing that the transnational migrant communities Appadurai relies on for his theory, are not always cosmopolitan. "It is unclear how many of these migrants feel that they belong to a world," writes Cheah, pointing to long-distance nationalism and insisting that the Global South is often left unreached by the transnational media and print networks that migrant communities create in the Northern hemisphere (1998, 37). Cheah and Robbins offer the concept of *cosmopolitics* to embrace the intertwined mechanics of nationalism and cosmopolitanism and to reenact the possibility of a universal ethics when global politics are in play (1998). Seyla Benhabib adds to this discussion by invoking a Kantian ethics of hospitality as the driving force for human rights policy in the global age of migration (2006). Though Benhabib makes a clear distinction between refugees and immigrants, she advocates for a rethinking of cosmopolitan practice that goes beyond theory to address the individual needs of those who choose to cross borders today. Human rights have understandably become an important concern of migration studies, especially with deaths by the thousands occurring annually in the waters of the Mediterranean and boats full of people still making their way toward French and Canadian coasts against all odds.

THE POETICS OF MIGRATION

As theories of migration have proliferated within the economic, sociological, political, anthropological, and ethical realms, the study of the poetics associated with the movement of peoples has come in disparate and disjointed forms, owing to a variety of subfields within the larger scope of migration studies. The sheer diversity of linguistic and cultural works that constitute the literary corpus born of migration has elicited very different critical responses. As we will see in chapter 1 and 2, this is somewhat due to literary categorizations that still use the nation-state and former colonial relationships as their determining criteria. Hence migration studies in literature has been confined to the context of various national literatures or postcolonial literature in general. Efforts to study the poetics of migration have been deployed in many languages and around different conceptual axes, nonetheless. Mireille Rosello has most importantly theorized the politics of immigration in France through the poetics of immigrant literature and film in *Declining the Stereotype: Ethnicity and Representation in French Cultures* (1998) and *Postcolonial Hospitality: The Immigrant as Guest* (2001). Rebecca Walkowitz's edited collection *Immigrant Fictions: Contemporary Literature in an Age of Globalization* (2006) took a critical step in divorcing the study of the literature of immigration from the one text/one nation-state model in order to analyze works across their "multiple geographies" (2006, 528) and within transnational literary systems. Walkowitz further draws on Leslie Adelson's analysis of contemporary literature in German to dissociate the term "literature of migration" from the ethnic origin of the author, extending it rather to writing that is "produced in a time of migration" (2006, 533). Other contributors to Walkowitz's volume isolate tropes linked to mobility which alter both narrative structure and genre within immigrant novels.[10] Scholars such as Carine Mardorossian have also defined migrant literature against the literature of immigration or

exile by claiming for it a stylistic and thematic rejection of the opposition between modern and traditional, home country and host country
(2002, 21).

Academic scholarship out of the French-speaking world has been less
concerned with modalities like those proposed by Mardorossian, looking rather for a taxonomy of topoi most commonly seen in the literature of immigration. Among these, questions of identity formation
across national boundaries and ethnic lines are most often isolated.
Christiane Albert's work in particular centres on discursive elements
within the text that explore forms of heterogeneity, multiculturalism,
and alternative notions of place ("hors-lieu"). Simon Harel (2005) on
the other hand focuses on the migrant psyche as expressed through narrative style, linguistic valence, and thematic approaches to immigration.
Indeed, identity remains a prevailing concern for scholars of migrant literature as critics like Pierre Ouellet (2003) and Danielle Forget (2004)
repeatedly play out the question of migrant identity formation and negotiation, ultimately pointing to the productive power of the literary
text as both discourse and ideology. Other scholars like Janet Paterson
(2004), Daniel Castillo Durante (2004), and the research group spear-
headed by Pierre Ouellet (2002) explore migration through questions
of alterity. Paterson's *Figures de l'autre dans le roman québécois* (2004)
sketches out the conceptual basis for a poetics of otherness, analyzing
the discursive forms that express alterity in Quebecois fiction. Castillo
Durante's *Les Dépouilles de l'altérité* (2004) is a philosophical reflection
on alterity's innate negation or the constant undoing that underlies the
very use of the concept. Pierre Ouellet's edited collection *Le Soi et l'autre*
(2002) examines how otherness is imagined, portrayed, lived, and theorized in literature, film, and art works in its relation to the crisis of the
self, or what Ouellet calls *l'incertitude*. The study of alterity brings to
the fore an important paradigm that underlies migrant subjectivity and
recasts the dichotomous relationship between the self and other as at
once relational, inflected with multiplicity, and evanescent.

Another field of literary analysis that falls within the general scope of
migration studies is that of exile literature. Edward Said defines exile as
"the unhealable rift posed between a human being and a native place,
the self and its true home" as well as "a condition of terminal loss" (1994,
137). Exiles, he remarks, are far more numerous in the present age due
in part to mass migrations (1994, 137–8), but nowhere does he confuse
exiles with migrants or the literature of exile with that of immigration.
The poetics he isolates and develops in various essays drawn from his

own experience as an exile express the permanence of the exilic condition, the ruptures that underlie it, and the critical distance it affords (2000). For Said, exile is most of all a form of resistance. Scholars like Anissa Talahite-Moodley bring together work about "exiles," "migrants," and even "cultural diversity," although she too cannot avoid demarcating the ways in which migrant sensibilities often deliberately reject the language of exile (2007, 152). Indeed, this terminological distinction can be a weighty one in literary terms where "exile" can sometimes connote a clichéd impossible return that colours the writing from within. Still many writers do not fall neatly within one category over the other, as migrant texts such as those by Leïla Sebbar, Ying Chen, or Régine Robin for instance betray a sense of mourning and loss that is reminiscent of at least part of Said's definition of exile.[11]

There are also scholars who have chosen to favour a shift in terminology from immigrant or migrant to diaspora. Carmen Husti-Laboye (2009) chooses to speak in terms of an African diasporic post-national community of writers whose sense of belonging escapes the nation, creating new transversal relationships in place of old filial ones. Joël Des Rosiers (2013), for his part, proposes the term *métaspora* in lieu of diaspora's longings for the past to inscribe migrant literary works in the cosmopolitan, itinerant esthetic space that the literary work inhabits. Husti-Laboye and Des Rosier's approaches recall that of Pascale Casanova's *La République mondiale des Lettres* (1999). Though Casanova does not depend on any notion of diaspora per se, her project is an ambitious rallying together of literature from the world over on its own autonomous esthetic and formal terms. In so doing, Casanova paved the way for many theoretical approaches to thinking about the internationalization of literature, including those laid out in this book. Casanova links the poetic choices of writers to their literary capital on the world stage, giving special attention to the role of Paris in its consecration of literary works from all over the globe.

It is difficult to evoke world culture in its relation to migration without taking a moment to consider the work of Caribbean cultural theorist Edouard Glissant, whose concepts of *Relation* (1990), *Poetics of the Diverse* (1995), and *Tout-monde* (1997) developed out of historical reflections on the Caribbean and resulted in a kind of global thinking that hinges on the experience of forced migration, displacement, and dispersal. In the last few decades, Glissant developed a pan-global system of thought that veered away from his earlier thinking about migration to, from, and within the Caribbean toward a utopic worlding of his initial concept of creolization. This conceptual move has been particularly useful for postcolonial theory in that it posits a form of non-imperial global travelling across cultures.[12] As such, Glissant has often been read by postcolonial scholars outside the purview of migration studies, even though his writing grows out of a fundamental migratory stance.

THE MIGRANT TEXT

Drawing on the body of work we have just seen in the study of migration, this book proposes "migrant" textual practice, not as a literary category but as a mode of writing that is independent of the ethnic or national origins of any given author. It therefore engages with a recent body of criticism that highlights the need to rethink nation-based models of literature in favour of ones that consider global networks, world literary canons, and the role of migration. The term "migrant literature" was first introduced in the early 1980s by French-Canadian critics searching for a moniker to distinguish the poetry and prose of a new generation of immigrants to Quebec who could neither be categorized as Canadian nor Quebecois, but it soon fell into trouble as a prejudicial marker of otherness that could not contain the variety of works that fell within its alleged parameters. Taxonomic efforts at containing this wayward literary category in Quebec, such as Simon Harel's *Le voleur de parcours: Identité et cosmopolitisme dans la littérature québécoise contemporaine* (1989), Clément Moisan and Renate Hildebrand's *Ces Étrangers du dedans: Histoire de l'écriture migrante au Québec (1937–1997)* (2001), and Luc Collès and Monique Lebrun's *La Littérature migrante dans l'espace francophone* (2007), either place too much emphasis on authorial identity or too little weight on authorial intentionality to conjure up a lasting literary definition. Furthermore, in their focus on literature in French, these works do not aim to make any broader claims for the genre of migrant writing as a whole. The migrant mode as we here conceive it considers the economic, poetic, and cultural strategies put in place by the individual agency of a given writer who chooses to narrativize the experience of migration.

The first part of this book is devoted to theorizing the migrant text, by clearing a space for it in existing literary theory. The migrant text should be conceived as a mode for studying literary texts that derives from and capitalizes on the experience of immigration. It is a mode of writing that flourishes in the blind spots of continental philosophy, the poetic evasions of critical theory, and the oft-repressed survival tactics of the global subject in late capitalism. Chapter 1 lays the groundwork for this claim in two ways: first by re-examining the legacy of World Literature (*Littérature-monde*) as a term for considering French-language texts; and then by re-appropriating and recasting the Quebecois term "Migrant Literature." A rehabilitated version of the term both addresses the limitations of Francophonie – French literature's current blanket category for the rest of the world – and characterizes the parallel waves of immigrant fiction that arrived in France and Quebec during the 1970s, 1980s, and 1990s. By tying new literary trends to the transatlantic politics of mass migration and accelerated globalization, this sociological and aesthetic model of migrant textuality expands the conventions of contemporary literary theory.

Chapter 1 begins by tracing the history of World Literature as a concept, from its German inception (Goethe's *Weltliteratur*) through its reappearance in anglophone debates in the late 1980s and, finally, to its recently proposed form in French. Unearthing the antecedents of this literary category helps to disentangle the legitimate concerns of this new Littérature-monde from the angry charges it levels against Francophonie. The examination of *Weltliteratur* considers not only early exchanges between Goethe and Eckermann in Germany but also considers Madame de Staël's use of the term to defend French literature in the late nineteenth century and Erich Auerbach's revival of it as a bulwark against the impending standardization of Western Cold War culture. These German-inspired works display a tension between the national and global that anticipates recent work on the pivotal place of translation in a global literary market. This is followed by an examination of some of the founding premises of the literary category known as Francophonie which has, until now, encapsulated all literature from the French speaking world that does not qualify as "French." A basic theoretical framework for the migrant text emerges from the above-mentioned analysis and is outlined at the end of this chapter.

Chapter 2, "The Migrant Undercurrents of Critical Theory," locates the migrant subject within the most influential theories of nationalism and post-colonialism. Through a series of against-the-grain readings of the literature on nationalism, it demonstrates how canonical texts conceive of nation, by and large, in terms of those who belong and those who do not. It then tracks the elusive figure of the migrant as it emerges in postcolonial theory, a concept that traverses the writing of many theorists as they critique and build on each other's work. My analysis of this wide swath of critical texts teases out three competing undercurrents in postcolonial thought: a poetics, a political history, and an economics of migration. It is at the intersection of these three axes, I contend, that a theory of the migrant text emerges.

Though the migrant is not always mentioned directly, its presence is felt across the development of critical theory. For instance, close readings of canonical concepts of nationalism show how and where the possibility of displaced peoples challenges the development of national paradigms, simultaneously embodying their focal point and their vanishing horizon. Postcolonial theory, which begins where these theories of nationalism leave off, does succeed in establishing a more productive concept of the migrant. From Homi Bhabha's poetics of hybridity, to Ranajit Guha and the Subaltern Studies Group's historiographic revisionism, to Graham Huggan's market-based economic reading – an interrogation of the most foundational postcolonial writings reveals that a more useful theory of literary migration only really arrives with the critiques of this first wave. Indeed, the pivotal theoretical moves for understanding the figure of the migrant beyond its poetic value arrive with Kwame Anthony Appiah's critique of postcolonial poetics as devised by a *comprador intellegentsia* and Arif Dirlik's positioning of postcolonialism in relation to the subject within capitalist society. These and other significant theoretical interventions help to extract the migrant subject from the realm of discursive idealism. Finally, Gayatri Spivak's work further complicates re-readings of colonial history that neglect the role of Western academic imperialism in postcolonialism. Indeed Spivak's critique uncovers the final twist in all of this – the migrant's own complicity in these games of power and influence. This chapter ends with considerations of a migrant exotic inspired by Graham Huggan's reading of postcolonial writers and texts as purveyors of an exotic that markets marginality.

Migrant texts in France and in Quebec connect intimately to conditions of literary production, marketing, and consumption. Drawing on Pierre Bourdieu's study of literary capital, chapter 3, "Creative Agency and Literary Markets," considers the often quite provocative ways in which the "otherness" or "foreignness" of migrant authors impacts the dissemination and consumption of their works in a literary marketplace. Through detailed analysis of the creative and commercial lives of individual novels, it highlights the financial impetus that drives migrant writing, analyzing the ways in which poetics and economics conspire to create the marketability of a literary genre. Although these types of intentionality are often a complicated prospect for literary critics, the theory of the migrant text proposed here draws on a socio-critical approach to consider how the creative agency of those who write migrant texts connects with the economic agency of those who sell it.

Based on specific examples within this literary corpus, the third chapter reconstructs the stories of their creation and dissemination in the marketplace through a sociological approach. It begins with a brief history of economic interpretations of literature from the nineteenth century onwards, examining the legacy of Romanticism, Formalism, and Marxism for literary criticism today. It then connects this body of theory to the actual paths of individual migrant works – drawing on interviews conducted with authors, editors, and publishers as well as on data relating to sales and marketing (from the research firm GFK in France and from a variety of government and corporate sources in Quebec). The chapter closes with reflections on the anecdotal and empirical insights gathered during research into the diverse publication track records of several immigrant authors in Quebec (Naïm Kattan, Dany Laferrière) and France (Azouz Begag, Dai Sijie, and Mehdi Charef). As we consider the task of the editor both from a historical perspective and a pragmatic one, the significance of the task of orienting the author's creativity for specific markets becomes apparent.

The second part of the book is devoted to the practice of the migrant text and begins with chapter 4, "Negotiating Culture." One of the key ways in which migrant texts turn foreign cultures into literary commodities is by invoking a sense of belonging in cosmopolitan communities, carving out ethno-cultural spaces from which their authors can speak. This chapter examines novels by Naïm Kattan, Dany Laferrière, Mehdi Charef, and Dai Sijie, analyzing the ways in which these four authors invoke the history, politics, and traditions of their respective communities and how they translate their experiences for French-speaking audiences.

Kattan's *Adieu Babylone* is a novel that enjoyed multiple literary lives, first in Quebec from Lapresse in 1975, then republished in France by Albin Michel in 2003 in the aftermath of the second Gulf war, translated into an English edition in Canada with photographs by Raincoast Books in 2005, and republished in Quebec by the Bibliothèque Québecoise that same year. The author's portrayal of the Jewish community in Iraq is thus transformed several times for different audiences, a process that becomes visible in the overlapping versions of his work, which include different forewords, different languages, and (in one case) photographs. By studying the different iterations of Kattan's first novel, we can thus see how he presents his Arab-Jewish identity in tellingly different ways for Quebecois, French, and Anglophone Canadian readers, enacting subtle shifts in his cosmopolitan renderings of Iraq's violent history and discriminatory politics. Similar techniques are at work in Haitian writer Dany Laferrière's debut novel, *Comment faire l'amour avec un nègre sans se fatiguer* (1985), which became an overnight sensation for VLB despite its seemingly crude content and overt exploitation of white racial stereotypes. Evoking an experience of oppression that he shares with his Québécois audience, the young author enacts a powerful critique of postcolonial conceptions of "hybridity" while seducing and provoking his readers to awaken their racial consciousness via a cutting sense of humour. In a similar vein, Mehdi Charef's *Le Thé au harem d'Archi Ahmed*, from Mercure de France in 1983, offers an example of the sort of cultural schizophrenia that sometimes plays out in migrant literature. France's first North-African immigrant or "Beur" author creates characters with conflicting experiences, as his protagonist's Algerian mother is marked as culturally other while her son is described as caught between two cultures. Migration is experienced here as a disassociated mode of life, where cultures at odds with one another become ultimately irreconcilable. In his first novel, Charef evokes the poverty of a generation of workers as a rallying point between Franco-Algerian immigrants and the French community at large, using this newfound alliance to offer a pointed critique of immigration politics in the Mitterrand era. Finally, Dai Sijie's first French novel, *Balzac et la petite tailleuse chinoise* (Gallimard 2000), actually both saved the author's fledgling cinematic career and marked an auspicious literary debut. In a story that extols the liberating virtues of French literature for a young Chinese peasant girl lost in the regressive politics of the Cultural Revolution, the novel carefully articulates a series of Sino-French cultural exchanges, packaging Chinese history in a consumable form for French audiences.

Chapter 5, "Linguistic Interference," suggests that an integral part of migrant texts is a sort of linguistic gymnastics that punctuates the narrative – from monolingual French apologies quarantining native languages to multilingual musings where readers are forced to arbiter a confusing mix of idioms. Works by Azouz Begag, Leïla Sebbar, Régine Robin, and Ying Chen offer instances in which other languages – Arabic, English, Hebrew, and Mandarin Chinese – appear and disappear within the French script. Studying their linguistic compositions as they undulate between clarity and subterfuge reveals buried sites of shame, guilt, and trauma on the one hand, and unearths the cold reality of financial viability and marketing functionality on the other.

Azouz Begag's *Le Gone du Chaâba*, published by Seuil in 1986, is perhaps the most successful novel of the first generation of Beur fiction to be published in France. In its literary use of dialectical Arabic, *Le Gone du Chaâba* becomes a functionally monolingual French text, relegating the protagonist's father/mother tongue to the sidelines in a gesture of political integration. Conversely, in *Je ne parle pas la langue de mon père*, which she published with Julliard in 2003, Leïla Sebbar revisits her childhood in Algeria through an ode to her paternal language – which she does not herself speak. Arabic thus permeates French with its marked absence in this migrant text, overturning colonial rule with the pull of absent patriarchy. Elsewhere, in Quebec, Régine Robin's *La Québécoite*, first published by Québec/Amérique in 1983, weaves English and Hebrew into French to create a slice of immigrant life in Montreal of the early 1980s and Paris of the early 1940s. In this case, the text's indecipherability to monolingual – or even bilingual – readers, combined with the narrator's own frustrations and inability to truly integrate anywhere, proffers a strong critique of French and Quebecois racism and the subtle forms of linguistic oppression operant in multicultural Canada. Indeed, the novel insists on the failure of plurilingualism while celebrating this very impossibility in the poetics of migrant textuality. Finally, Ying Chen's *Les Lettres chinoises*, first produced by Leméac, 1992, is an epistolary novel between Chinese characters but written entirely in French. The Chinese language is thus both everywhere and nowhere to be found in a text that presents us with what I call a "poetics of linguistic difference." While Begag and Sebbar both compose novels that play on the political and creative capacities of linguistic restraints or limitations, Robin and Chen deploy poetic strategies to take on the practical challenges of multilingualism, each highlighting the challenges of maintaining relationships through traumatic memories (the Holocaust and the Cultural Revolution respectively) and the difficult process of integrating into another linguistic culture.

Finally chapter 6, "Migrant Feminisms," takes up questions of gender identification that also populate migrant texts, focusing on the specific sort of multicultural and queer feminism that arises out of the work of these narratives. Reworking Susan Friedman's notion of migratory feminism, the literary strategies analyzed here foster a sensibility that crosses cultural and linguistic divides, undermining the body politic through female individuation and emancipation from the oppressive power structures of the nation-state. At the same time, we see in the works of writers like Régine Robin, Ying Chen, Leïla Sebbar, and Calixthe Beyala, a type of cosmopolitan consciousness that refuses to align itself with extant female perspectives in either its ethnic community of origin or its adopted homeland.

Because all of these writers offer a series of migrant works, this chapter constructs a theory of migrant feminism that addresses the charges levied by multicultural feminists across generations, nations, and continents. Régine Robin's *La Québécoite* (1983) goes so far as to depict migration itself (Jewish, Polish, French) as a specifically female-centred poetics that responds to the dynamics of political exclusion in Canada and France. For her part, Chen takes on concepts and symbols of Chinese womanhood in an ongoing, virulent critique of female oppression that appears in novels like *Les Lettres chinoises* (1993). In *Je ne parle pas la langue de mon père* (2003), Sebbar engages French colonial politics in Algeria and their forgotten legacy in current day France, focusing in particular on the vexing place of women in this fraught legacy of displacement. In her novel *Femme noire femme nue* (2007) published by Albin Michel, Beyala brings various strands of African-American feminist thought together with First World Feminism in order to critique African conceptions of womanhood. As a group, these writers have carved a collective place within French-language literary circles, contemporary women authors who cull a new literary mode – the migrant text – to make way for feminisms that artfully navigate the politics of cultural dissonance.

TOWARD A GLOBAL FRENCH LITERATURE

By doing away with old nationally inflected categories, the migrant text suggests an opening to study literature as it moves between – and not *in-between* – national, cultural, and linguistic spaces, thus expanding the reach of contemporary French literature to global proportions. We could not possibly have brought to bear all of the migrant texts in French that deserve to be studied as a part of this project. Yet the textual examples analyzed here are suggestive of a larger trend within French literature that even extends beyond the linguistic moniker "French." Writing that draws on, delves into, and capitalizes on the experience of migration is common to English, Spanish, Catalan, and German literature today – to name only a few of the many languages of choice – as increasing numbers of authors elect to write in a language that is neither their first nor the one that is tied to their country of origin. Others, having encountered or lived through migration, return to their native languages to put their experiences into words. Within this growing corpus of texts in all languages lies a paradoxical relationship to the nation that plays itself out in every part of the writing and publication process, from composition to editing, production to distribution, and marketing to sales.[13] The examples I put forward within the French-speaking contexts might thus be supplemented by others in neighbouring countries and idioms because to speak of the migrant text as a mode only available to French-language immigrant writing is at once closing the very doors we endeavoured to open.[14]

As a literary mode, the migrant text here takes on transatlantic proportions, linking the two most powerful French-language publishing industries, that of France and Quebec, and then including smaller publishing venues on the European and African continents whenever possible. Moreover, the category cannot be defined solely in relation to an author's immigrant status within a host country but is rather a function of the literary text itself. Migration manifests itself in the themes, tropes, and textual strategies of the literary work regardless of the author's citizenship or country of birth. Thus a writer like Franco-Algerian Azouz Begag or Sino-Canadian Ying Chen may have works that can qualify as "migrant" novels or plays, while others do not.

The migrant text – as this study conceptualizes it – does not compete with national literatures, rather it sidesteps them. It is a deliberate circumvention of the paradigms of nationhood and nationality – whether to question, critique, or simply escape their grasp. Yet it neither denies the existence of the nation-state, nor disregards its overarching influence in defining identity and structuring belonging. In fact, this is a mode that often engages with notions of rights and citizenship; it is concerned with the possibility of cosmopolitan ethics and multilingualism in systems that advocate homogeneity and monolingualism. At the same time, migrant texts are written, published, and first circulated within the nation-state and as such always carry with them the traces of exoticism and otherness that allow for their creation and dissemination in the national, and later global literary marketplace. They are after all cultural products of global capitalism as much as an outgrowth of the contemporary nation-state.

The migrant text moves away from colonial and postcolonial frameworks, which have for too long cast a shadow on all literature from the Third World and former French colonies. It is a departure from the politics of oppression and resistance tied to old colonial regimes; its battles are now of a different order related to mass migrations, ethnic war zones, dictatorships and democracy, rights of citizenship, and the struggle against various forms of discrimination based on race, class, gender, or sexual orientation. Economic and political exploitation figures prominently as does the clash of languages and cultures. Of course, this textuality does not exist in a historical vacuum, and the ghosts of colonialism certainly hover close behind, but it is no longer fruitful to rehash the texts of immigration through theories of postcolonialism that posit the migrant as an ideal of hybrid culture, as we will see in chapter 2, rather than the complex and contradictory reality that it embodies today.

The migrant text is finally an opening toward other categories and an invitation to find new approaches for studying literature, to mobilize creative and innovative strategies for analysis and criticism. Travel writing, a field experiencing a rebirth in recent times, actually shares much common ground with a migrant textuality. Indeed, many works may well fall within both realms, thereby increasing their potential for academic scrutiny. It is perhaps the rigidity and hegemony of the Francophone enterprise that writers, critics, and scholars alike have found most constricting, and in its stead we can only have open global categories that confront the alternating threat and promise of homogenizing modernity and inter-cultural difference. It is in an effort to define one such mode that the following chapters stake a claim.

PART ONE

Theory

I

From *Weltliteratur* to the Migrant Text

INTRODUCTION

If world literature was a natural outgrowth of postcolonialism in the wake of nationalism's far-reaching claims over migrant bodies, cultures, and texts, it is a term that is often loosely applied to everything from Homer to Molière, and Jorge Luis Borges to Anita Desai. Despite its all-encompassing character, however, the concept continues to hold sway in academic circles today because it symbolizes a theoretical move out of more constrictive categorizations of literature, whether by country or hemisphere, economic centre or former colonial empire. The limitations of previous bodies of theory, two of which we discuss in the following chapter, are especially evident when one considers writing that escapes the confines of nation and postcolony. Yet while in theory World Literature is truly a global category, its practice has paradoxically involved a partitioning of literature along linguistic and hemispheric lines. Critics of World Literature thus point out that the majority of texts that fall under this new rubric as it is taught in most American universities today are either Greek or Latin classics taught in translation or works of English literature (Siskind 2010). As a result, while classes in world literature pepper the course bulletins of most English departments, they are rare in departments of French, Italian, Spanish, Portuguese, German, or even African or Asian literature. Indeed, the absence of an equivalent term in other languages (except the original German and the efforts to render it into French that we will soon discuss), point once again to the concept's limited praxis, though its theoretical openings continue to seduce, suggesting new possibilities for the former pariahs of canonical literature.

French literature, carefully segregated into works from France and those from the Francophone world, is perhaps most ripe for an entry into World Literature, as the 2007 *Manifeste pour une littérature-monde* and its forty-four signatories professed.[1] "Le monde revient," wrote Michel Le Bris, arguing against a France-centred approach to literature in a manifesto that was published in France's *Le Monde* newspaper on 16 March 2007 and signed by Francophone writers the world over. To recognize its global implications, one had only to read the names of the various signatories of the manifesto (Tahar Ben Jelloun, Maryse Condé, Édouard Glissant, Jacques Godbout, Dany Laferrère, Alain Mabanckou, Anna Moï, and Dai Sijie, among others). The time is now, argues Le Bris, for the world to make its return into a French literary canon too often compartmentalized from its relation to the nation-state and colonial history. For French literature "from the periphery," as LeBris calls it, 2006 was a watershed year, with works from the Francophone world securing the Goncourt Prize, the Grand Prix du roman de l'Académie française, the Renaudot Prize, the Femina Prize, and the Goncourt des lycéens Prize (Le Bris 2007). Le Bris thus called for a World Literature in French – citing the model of the Anglophone world and calling on the examples of Kazuo Ishiguro, Ben Okri, Hanif Kureishi, Michael Ondaatje, and Salman Rushdie – to do away with the colonial vestiges that plague French literature in order to induct the recent awardees, the signatories of the manifesto, and all French writers into a new *Littérature-monde*. Le Bris's manifesto was met with fierce opposition, especially from the defenders of the political and literary institution of *Francophonie*, who accused LeBris of historical shortsightedness.[2] Indeed LeBris's text is replete with historical oversights, including the politically charged failure to recognize the importance of *Francophonie* as a bastion of resistance to French colonial rule and a superficial treatment of World Literature that did not consider its complexities and history. Specifically, no mention is made of World Literature's German antecedents, as it was Johann Wolfgang von Goethe who first coined the term in writings that date back to 1813 through 1827, in a language, as we shall see, that always took on an elusive character with regards to *Weltliteratur* as he termed it. Furthermore, as proponents of *Francophonie* argue, there are important distinctions to be made between what was formerly known as Commonwealth literature and the Francophone literary system, itself the result of a long-waged battle against the French colonial empire.[3] These factors, as I will show, complicate the viability of *Littérature-monde* as a literary category but point nonetheless to a pressing need for new approaches to the study of Francophone literature.

In this chapter, I will begin by tracing the history of a concept – from its German inception, through its German and Anglo-American interpretations, to its currently proposed French form – in search of what it might mean to speak of a "world" when literature is at stake. I will then propose an alternative way to theorize French literature, appealing to broader frameworks such as globalization and migration studies and building on what has come to be known today as *Littérature migrante* or Migrant Literature in the Franco-Canadian academy.

GOETHE'S WORLD

Goethe's first references to world literature appear in his speech to the Freemasons Lodge in 1813, where he links the development of world literature to the art of translation (Strich 7). Goethe argues that by reducing the text to its bare form and surrendering its national characteristics, the translation transcends one language and one nation to belong to another. Foreigners such as Shakespeare can thus be Germanized, just as Germans like Goethe himself can be Anglicized, Francized, and so forth. For Goethe then, world literature is essentially a form of exchange that takes the nation-state as its basis. Indeed, it is no coincidence that Goethe made use of the language of economics to define *Weltliteratur* since it was, in his sense, an intellectual barter that followed the model of the international market (Strich 28). As Goethe further nuanced his idea during his conversations with Eckermann in 1827, *Weltliteratur* as literary transaction was no longer intended to benefit the nation-state as much as mankind in general, and every thinking person had a role to play therein: "National literature is now rather an unmeaning term; the epoch of *Weltliteratur* is at hand, and everyone must strive to hasten its approach" (1930, 165). A year later, in his *Uber Kunst und Altertum* (1828), Goethe added a spiritual dimension, no doubt inspired by Hegel's *Phenomenology*, to the exchange of literature as facilitated by the figure of the translator: "And thus every translator is to be regarded as a middle-man [*Vermittler*] in this universal spiritual commerce [*allgemein geistigen Handels*], and as making it his task [*Geschafft*] to promote/further this exchange [*Wechseltausch*]: for say what we may of the insufficiency of translation, yet the work is and will always be one of the weightiest and worthiest matters [*Geschaffte*] in the general concerns of the world" (1901, 427–8). Here, Goethe's use of "the world" does not coincide with the globe or point to the sum of all nations. Rather, it consists of a community of people who are intent on furthering human understanding and tolerance through the exchange of literature. *Weltliteratur*, as Pheng Cheah points out in his reading of Goethe, is therefore a normative activity

(2008, 29). It is the becoming of a new social order, a human network of sorts that spans the globe and is possible only through literature, which is in turn facilitated by trade and commerce. In other words, Goethe saw *Weltliteratur* as the key that unlocks the door to a global literary culture, one where universal values unite people across geographical and political lines.

Goethe believed that of all nations, France was likely to gain the most from the advent of *Weltliteratur*. One reason for this was France's already well-disseminated culture of manners that Goethe believed had extended the influence of the country well beyond its borders. At the same time, he thought that nineteenth-century France, unlike Germany, had closed itself off to any foreign influences and would be greatly enriched by opening itself up to other literary influences (Strich 29). Finally, Goethe greatly appreciated French literary criticism as exemplified in *Le Globe*, a journal founded in 1824 "aimed at making known to the French public all important scientific, literary and philosophical works" (Strich 196). In many ways, French literary culture seemed best prepared, in Goethe's view, to participate in the creation of a "world."

Paris of the nineteenth century was indeed a haven for many émigré writers and various European literary and philosophical works were being read in translation (Casanova 2007). Both Goethe and his predecessor Herder were widely read in France and the French writer Edgar Quinet would even proclaim the idea of world literature in his essay *De l'unité des peuples modernes* (1838). However, as Fritz Strich shows in his study of Goethe's legacy, it is a teleologically inspired humanism that arises in France following the model of Goethe's *Faust* with works such as Lamartine's poem *La Chute d'un ange* (1838) and Hugo's *Légende des Siècles* (1859) rather than the exchange of literatures that Goethe imagines as constituting a "world." As Strich notes, the French works maintain a strict and traditional sense of French form while articulating general ideas on shared human values.

Most significant for the reception of Goethe in nineteenth-century France is Madame de Staël's *De l'Allemagne* (1813), in which she reconsiders his concept of *Weltliteratur* without using the term per se. In Goethe's openness to other literatures, de Staël sees a model to remedy the sterility of French works of her time: "Toutes les fois que, de nos jours, on a pu faire entrer dans la régularité française un peu de sève étrangère, les Français y ont applaudi avec transport" (1906, 4). [In our days, whenever a little foreign leaven has been allowed to mix itself with French regularity, the French have themselves applauded it with delight (1850, 149).] She goes on to cite Rousseau, Bernadin de Saint Pierre, and Châteaubriand as inspired by the type of versatility championed by Goethe in the German tradition: "Sa poésie prend facilement la couleur des contrées étrangères; il saisit avec un talent unique ce qui plaît dans les chansons nationales de chaque peuple. Il devient, quand il le veut, un Grec, un Indien, un Morlaque" (1906, 49). [His poetry easily assimilates itself with foreign countries; he seizes, with a talent perfectly unique, all that pleases in the national songs of each nation; he becomes, when he chooses it, a Greek, an Indian, or a Morlachian (1850, 228).] Even so, De Staël's chief concern remains the sovereignty of French literature. She repeatedly cautions against imitation (1906, 20–1, 25), confident of French superiority where taste and style are concerned (Blankenagel 1925, 148). French thinkers of the nineteenth century consistently read Goethe as first and foremost a promoter of national literature. As a result, *Weltliteratur* eventually falls by the wayside in French literary thought and though foreign influences are present in many French works of the nineteenth and twentieth century, Goethe's "world" no longer holds currency in the discourses surrounding literature.

In Germany, however, *Weltliteratur* remained a topic of discussion and in 1952, Erich Auerbach sees its relevance once more in the context of a world in danger of homogenization: "The presupposition of *Weltliteratur* is a *felix culpa*: mankind's division into many cultures" (1969, 2). In his essay *Philologie der Weltliteratur*, Auerbach expresses concern over the cultural standardization of the Western hemisphere at the height of the Cold War: "All human activity is being concentrated either into a European-American or Russian-Bolchevist pattern" (1969, 3). He warns against the dawn of a single literary culture among only a few literary languages. The task of *Weltliteratur* at the dawn of the global era as we now know it was, in Auerbach's terms, to expand a "world" that was too quickly contracting. "Our philological home is the earth, it can no longer be the nation," concludes Auerbach (1969, 17). This statement should not be interpreted as a complete rejection of national literature; quite to the contrary, he believed in the extreme worth of a nation's literary treasures. Like Goethe, he envisioned *Weltliteratur* to be at its strongest when building outwards from nation toward the "world." At the same time, he interprets Goethe's concept in its post-national and perhaps even post-global sense: the world is getting smaller and it is the task of every thinking person to expand it.

NEGOTIATING THE WORLD

The move from *Weltliteratur* to World Literature in the Anglo-American context is a relatively recent phenomenon that has emerged in response to the growing challenges of globalization. In opposition to Auerbach, whose concern was with a shrinking universe, theorists like David Damrosch and Franco Moretti are rethinking Goethe's concept in light of the vast expansion of the global literary scene. Damrosch reads Goethe through Marx and Engels, pointing to a network of exchange and defining the "world" as a mode of circulation and reading that literature falls in and out of as it moves "beyond its linguistic and cultural point of origin" (2003, 6). Perhaps most crucial to his departure from Goethe is Damrosch's emphasis on the phenomenology of the work of art over its ontology. For while Goethe employs a language that places ontology at the heart of world-making, not all works of literature can aspire to this noble calling. Damrosch pursues a more democratic model, opening his "world" to various forms of high and low literature, as well as to the ebb and flow of market-driven economies and the literary works they sanction. By privileging phenomenology, Damrosch's "world" also moves away from the canon of English literature to texts written by lesser-known authors in lesser-known parts of the globe. For while Goethe does liken *Weltliteratur* to the international marketplace, he neither anticipates the vast expansion of global capitalism nor foresees the selection processes by which works of art rise and fall in today's literary market.

Moretti defines the "world" in a similar fashion to Damrosch by accounting for massive global inequalities that Goethe or Marx and Engels never could have imagined. For the authors of the *Communist Manifesto*, world literature accompanies the emergence of a global proletariat whereby "national one-sidedness and narrow-mindedness become more and more impossible," and a new world consciousness is born (1954, 421). Inherent to their concept of world literature is the underlying equality of all local literatures. Moretti, however, draws on Immanuel Wallerstein's world-systems theory, pointing to the unequal co-existence of a literary core and periphery where the latter is often ignored when it interfaces with the former. As literature and culture from the periphery make a bid for the "world" they invariably intersect with a literature and culture from the core that tend to reject them. As a result, Moretti points to the ways in which literature from the periphery seeks out a compromise by borrowing from the core: "the modern novel arises not as an autonomous development but as a compromise between a Western formal influence (usually French or English) and local materials" (2004, 58). Literature from the periphery contributes something recognizably familiar and intriguingly unfamiliar to warrant its acknowledgment by the core and endorsement of its participation in World Literature. This is, of course, of great relevance to the French model, which we shall return to later.

For Goethe, the acknowledgement of literary masterpieces from other countries, and especially from the non-Western world, involves both literal and figurative translation and a translator whose multilingual skills make him or her a sacred purveyor of *Weltliteratur*. Recent Anglo-American theorizations of World Literature by Moretti and Emily Apter seek to demystify the work of the translator by pointing to the impossibilities that belie any act of translation. Tracing the work on comparative and world literature by Leo Spitzer during his exile in Turkey, Apter argues that they signal "a paradigm of *translatio* ... that emphasizes the critical role of multilingualism within transnational humanism ... a policy of nontranslation adopted without apology" (2004, 104). Her theory of World Literature thus centres around the reality of "untranslatable" texts, the deciphering of which include mistranslation, neologism, semantic dissonance, and collective authorship (2008, 597). Drawing on literary projects by Barbara Cassin and Moretti, Apter rejects a simplified understanding of translation that fails to recognize its endemic failure in praxis.[4]

In its transformation from *Weltliteratur* to World Literature, Goethe's thought also dovetails with many of today's theories of globalization. Current debates surrounding globalization question global capital's impact on the sovereignty of the nation-state and national culture. In other words, theorists study the ways in which national and global paradigms come into contact with one another in order to scrutinize and debate one's effect on the other. Where economists and theorists of nationalism like Anthony Smith argue that national culture inhibits global culture, which is at once ahistorical, memoryless, and timeless, others such as Arjun Appadurai and John Tomlinson point to the complex connectivity and deterritorialization that is at work in the global, insisting that global culture need not and does not necessarily build on national culture. In many ways, Goethe's ambiguous concept prefigures these debates as he wavers between the preponderance of the nation and the urgency of world-making. What has been erased in our hyper-globalized discussions of World Literature, nonetheless, is the spiritual [*geistigen*] aspect that Goethe intended for it, a register of language that has been left out in recent writing on the subject but that made a brief appearance around the formation of the Francophone literary system in the period following decolonization and early independence.

A SPIRITUAL CONNECTION

In the French context, a spiritual element returns, strangely enough, in the very phenomenon against which the authors of *Littérature-monde* proposed their new concept. Xavier Deniau's history and defense of *Francophonie* defines the term as a cultural community and one of the meanings he ascribes to this particularly nebulous grouping of peoples is a spiritual and mystical one. Commenting on de Gaulle's speech at the UNESCO meeting of November 1966, Deniau writes: "Ainsi se définissent des familles spirituelles plus riches de leur héritage partagé ... Cette notion d'idéal communautaire, de partage, nous conduit à examiner une évolution du sens spirituel du mot francophonie que l'on pourrait qualifier de 'mystique'" (1983, 19). [Hence spiritual families are enriched by their shared heritage ... This notion of ideal community, of sharing, propels us to examine the evolution of the spiritual meaning of the word *francophonie* that we may qualify as mystical.][5]

In a language vaguely reminiscent of Goethe's *Weltliteratur*, Deniau argues against any form of hegemonic neo-colonial manipulation, citing Léopold Senghor, Saint-John Perse, and Aimé Césaire as marking the poetic advent of *Francophonie*, which in this optic takes on the appearance of a French equivalent of Goethe's "world."

Poetry, for Goethe, is the privileged form of *Weltliteratur*: "I am more and more convinced that poetry is the universal possession of mankind" he told Eckermann (1930, 165). Likewise, for Deniau, Francophone poetry fosters a spiritual communion through the universality not only of poetic form, but of the French language. The spiritual vocation that is here ascribed to *Francophonie* finds its roots not only in a discourse that hails back to Renaissance poet Joachim Du Bellay's *Défense et illustration de la langue française* (1549), as well as to Antoine de Rivarol's 1784 treatise *Discours sur l'universalité de la langue française*, but later to the writings of Senghor, Senegal's first president. A fervent believer in *Francophonie* as a political and literary institution, Senghor argues in favor of its ability to promote a universal humanist model of cooperation between nation-states through the shared medium of the French language. Like those before him, he sees extraordinary potential for humanism in the beauty of French verse:

La beauté du français, de sa poésie, ne vient pas du pouvoir imaginant des mots, qui se sont dépouillés du concret de leurs racines; elle vient de la musique des mots et des phrases, des vers et des versets: de leur rythme et de leur mélodie ... Ce long arrêt à la poésie. Pour dire que la langue française est *culture*, c'est-à-dire esprit de civilisation, fondement d'un humanisme qui ne fut jamais plus actuel qu'aujourd'hui. (1977, 84–5)
[The beauty of French, of its poetry, does not derive from the imaginative power of words, that have been stripped of their concrete roots; it comes from the musicality of words and sentences, of lines and verse: from their rhythm and their melody ... This long pause on poetry. To say that the French language is *culture*, that is spirit of civilization, foundation of a humanism that has never been more relevant than it is today.]

More than any other advocate of *Francophonie*, Senghor consistently resorts to metaphoric language to present the Francophone cultural venture as one of spiritual connectedness that eventually moves the world beyond nations, continents, and races. He speaks of a "symbiose d'énergies dormantes," latent energies that are awakening through *Francophonie* to a complementary warmth ("chaleur complémentaire") among peoples (1962). Senghor's reasons for promoting such a spiritual community were not to prolong the French colonial empire so much as to preserve Africa from inevitable balkanization into separate and warring states. Senghorian universalism was a part of his pan-Africanist dream to avoid the very tribal wars and predictable migrations that have resulted in the political instability so characteristic of postcolonial Africa today.

Quebecois journalist and writer Jean-Marc Léger was another supporter of *Francophonie* who shared a belief in the organization's spiritual potential. As the first secretary general of the AUPELF (Association des universités partiellement ou entièrement de langue française), Léger continually sought support for the teaching and propagation of the French language. The goal was to create greater opportunities for cooperation in the French-speaking world, thereby countering the threat of "Anglomania" and Americanization through a shared linguistic heritage: "La francophonie doit être d'abord un état d'esprit et elle ne peut l'être qu'à partir d'une connaissance intime, approfondie de la langue commune, qui doit être ressentie par l'ensemble de ses locuteurs comme une sorte de patrie spirituelle" (1987, 49). [Francophonie must first be-

come a spiritual state and it can only be so out of an intimate, deep
knowledge of the common language that must be experienced by all of
its interlocutors as a sort of spiritual homeland.] Léger's faith in Francophone solidarity was motivated by his own nationalist leanings in
Quebec. Battling a federal government often looking to intercept Quebec participation in Francophone conferences without its approval,
Léger's position is steeped in a nationalist agenda different from the
universalism of Senghor. *Francophonie* was nonetheless a common
means to particular ends and its strength for Léger, as for Senghor, lay
in the profound spirit of unity that it would foster among diverse national participants.

The belief in a Francophone community was subject to criticism
right from the outset. Scholars such as Guy Ossito Midiohouan and
Ambroise Kom reveal repeatedly the neocolonial bid for power that
lay behind the multitude of organizations, conferences, and literatures
to which *Francophonie* gave rise. Their critiques spare neither French actors like de Gaulle nor Africans like Senghor and Habib Bourguiba,
then the president of Tunisia and a zealous promoter of the Senghorian idea of a Francophone community. Midiohouan and Kom's claims
rely heavily on anti-colonial and postcolonial arguments anchored in
the national autonomy of newly independent states. While these critical approaches raise important questions about the colonial legacy of
Francophonie, they do not suggest more than an African communion
of shared oppression and emerging literatures.

IN RUSHDIE'S FOOTSTEPS

Michel Le Bris and the other signatories of the 2007 *Manifeste* reject
the notion of a so-called "spiritual community" of *Francophonie*, which
they claim consigns them to an outer periphery of the literary world.
They prefer instead to draw on the Anglophone example of World Literature as a way out of colonialist power plays. Their manifesto imitates
the model of another manifesto-type essay written by Salman Rushdie
in 1983 entitled "Commonwealth Literature Does Not Exist" – later
hailed as the work that led to the demise of that notion among the Anglophone literary establishment. In obvious anger, Rushdie argues that
Commonwealth Literature is an exclusionary ghetto that serves to
"change the meaning of the far broader term 'English literature' – which
I'd always taken to mean the literature of the English language – into
something far narrower, something topographical, nationalistic, possibly even racially segregationist" (1992, 63). Rushdie goes on to liken the

Commonwealth to a chimera: "but you will recall that a classical chimera was a monster of a rather special type. It had the head of a lion, the body of a goat and a serpent's tail. This is to say, it could exist only in dreams, being composed of elements which could not possibly be joined together in the real world" (1992, 63). In a scathing critique of Commonwealth Literature, Rushdie argues that Commonwealth literature is an imposed category that subordinates new works from outside the UK and the United States to colonial history rather than to celebrate the new literary freedom of a world language. To bolster his point, Rushdie argues for a "remaking" of the English language, citing the example of a younger generation of writers in India who no longer think of English as anything other than an Indian language. In response to those who defend Commonwealth Literature as a diversity of national traditions under the English banner, Rushdie dismisses the discourse of authenticity as "the respectable child of old-fashioned exoticism," (1992, 67) which has every author accountable to his or her culture of origin instead of to actual literary work. In a similar fashion, many of those who today defend *Francophonie* are open to criticism that their apparent legitimization of writers from the margins is couched in a questionable discourse of authenticity. Rushdie's model is therefore a telling one for the writers of the *Manifeste pour une littérature-monde* and, while they do not cite his essay, his name is synonymous with the end of the Commonwealth and the dawn of World Literature.

ACKNOWLEDGING THE WORLD

Against this backdrop, what kind of a "world" do the proponents of *Littérature-monde* have in mind? In the essays they compiled *Pour une Littérature-monde*, Le Bris and Rouard suggest what *monde* might mean for writers of the French-speaking periphery who, in Moretti's terms, have for too long been at the mercy of the core in terms of critical and public recognition. Le Bris's essay begins by referring to the watershed year of 2006, when five of France's most prestigious literary prizes were awarded to non-French authors. He refers to this momentous feat as a "révolution copernicienne" [Copernican revolution], signaling the end of the core-periphery model and the advent of a new system of literary world relations. The centre has been dispersed, he announces, "fin de la Francophonie. Naissance d'une littérature-monde en français" [The end of francophone literature – and the birth of a world literature in French (Hargreaves et al. 2010, 296)]. In Le Bris's exclamation "le monde revient ... N'aura-t-il pas été depuis longtemps le grand absent de la littérature française ?" [The world is returning ... Wasn't the world always conspicuous by its absence in French literature? (297)], it is difficult not to hear echoes of both Goethe's and De Staël's warnings against the isolationism of French literature. In his longer essay in the edited volume, Le Bris begins outlining a possible definition for his newly minted concept. He draws almost exclusively from the anglophone model of World Literature, highlighting hybridity, *métissage*, and migration. He writes metaphorically of literature's rebirth through the multiplicity of cultures and languages and of the absence of a centre. Goethe's humanism is not far off from the "world" Le Bris imagines, as it appears above all to be a meeting of literatures from all over the globe, a rejection of literary nationalism full of idealism and excitement at the prospect of freedom from alienation for the formerly francophone writer.

Unlike *Weltliteratur*, Le Bris's *Littérature-monde* is a political stance against the cultural imperialism of France, and as such it is closest to the anti-Commonwealth movement that preceded it in the Anglophone world. The concept is both a deliberate attempt at levelling the playing field and a call to France and to French literature to open itself up to the world. Just as Goethe once believed that France, of all nations, had most to gain from *Weltliteratur*, so do the contributors to *Pour une Littérature-monde* believe that France has everything to lose without it. The move here is akin to De Staël's, only this time it hails from the outside. For the various contributors to the edited volume, *Littérature-monde* is less about world-making than about embracing a "world" that already is. Tahar Ben Jelloun, for instance, speaks of the privilege of inhabiting two cultures and languages while Anna Moï embraces the fact that she is labelled as Other and Dany Laferrière marvels at the diversity of his cosmopolitan encounters when travelling. The multiplicity of voices results in a plethora of "worlds," most left undefined but waging war against any notion of purity, whether cultural or linguistic. In perhaps the best summary of Le Bris and Rouard's collection of essays, Alain Mabanckou writes: "La littérature-monde est le concert de la multiplicité d'expériences, la reconnaissance de la force de l'art dans ce qui apparaît comme le 'désordre de la vie'" (2007, 64). [World literature in French is the culmination of a multiplicity of experiences, the recognition of the power of art in what appears as the "disorder of life" (2009, 149).] There is a unity of tone in the variety of experiences the collective authors narrate, and the French language serves as the only common denominator linking all their writings together. Most importantly, the volume itself suggests a refusal of centre-periphery relations represented by the institutions of *Francophonie*.

At its best, the "world" implied by the relatively small body of literary and critical writing on *Littérature-monde* is suggestive of a post-Francophone consciousness rather than the dawn of a new literary era. If anything, *Littérature-monde* signals the crisis of *Francophonie* as a literary category and mode of analysis. Just as World Literature has invited many methodological essays by scholars of Rushdie, Ondaatje, and Kureishi, *Littérature-monde* should do so for scholars of Abdourahmane Waberi, Nancy Houston, and Dai Sijie. For World Literature, Moretti proposes the bold strategy of "distant reading" (as opposed to close reading) as a way to "focus on units that are much smaller or much larger than the text: devices, themes, tropes – or genres and systems" (2004, 151). Likewise, *Littérature-monde* is an invitation to read across nations and languages, to find new and innovative ways of bringing texts together. Drawing on *Littérature-monde*'s German and English antecedents, it is also a call to consider the life of a work not only in its original language but also in translation, as it rides the ins and outs of market economies and participates in social and literary networks that exceed its national scope. Above all, *Littérature-monde* is an opportunity for scholars of French literature to think beyond colonial and postcolonial rubrics to the realities of migration, globalization, cosmopolitanism, and multilingualism.

LITERATURE IN THE GLOBAL ERA

To approach literature from the vantage point of globalization and migration is to enter several debates about the nature and timing of a global world and migrating peoples. Is globalization a consequence of modernity (Giddens 1990), or is it a condition of divergent modernization (Robertson 1992)? Is it synonymous with homogenization, according to a Marxist-functionalist reading, or is it in fact the very postmodern heterogeneity that inter-culturalists have been defending all along (Bhabha 1994; Hall 1992; Clifford 1988)? Is migration a geopolitical phenomenon of the twentieth century that is dependent on the prior existence of the nation-state (Basch, Schiller, and Blanc 1993), or should it be traced back to its first manifestations some two million years ago in the Harappa region (Pieterse 2004)? To consider literature's place at the intersection of present-day global and migratory processes is not a disavowal of the ways in which literature has historically been a heterogeneous cultural product. Rather it is an acknowledgement of the sweeping literary categorizations that accompanied the birth of the nationalist project in the nineteenth century, categorizations that have made it next to impossible to speak of a literary work today without placing it within the geopolitical confines of its "home" country. As we have seen, even global institutions such as the Commonwealth and *Francophonie* have grown out of the preponderance of the British and French nation-states and still today the linguistic marker "French" remains inextricably tied to national identity in France.

However, as Jan Nederveen Pieterse argues, during the past four decades, there has been a shift; "nation-state pathos has been receding and in its stead have come globalization, regionalism and an 'age of ethnicity'" (2004, 33). Economists and theorists of cultural studies trace the recent acceleration in global processes and movement to the 1970s, a period that corresponds with the growth of new media, banks, and technologies along with the rise of advertising and consumption. Concepts such as McDonaldization and Disneyfication run up against notions of hybridity (Bhabha 1994; Pieterse 2004) and deterritorialization (Deleuze and Guattari 1980; Tomlinson 1999) as theorists attempt to describe the cultural ramifications of mass migrations and mediation. Nonetheless, as Arjun Appadurai (1990) points out, the nation-state continues to remain a significant player although its own discourse of homogenization now competes with that of other global actors.

The 1970s were a key period where political legislation in matters of immigration were concerned both in France and Canada. Quebec created a ministry of immigration in 1968, two years after Maurice Duplessis's nationalist party came into power and the very year that Quebec's secessionist Parti Québécois was created. In the decade that followed, the provincial government began taking a variety of linguistic and cultural measures to ensure the integration of immigrants into Francophone rather than Anglophone communities of Quebec. In other words, by the late 1960s, the Quebec government faced an increasing influx of immigrants and a dire need to devise legislative policy to protect the viability of its claims to national sovereignty.

The most recent phase of mass migration to France goes back to the period from 1950–1974, a time frame that coincides with decolonization, independence, and a deficit in France's blue collar workforce that led to an open-door immigration policy. Migrant workers from France's ex-colonies were hence automatically granted the *carte de séjour* to live and work in France. As soon as the French economy picked up in the early seventies, however, the Giscard government imposed a complete stop on immigration and, in 1974, began implementing a series of measures to persuade migrant workers to return to their countries of origin. Coincidentally, these policies came on the heels of Jean-Marie LePen's newly created far-right nationalist party, the Front National, in 1972. A few years later, due to pressures from the left, Giscard's right-wing UDF voted in the *Loi sur le regroupement familial* in 1976, allowing immigrant workers to sponsor their families over to France. What ensued was more rather than less immigration and the continued strengthening of nationalist groups such as the Club de l'Horloge and, of course, the Front National.

As the decade that ushered in the global age and the first mass migrations to France and Quebec, the 1970s also marked an important change in the literary politics and output of the French-speaking world. It was in 1970, ten years after the independence of most of France's colonies, that *Francophonie* was created under the then aegis of ACCT (Agence de coopération culturelle et technique), later to become the OIF (Organisation internationale de la Francophonie) in 1998. This political initiative conformed to the changing dynamics of a post-colonial world in which the legacy of de Gaulle, Senghor, Bourguiba, and Hamani Diori was giving rise to a global community of French speakers. At the same time, French-language literature was undergoing a significant transformation. While post-independence literature had been deeply anchored in postcolonial paradigms, wedded to a national sense of place, French language literature was slowly taking a turn toward the world. A first generation of immigrant authors to France and Quebec began publishing in French, blending their voices with those of native French and Quebecois writers of the 1970s. In Paris, Moroccan Tahar Ben Jelloun published his "roman-poème" *Harrouda* (1973), followed by several other works including *La Réclusion solitaire* (1976) and *Moha le fou Moha le sage* (1978). In the same time span, Algerian Nabile Farès came out with *Yahia, pas de chance* (1970), *Le Chant d'Akli* (1971), *Un Passager de l'Occident* (1971), *Le Champ des oliviers* (1972), and three other novels before the decade was over. In Montreal, Iraqi Naïm Kattan made his literary début with *Adieu Babylone* (1975) while Haitian Émile Ollivier published a two-part novel *Paysage de l'aveugle* (1977) in Montreal. These works for the most part are reflections on immigrant life and the difficulties of negotiating identity across nations. As the institutional wing of *Francophonie* took shape in the name of the global, so-called "Francophone" literature was already unearthing *Francophonie*'s limitations as a literary category, its imperialist prerogatives, and its profound inability to make sense of transnational and cross-cultural literary ventures.

MIGRANT LITERATURE

By the early 1980s, it was clear that a new generation of French-language immigrant writers was emerging both in France and Quebec. In France, publishing houses, critics, and scholars alike continued to categorize this literature according to the home countries of the authors, but scholars in Quebec responded to the challenge by devising a new literary category. Since Quebecois scholars and critics had always rejected the literary term of *Francophonie* as a neo-colonial construction, preferring the categories of Quebecois and French literature instead, it was evident that this new literature could not be lumped into national groupings when the novels clearly exceeded the scope of one country's literature. The first two novels of Franco-Jewish author Régine Robin, *Le Cheval blanc de Lénine* (1979) and *La Québécoite* (1983), take us to Poland, France, and Canada, all countries that were home to Robin at some point in her life. Similarly, Haitian-Canadian writer Dany Laferrière, whose many novels include *Comment faire l'amour avec un nègre sans se fatiguer* (1985), *Éroshima* (1987), and *L'Odeur du café* (1991), inflects his prose with references to Haitian, African-American, and Quebecois culture, politics, and history – flirting with national allegiances that span the entire North American continent and beyond.

To account for the growing number of immigrant authors and playwrights moving away from nationalist tropes and exploring new relationships to culture and language in Quebec, critic Robert Berrouët-Oriol devised the term *littérature migrante* in 1986 to account for what he called "le caractère apatride" [the stateless character] of this new literature. The expression quickly struck a chord in critical and scholarly circles in Quebec, and others such as Gilles Dupuis and Simon Harel began offering both a taxonomy and critique of its usage. In his work, Harel notes recurrent themes surrounding identity and the politics of place, a different relationship to language and, most notably, an ethics of difference based on the trauma of migration:

> Le trauma se dit mal, puisque c'est la capacité même de se souvenir qui fait l'objet d'un déni implacable. Pourtant, l'écrivain migrant ouvre un espace enfoui au-dedans de soi. Il faudrait alors envisager une autre forme de témoignage, puisque le sujet migrant est le porteur de l'envers de la mémoire officielle qu'il dénonce par son écriture: refus de la mémoire nationale de la communauté d'accueil; refus de la commémoration passéiste que requiert de son côté la communauté ethnoculturelle. (2005, 63)

[The trauma is difficult to express, because it is the very capacity to remember that is the object of an implacable denial. Nonetheless, the migrant writer opens a repressed space within him or herself. One must then envisage a different kind of witnessing, since the migrant subject carries the reverse of the official memory that he or she denounces in writing: a refusal of the host community's national memory; a refusal of antiquated commemorations that requires a given ethno-cultural community.]

Central to Harel's definition of migrant writing is a work's refusal to position itself within the national memory of the host country or that of the ethno-cultural diasporic community from which it hails – an aspect that distinguishes it from diasporic literature.

Wary of how the term *Francophonie* served to separate literature from the periphery from that of the centre, Harel warns of the nationalist exclusion of literature from the margins in Quebec: "Parlant d'écriture migrante, le discours dominant se donne les conditions exotiques d'un rêve qui est une plongée dans l'imaginaire de l'Autre (2005, 62)." [Speaking of migrant writing, the dominant discourse grants itself the exotic conditions of a dream that is immersed in the imaginary of the Other.] Migrant literature might this way take on the problems of *Francophonie*, offering yet another literary category that bids for the world with a hidden nationalist agenda. Moreover, authors such as Italian born Marco Micone have little in common with the likes of Haitian-Canadian author Emile Ollivier, argues Harel, and it is nothing short of racial prejudice that has us placing them in the same literary category. Carine Mardorossian has also warned against the concept's clichéd use when applied unilaterally to all works written by contemporary exiled writers or texts about the immigrant experience. In recent years, critics such as Gilles Dupuis have suggested alternate ways of qualifying this body of writing, drawing on terminological nuances suggested by Pierre Nepveu (1988), Robert Berrouët-Oriol (1992), Clément Moisan and Renate Hildebrand (2001), as well as Daniel Chartier (2002) and dropping the word *littérature* in favour of *écriture(s)*. Dupuis's resulting *écritures transmigrantes* (2006) is a further lexical move away from both "literature" and "migrant" in an effort to bridge the politicized gap between native and immigrant in Quebec.[6] Yet as the notion of migrant writing falls into oblivion with some critics in Quebec, it continues to enjoy currency in Europe and the US in a second wave of criticism that has risen over the last decade in response to a large body of work that calls for a different analytic paradigm.[7]

To propose the migrant text as a literary mode in the light of *Francophonie*'s overreaching claims and the *Manifeste pour une littérature-monde*'s appeal for a new worlding of French literature is not to ignore the important warnings raised by critics like Harel or Mardorossian but rather to redefine the term in their wake. My suggestion, first of all, is that the advent of a global era in the study of literature must bring with it changes in the ways we approach literary texts. Harel's concerns in fact echo those of theorists of globalization such as Tomlinson and Appadurai; empire and the nation-state never linger far behind claims for a worldwide, open network of literary circulation. Yet the only way to undermine the pervasive power of such closed systems of thought is to devise more fluid categories that flow in and out of each other.

The Migrant Undercurrents
of Critical Theory

NATIONALISM: AN INTRODUCTION

Any theoretical positioning of migrancy[1] must endeavour to situate its subjects within the realm of "movement" itself, outside paradigms that aim to fix people in determinate places. Nationalist frameworks, though they often find themselves endangered by the onslaught of globalization, continue to be pivotal in the emergence of new identity formations and social definitions and hence are at the centre of any discussion about the viability of the migrant condition.[2] The appearance of actual new nation-states may have decelerated over the past fifty years, but the power of nationalism lives on in the abundance of ethnic, cultural, and religious communities that depend on national identity as a way to establish their own territory and political autonomy.

Theories of nationalism first flourished at the end of the nineteenth century, just as the first colonies claimed independence. Lord Acton and Ernest Renan are most often cited as the precursors of modern theories of nationalism. In Great Britain, Lord Acton wrote in 1860 about the new, irresistible power of nationalist forces with no end in sight, quite different from egalitarianism and communism, movements for which he saw clear expiration dates (1967, 134). For Acton, the goal of nationalism is to establish the legitimacy of the great colonial empires, which had been called into question by the arrival of new independent countries on the international scene.[3] But what Acton highlights with great precision is the sheer attractiveness that nationalism would exert upon his fellow citizens – something he thought would prove awfully hard to resist (2000, 17–38).

Twenty years later, the French theologian Ernest Renan came up with the very first definition of the nation, borne of his effort to explain the developmental trajectory of Western Europe since the fall of the Roman Empire. Renan denounces, first and foremost, all of the non-foundational elements of the nation, including race, religion, and language. The nation is, for him, a soul – a spiritual principle based on establishing a shared past full of memories and a present effort to validate that heritage: "Une nation est donc une grande solidarité, constituée par le sentiment des sacrifices qu'on a faits et de ceux qu'on est disposé à faire encore" (1882, 27). [A nation is therefore a large-scale solidarity, constituted by the feeling of the sacrifices that one has made in the past and of those that one is prepared to make in the future (Eley & Suny 1996, 53).] It is from this form of "daily plebiscite" that Renan envisions the roots of a nation, even though he recognizes the importance of geography and religion in the establishment of societies. Broadly against individualism, he sees the basic principle of the nation as a fundamental need of humanity, despite the "historical error" that will always characterize it.

Since Acton and Renan, theories have proliferated about the roots of the modern nation and the reasons for its development. Some insist that it remains a purely Western creation, while others explore its antecedents outside Europe. Among all of these theories, a handful of theorists have offered the most conclusive answers to these questions – Otto Bauer, Benedict Anderson, Richard Handler, Ernest Gellner, and Eric Hobsbawm. The paragraphs that follow seek to isolate the role of migrancy in these influential conceptualizations of the nation.

BAUER'S "COMMUNITY OF DESTINY"

In 1907, Otto Bauer, then the head of Gestamtpartei, the Austrian Social-Democrat party, became the most important theorist on the question of nationalism when he published *Die Nationalitätenfrage und die Sozialdemokratie*, translated into French in 1987 and English in 2000 as *Social Democracy and the Nationalities Question*. As a Marxist, Bauer's goal in writing the book was to raise national consciousness about the concerns of the working class. The nation, for Bauer, forms a community that, by definition, lives in "profound reciprocal interaction" – phrasing he borrows from Kant (1987, 140). National identity appears in the ways in which each individual reproduces and lives this sense of community. Throughout history, explains Bauer, each individual recognizes the communal identity that he shares with his compatriots. Capitalist exploitation, on the other hand, works to alienate both the dominant and the working classes from national consciousness. Consequently, the process of assimilation that is necessary for achieving the national cause is only possible in a socialist framework, which has as its goal the "nationalization" of the proletariat. In this way, Bauer advances the following definition of the nation: "a totality of men united through a community of fate into a community of character" (1987, 160). In other words, common experiences give rise to a national character shared by all. As examples, Bauer cites both Germany and Austria – and as a counter-example, he cites the Jewish nation. Jews do not qualify for Bauer's national model because of their remarkably prolonged and dissipated history of migration.

For the purposes of our study, the Jewish example presented by Bauer is of particular importance, because he abandons it as yet another way in which capitalism effaces all national distinction. In other words, Jews can never constitute a nation, according to Bauer, because they are an ethnic and religious community that succeeds in assimilating into other communities – hence impossible to isolate as a distinct national community. From this perspective, migrants can be claimed by the nationalist project if they manage to assimilate into the host nation, or if they find former national compatriots among the diaspora of the host country. Without this, migrants would be left to the whims of industrial capitalism, for which ethnic, religious, and linguistic descriptors have absolutely no value.

Bauer's nationalist project, inspired in part by that of the famous Austrian Chancellor Karl Renner, seeks as its last goal a way to rally diverse nations beneath the same state apparatus. This state then serves as a historical and institutional shell, which houses a multiplicity of nations as they wait out the eventual disappearance of all states.[4] Ephraim Nimni, in his forward to the English translation of *Die Nationalitäten-frage und die Sozialdemokratie*, notes the pertinence of this work for the Canadian situation. Bauer's is a sort of "multiculturalism" *avant la lettre*, one which for Nimni offers a useful way to articulate the terms of Quebecois national identity as well as that of other minority populations in Canada (2000, xxx). This means recognizing many nations under the aegis of one state, all of them lacking the autonomy that customarily comes along with territorial secession. The "national" title is sufficient then for giving each nation the right to preserve its identity, culture, and language without fragmenting the country. Nimni's interpretation of Bauer, however, neglects the importance of a disappearing state apparatus in the imminent destruction of capitalism, at which point the immigrant is once again left to the mercy of competing, warring nations. Indeed for Bauer, the state was by nature impermanent and as such just a temporary way of quelling differences that could only be reconciled through proletarian revolutionary unity.

ANDERSON'S "IMAGINED COMMUNITY"

It would take seventy-six more years before a second decisive theory of nationalism would appear in the West, but this time capitalism would not be cast as a villain. In his celebrated work *Imagined Communities: Reflections on the Origins and Spread of Nationalism*, Benedict Anderson defines the nation as "an imagined political community" (1983, 6). This community is imagined because it unites people who do not know each other and who will never cross paths, but who retain all the same a strong feeling of conjoined identity. The only connection between them is a past that, while it is often fictitious, nevertheless justifies their association with one another. Anderson's nation is both limited and sovereign, in that it makes no attempt to include all of humanity; at the borders of one nation there simply lie several others. In the Andersonian sense, then, national consciousness replaces all other cultural concepts of identity formation, which lose their influence over the now national subject. In place of religion, dynastic rule, and the immeasurability of time comes capitalism, bringing with it new forms of communication technology, a henceforth linear conception of time, and various vernacular languages. Anderson suggests that it is these changes that brought about a new national consciousness to supplant all other forms of identity creation.

Anderson barely mentions the immigrant and diasporic populations of a given nation in his work. Since his view of nation is not bound by geography, however, it seems tailor-made to include those subjects who, though they may physically distance themselves from the centre of the nation, continue to adhere to the collective imaginary of the community to which they hope to belong. If there exists no such desire for belonging and no such espousal of an imaginary, as in the case of migrants who reject all national attachments and refuse the fictive camaraderie that binds them to their supposed co-nationals, then Anderson's theory does not account for their presence as the nation has no way of polling its subjects in any case.

GELLNER'S INDUSTRIALIZED SOCIETY

It is next to impossible to consider Anderson's theory without also thinking about the work of anthropologist Ernest Gellner, whose book

Nations and Nationalism came out the same year as *Imagined Communities*. Gellner theorizes nationalism as "a principle which holds that the political and national unit should be congruent" (1983, 1). In so doing, Gellner navigates the epistemological difficulties of defining the nation by proposing a practical explanation rather than an ideological one, a move that helps him to conceive of the nation *a priori*. He maintains that nationalism is symptomatic of the modern life of the state, and distinguishes between three phases of human history, the third of which for him is (as for Anderson) the industrial phase. In the transition between the agro-literate phase of history and the industrial one, the elite find use in the imposition of cultural homogeneity, as the management of labour requires an impersonal and direct form of communication – one that does not allow for workers to differentiate themselves culturally. From this is born a sort of egalitarianism that rewards those who distinguish themselves through education and specialization, rather than through filial or personal relationships. Nationalism thus emerges when the State fuses with a high culture – created by the elite – which becomes normative due to the standardization of education. This sort of nationalism demands a loyalty veiled as economic competition.

For the purposes of our study, Gellner's theoretical model, though often mentioned apace with Anderson's, deserves separate consideration. This is because Gellner signals the importance of a cultural homogeneity that is imposed from above and which, eventually, prompts the emigration of those who wish to integrate the culture – i.e. the standardized and centralized educational system – of another nation state. In concrete terms, the economic pull of one state with respect to another, and the migration that ensues, represents a change in national allegiance, whatever the "imaginary" penchants of the migrant might be. Gellner hence complicates Anderson's theory with a dose of economic, political, and social reality that may often confuse a migrant's sense of national belonging. This particular industrialist theory of the nation is to be distinguished from Bauer's multicultural model in that Gellner does not anticipate any imminent dissolution of the modern state apparatus. In the capitalist paradigm wherein nation-states flourish, migrants cannot therefore hope to escape the various nationalisms that abound, and this even if the characteristic movement of migrancy might seem to suggest so. This institutional and rigid view of nationalism thus establishes quite a counterpoint against Anderson's fluid and amorphous one. Gellner's model offers no exceptions, even to migrants who by definition seek to evade the grasp of an original nation.

HANDLER'S POSSESSIVE INDIVIDUALISM

In 1988, Richard Handler corroborated Gellner's principle of national homogeneity in his study of Quebecois nationalism: "In principle national being is defined by a homogeneity which encompasses diversity: however individual members of the nation may differ, they share essential attributes that constitute their national identity; sameness overrides difference" (1988, 6). Handler develops a theory of nationalism via his study of the Quebec nation, in which he emphasizes the importance of individualism, a phenomenon he suggests is unique to modern Western society. Following the metaphor of a "collective individual," based on the notion of human individuality, the members of a nation end up sharing a communal "essence" despite their various differences. Each individual expresses his or her "being" or personal character by making a choice. This choice is an external manifestation of being, and it derives from the concept of property or possession: "Property is what results from choices – products that exist in the external world yet remain linked through proprietorship to the self that created them" (1988, 51). From this is born, for Handler, the notion of distinct cultures belonging to each nation. The Quebecois nation possesses a distinct culture, which as a result gives life to its nation. Handler writes, "To lose one's culture, or to abdicate responsibility for cultural creation and autonomous choice, is to renounce life itself" (51). Indeed, for Handler, the conception of a national "essence" is as natural as it is inevitable. One does not choose a national identity; rather one acts according to what is naturally prescribed by this identity: "To be Québécois is to act/choose/create Québécois, and to act/choose/create Québécois comes naturally to those who are Québécois" (47).

It is easy to assume that the immigrant would be excluded from Handler's theory of Quebec nationalism. For instance, the common expression "Québécois de souche" distinguishes between those people who have ancestors among the original French colonists and those who were more recent arrivals to the province. Migrants are destined to become part of this "natural" order only over time, integrated – whether through mixed marriages or other circumstances – into the national Quebecois body. This process of naturalization is nevertheless compromised by what Handler calls the "negative vision" of the Quebec nation – one that sees itself as threatened by external forces, by those "others" who put it at risk of pollution, or even extinction. In Handler's view, diversity and heterogeneity are significant obstacles for Quebecois national identity and immigrants must be assimilated as quickly as possible. Such a theory of nationalism would well explain Quebec's immigration policies from the 1970s onward that promote sudden and significant measures to address the immigrant question.

HOBSBAWM'S POLITICAL MODERNISM

In 1990, the British Marxist Eric Hobsbawm published *Nations and Nationalism since 1780*, a work that, along with others, earned him renown as one of the most important historians of the twentieth century. Though Hobsbawm borrows his definition of the nation from Gellner, he uses a rather different historical division of national movements (1992, 6). Instead of pre-agrarian, agrarian, and industrial stages of human history, Hobsbawm employs the tripartite division of the Czech historian Miroslav Hroch to explain the development of nationalism. According to Hroch, the first phase of nationalist movements is purely cultural. Originally conceived in Europe in the nineteenth century, these movements were of no real national or political consequence. The second phase is characterized by the appearance of nationalist militancy and ensuing political mobilization. Finally, in a third and final phase, nationalist programs gain the support of the masses. For his part, Hroch's work focuses on the second stage, while Hobsbawm dwells on the third – and in particular on the transition into this final phase of nationalism. His critique of Gellner lies in what he sees as a "top-down view of modernization," one that he would like to counteract by looking at similar processes from below – from the perspective of ordinary people who are the targets of the propaganda and oppressive tactics of governments (1985; 11–12). Unlike Gellner, who explains the emergence of nations as a function of industrialization, Hobsbawm analyzes the same events through the lens of political modernization. In Europe of the nineteenth century, contact between the State and the people became more and more common as those in power sought to secure the loyalties of the population, and in so doing, legitimize the modern state apparatus.

Though *Nations and Nationalism* is an empirical study of multiple countries and ethnicities, France stands out as a singular example because the French Revolution is a remarkable pivot point for Hobsbawm's conception of political modernization. Since the Revolution, French citizenship involves an implied consent to linguistic uniformity, a principle that has become foundational to their nation. Despite the diverse languages spoken in France at the time of the Revolution, the acquisition of a now standardized French language became the sin-

gle most important requirement for belonging to the French nation
and, by extension, for membership in its citizenry. The Jacobins would
see it as the ultimate way to keep the old regime away from civil service. The word *patrie* would now acquire a connotation in France that
was borrowed from the American and Dutch revolutions of 1783,
where the patriots of 1789 bore witness to their love of country in a
shared desire to renew it through reform and revolution. It is in this
way that Hobsbawm emphasizes the political nature of the nation
borne of patriotic sentiments: "And the *patrie* to which their loyalty lay,
was the opposite of an existential, pre-existing unit, but a nation created by the political choices of its members who, in doing so, broke with
or demoted their former loyalties" (1992, 87). According to historian
Ernest Lavisse, this is the greatest contribution of France to world history – that is, a "nation that recreated itself by its own devices."[5] Since
that time, the definition of citizenship has been congruous with nationality itself, as one and all became citizens of the New Republic. Despite the varying annexation dates of France's multiple regions – the
last of which were barely a century old at the time of Revolution –
the inhabitants of France's different regions now enjoyed a new-found
sense of nationality defined by one single marker: the French language.
French nationalism, at this point, was still quite a way off, since the
French Republican model rests on the very idea of a fallible nation that
must *renew* itself. The people remain its core value, regardless of their
multiple histories, ethnicities, and maternal languages.

For Hobsbawm, the modern French state took form in the era that
followed Revolution, as subsequent governments strived for uniformity on French territory (1992, 80). The French government, much like its
European neighbours, hardly hesitated to use nationalism as a way to
unify itself against a more defined enemy, evoking "natural frontiers"
(*frontières naturelles*) and the notion of "indivisibility" (*une et indivisi-
ble*) to reinforce the territorial dimension of national identity. Resort-
ing to means such as obligatory education, military service, and voting
privileges, the state apparatus became inseparable from its people, weav-
ing lasting connections between its citizens and their government. Public function also grew in order to allow for the increasing number of
government programs connecting a people to their governing bodies.
In 1906, for instance, the number of French citizens working in public
services had already grown to 500,000 (1992, 82). The less one escaped
the government's reach, the more one subscribed to the "imagined
community" and the resulting nationalism.

THE CODING OF NATIONALISM IN FRANCE

Post-revolutionary nationalism, as Mette Zolner points out in her analysis of the construction of the French nation, extended as far as the colonies, where France took on a *mission to civilize* the indigenous peoples of Africa, America, and elsewhere (2000, 28). Zolner's analysis adds an interesting appendix to Hobsbawm's work, as it explores the nationalist roots of the recent immigration problems encountered by France. Zolner distinguishes between a nationalist discourse and a counter-nationalist one, both formulated during the nineteenth century (2000, 31).[6] As we have seen, the Republican model perpetuated by the French Revolution conceives of the nation as a political community where each individual participates voluntarily and by rational choice and right. The counter-national, for Zolner, appears in the period of economic and social crisis around the loss of Alsace-Lorraine. In her account, French counter-nationalism defines the nation as an ethnic and religious community in which people inherit position and privilege. Conceived by French doctrinary thinkers like Maurice Barrès and Charles Maurras, counter-national discourse subordinates the individual to collective law in order to reinforce a sort of history composed of traditional values and familiar sources of authority. Against an urban and diverse France, counter-nationalism offers a rural and Catholic depiction. But the dichotomy between these two divergent positions is not always quite so evident. Despite the fact that they confronted one another during certain historical periods – and particularly during the Third Republic – Zolner explains via the work of Michael Winnock that at other moments they can be confused in the words and actions of a single politician, like an Edmond Michelet or a Charles Péguy.[7] What always distinguishes the two rival discourses, however, are their positions on the Other – that is to say, the Other of France. Following Zolner's analysis of the two discourses in terms of coding, we see that Republican discourse assimilates the Other whereas the counter-national excludes it: "Thus, while the former coding was open to including peasants, Protestants, Jews, Catholics, colonised peoples and immigrants, the latter was closed, excluding the same categories as well as Cosmopolitans, Francsmaçons and others" (2000, 34). Zolner cites the cyclical resurgence of counter-national sentiment during the Dreyfus affair as well as around the xenophobic crises at the end of the nineteenth century and the 1930s clashes between French and immigrant workers. The culmination of all this, of course, came about with Vichy, which abolished the citizenship of Jews and foreigners, who had finally earned it only one century earlier. Nevertheless, the two discourses share a basic preconception that makes difference fundamentally antagonistic to the idea of nationhood. The Other is irreducible for those who follow the counter-national, whereas she or he is malleable for Republicans. In both cases, though, the homogeneity of the nation is an indispensable part of an imagined French community. French colonial expansion and its *civilizing mission* fall, for Zolner, under this same sort of pursuit of national homogeneity. Ultimately, her research probes rhetorical constructions in order to explore debates around the issue of colonialism and to demonstrate that at the turn of the twentieth century, the French were much more concerned with territorial acquisition overseas – to compensate for the traumatic loss of Alsace-Lorraine – rather than dealing with their immigrant populations at home. This in turn led to a renewed sense of nationalism bent on expanding French dominion by integrating new territory, the human toll of which was only confronted from the 1970s onwards and still continues today.

POSTCOLONIALISM: AN INTRODUCTION

While theories of nationalism have tried to contain migrants in explicit and implicit ways, postcolonial theory since its inception in the early 1970s has looked to the migrant as a somewhat salutary figure – one that best embodies the condition of those who seek not only to escape colonial paradigms and neocolonial oppression but to avoid the grasp of any totalizing entity such as the nation-state. The work of Homi Bhabha is instrumental in bringing this figure to the fore, as in *The Location of Culture*, wherein the "migrant" subject incarnates a progressive form of hybridity that can evade the hegemony of colonial discourses divided all-too cleanly between European colonial and non-occidental subjects. Bhabha's eloquent articulation of this problem has roots in the development of postcolonialism as a field of inquiry. To begin our search for the role of the migrant within this contemporary paradigm, we must begin by navigating the writings that founded a vast and nebulous domain that has been best characterized by passionate disagreements between its most fervent supporters.

In a 1972 article describing the role of a decolonized Pakistani state, Hamza Alavi proposed the word "postcolonial" as a replacement for "Third World," itself derived from the 1950s French term *tiers-monde* (1972). Like many of his contemporaries, Alavi used "postcolonial" to refer to states that gained independence after the dissolution of the colonial empire in Asia and Africa, but he added several important distinctions.[8] For Alavi, postcolonial states share two fundamental capitalist principles – an underdeveloped government system (supported by an overdeveloped indigenous bourgeoisie) and a society dominated by three main classes: a metropolitan bourgeoisie, an indigenous bourgeoisie, and property owners (Ahmad 1995). In response to this bipartite definition, other theorists launched a polemic. Among them was Aijaz Ahmad, who argued that Alavi's claims were far too based on the Pakistani situation. Ahmad points to Algeria, India, and Egypt as counter-examples, but it is Turkey that provides him with his own hypothesis. He rejects the idea that there is a government organization somehow "typical" of post-colonial states. Rather than speaking of the post-colonial as a condition uniting the newly independent, former colonies, Ahmad insists that all they share is a newfound, contradictory place in the global capitalist order.

Roughly concurrent to the Alavi-Amad debate about the temporality and definition of the post-colonial state, another discussion was emerging in the wake of May 1968 among post-structural theorists. Inspired by the fervor they saw in anti-colonialist movements, they began to discuss how to view the new cultural status of the "Third World." Many of them, according to Robert C. Young, viewed the Third World as an exciting new stage for the global proletarian struggle: "The common assumption [was] that the revolutionary stage had moved to Third-World struggle, that revolution would be made not in Paris, Rome, Berlin but in Johannesburg, Hanoi and Santiago" (2004, 114). In *White Mythologies*, Young traces a history of post-colonialism whereby what we will term a "second" polemic arises from a combination of anti-colonialist movements and post-structuralist theory that is both North American and European of lineage and which is no longer simply Marxist but Mao-inspired. It was a more general theoretical intervention, galvanized by the political groundswell against the hegemonic ideology of the colonial, capitalist Western powers. Here, questions concerning the postcolonial condition gradually took precedence over the terms of the earlier debate about the postcolonial state. Among these, two became foundational – one modelled by Indian historiographers belonging to the Subaltern Studies Group, and the other by literary theorists of what we might call a postcolonial "poetics." While both versions characterize the postcolonial as a struggle against colonialism via the recognition of specific historical situations, the first (Subaltern Studies) does so through revisionist, nationalist history, while the second (Bhabha et al.) approaches similar questions from the perspective of a transnational poetics of "hybridity." In either case, though, the "post" signals a purposeful and *meta-temporal* move away from the colonial – one that was first articulated in the influential work of Edward Said.

SAID'S ENLIGHTENED MIGRANT

In *Orientalism*, Said works to unveil a binary system of thinking in the Occident that groups all Third World countries into a fantasized "Orient." In a Nietzschean vein inspired by Foucault, Said evokes the mythical Other created by an Occident in search of legitimizing discourses by which to understand, control, manipulate, and even assimilate difference. His critique of this fundamental opposition in Western thought can be seen as a sort of first premise for postcolonialism today. Put simply, we must move beyond the notion of anti-colonialism to find a reality no longer defined by a dialectic born of opposition, but by a call to historical and political consciousness for all people of the world (1979, 328). *Orientalism* succeeds in revealing the profound complicity between received ideas and powerful institutions in the West, and Said's great contribution remains his illumination of the ethnocentrism inherent to much of Western scholarship and criticism, which tends to re-impose its own ideologies despite its attempts to respond responsibly to the Third World. Such a politicized situation can only be remedied, Said argues, through a more situational type of writing that engages directly with the socio-cultural position of the writer. The goal of *Orientalism* is to reverse preconceptions about what was called "the Orient" and to strip theoretical, historical, and political language of a facile dualism between East and West. No doubt, Said's work succeeds in building a profound distrust of the term "Orient" itself – one that remains with us today, even beyond the academic world.

Despite the general eloquence and strength of his argument, Said proves unable to completely shed the totalizing discourse that he theorizes so successfully in *Orientalism* and thereby encounters a methodological problem. In evoking a mythic "Orient" created by the Occident, he submits that there must also be a *real* Orient to which said "Orientalists" will never have access. He thereby implies that access to the Orient is not always blocked, and allows that one solution to the problem might occur through the notion of "human encounters." As James Clifford emphasizes, the very humanism through which Said hopes to escape the orientalist trap, is actually laden with Western principles (1998, 255–76). In his critique, Young follows suit by showing that Said presupposes an elite, European, intellectual culture since he rejects the complicity between "culture" and the State (2004, 172). Said subscribes, therefore, to the same knowledge paradigms that he reproaches. As a consequence, Said's response to that which he opposes appears fundamentally ambivalent.

Nevertheless, our goal here is less to revisit the polemics surrounding *Orientalism* than to uncover Said's vision of the immigrant as it is implied in this foundational text of postcolonial theory. The figure of the migrant appears, it turns out, in the task that Said lays out for the enlightened critics of Orientalism. For instance, in citing Auerbach, from whom he borrows a great deal of his humanism, Said writes: "The man who finds his homeland sweet is still a tender beginner; he to whom every soil is as his native one is already strong; but he is perfect to whom the entire world is a foreign land" (1979, 259).

We begin to find here a special theoretical place forged for the intellectual, one characterized by a state of perpetual *migrancy* or cosmopolitanism. Through Auerbach, Said hence takes us from nationalism to a new state of being, born of emigration and its persistent state of alienation, which permits a type of human experience that lies beyond the bonds of national alliances. In other words, it is only by transcending the ideological claims of nationhood that one can think and situate oneself outside the norm. It is in this way that Said's intellectual, thriving on her critical conscience, manages to evade the determinate nature of a cultural system that, among other things, created Orientalism.

BHABHA'S POETICS OF MIGRATION

Without explicitly invoking migrancy, Said's borrowing from Auerbach thus presents the fundamentals that would later inspire Bhabha to fashion his own postcolonial conception of the migrant subject. In his critique of the work of Said, Bhabha pushes Said's reasoning to its limits. While probing the ambivalence created by the distinction between what Said calls "manifest" Orientalism and "latent" Orientalism, Bhabha highlights two separate usages of the term – one intended as a *discipline* and the other as a *spirit*. In this way, Bhabha shows the crucial conflict that is inherent to Western powers, and one that the colonial enterprise squarely reproduced. The basis of colonial discourse, for Bhabha, is hence contradictory – the colonial subject is every bit as divided in its representation of self as is the representation of its object, the colonized. Bhabha rereads Said through a psychoanalytic lens, from which the latter had borrowed terms without pursuing the analysis. Via the concepts of stereotype and fetish, he introduces what he calls the "structural link" and the "functional link" in Said's work, both of which overlook, for Bhabha, the manner in which the colonial subject disavows difference:

> The construction of colonial discourse is then a complex articulation of the tropes of fetishism – metaphor and metonymy – and the forms of narcissistic and aggressive identification available to the Imaginary. Stereotypical racial discourse is then a four-term strategy. There is the tie-up between the metaphoric and the masking function of the fetish and the narcissistic object-choice and an opposing alliance between the metonymic figuring of lack and the aggressive phase of the imaginary. One has then a repertoire of conflictual positions that constitute the subject in colonial discourse. (1990, 204)

Orientalism omits what Bhabha calls the colonizer's "strategy of disavowal," since it occupies a position identical to that of Said himself. In Bhabha's reading, it is inevitable that Said falls into the very ambivalence he criticizes. For if Said falls into contradiction, it is because he neglects to situate himself in the in-between space that Bhabha's work strives to legitimize through the figure of the migrant.

By now renowned as *the* critique of the postcolonial condition, Bhabha's theoretical model for reading ambivalence challenges other contemporary postcolonial theorists, among them the influential volume by Bill Ashcroft, Gareth Griffiths, and Helen Tiffin, *The Empire Writes Back: Theory and Practice in Post-Colonial Literature*. Whereas Ashcroft and his colleagues seek to define a geopolitical and literary field for post-colonialism, Bhabha challenges such a categorization since it promulgates a cultural conscience for formerly colonized countries that is, in the end, quite national. In place of this, Bhabha suggests, postcolonialism should embrace a transnational approach, since it concerns itself less with emancipation at the national level than with a complete reversal of hegemonic colonial discourse on a global scale. To this end, he proposes a mimetic model that emerges in a series of articles, first called "mimicry" and then fetishism, hybrid, hybridization,[9] and finally paranoia.[10] In proposing this string of terms, Bhabha refuses to designate his own privileged position, choosing instead a place of ambivalence rather than anchoring himself to a univocal discourse that would go against his larger project. Young compares this theoretical maneuver to a performative narration: "Each essay can be seen as illuminating specific moments in the ambivalent and cumulative apparatus of colonial discourse ... Each text is both placed in its historical moment and gradually shifted from any single determination or linear development as Bhabha elaborates the complex problem of his reading" (2004, 186). This interpretation highlights the deliberate complexity of Bhabha's position on colonial discourse, as well as the difficulty it presents for readers, embracing a set of terms that are most characterized, in the end, by shifting meaning. Not surprisingly, this is the angle that most of Bhabha's critics take on his writing, arguing that a thesis is impossible to extract without recourse to ambiguous language. Even so, it is by uniting the form of his writing with the form of his thought that Bhabha escapes the contradiction and avoids participating – at least stylistically – in the hegemony that his argument rejects.

In the introduction to *The Location of Culture*, Bhabha makes use of the Freudian notion of *unheimlich* to present his vision of the liminal and contingent space of the *hybrid*. He calls into question a concept of homogeneous national culture, and proposes a postcolonial aesthetic based on movement and translation. At the centre of this evasive model, Bhabha theorizes a "migrant" subject who embodies the hybrid and inhabits the in-between, one of Bhabha's chosen few who is capable of personifying the ambivalence of a Third space. Bhabha evokes the example of displaced and minority populations who are not contained by the *Heim* of the nation – among them "migrants" (1994, 164). For Bhabha, even the "anti" falls back on the very notions it opposes, thereby reinforcing nationalist cultural imperatives and recycling their totalizing superiority. The migrant is therefore the centre of a new cultural paradigm, capable of seeing two sides without ever putting down roots. Postcolonial discourse is anchored in these stories of cultural displacement and the lives of those who are exiled by History. As such it contributes to a re-examination of the concept of culture itself, re-writing it from a position of marginality: "The affective experience of social marginality – as it emerges in non-canonical cultural forms – transforms our critical strategies. It forces us to confront the concept of culture outside *objets d'art* or beyond the canonization of the 'idea' of aesthetics, to engage with culture as an uneven, incomplete production of meaning and value, often composed of incommensurable demands and practices, produced in the act of social survival" (1994, 172). Culture, in this sense, becomes a strategy for survival, one to which the migrant must cling in order to traverse the chasm between nations. In this sense, culture is both trans-national and "translational" – or, put differently, the transnational aspect of culture resides in the very act of translation that defines it. Bhabha prefers the cultural transformations and dislocations purveyed by phenomena like migration, diaspora, and displacement to the unifying discourse that underlies myths like "nation," "peoples," and "folkloric authenticity" because he insists that the particularities of culture linked to a people/nation/country are nothing short of illusion. Postcolonialism, for Bhabha, derives from a pluralism or a relativism enacted by the condition of the migrant – who, hybrid by nature, represents its apotheosis.

Bhabha's model serves as the basis for many postcolonial critiques that come in its wake, mostly because it offers an alternative to binary thinking between the West and the Third World, conjuring a liminal space for postcolonial literature. At the same time, because of the ambiguity of Bhabha's own writing, critics often seek to nuance the view that his work deploys. In the following paragraphs, we will look at the responses of certain Western intellectuals to this vein of post-colonialism influenced by Bhabha. We would be remiss not to point out that all of the literary theory covered to this point comes from the American academy, even though many of the authors are originally from the Third World. By the same token, the inspiration for their texts can quickly be traced to French post-structuralism – Derrida, Lacan, Foucault – and the German philosopher Nietzsche. In other words, the reversal of colonial archetypes proposed by post-colonial thinkers remains strongly anchored in Western thought. Our goal in studying the critics that follow is to reveal the conflict between the poetics that Bhabha proposes, on the one hand, and the veiled history for which this theory can be criticized on the other – i.e., the prominence of American academe in the very definition of postcolonial studies. We will begin by looking at the collective work of the *Subaltern Studies* group which represents, for us, the neglected element of the aesthetic postcolonialism of Bhabha and his predecessors. The role of this group becomes even more important in the confrontation between East and West, which continually resurfaces in the work of many postcolonial critics.

Benita Parry, for instance, finds in Bhabha's postcolonial theory a way to reconfigure identity. She points to the precedence of a diasporic point of view in the work, for example, of the poetic representation of German revolutionary Rosa Luxembourg and critic Walter Benjamin, as well as in the art of American artist R.B. Kitaj: "Identity is now perceived as multi-located and polysemic – a situation that characterizes postcoloniality and is at its most evident in the diasporic condition. An uninhibited statement of the gratification of inhabiting many cultures, and identifying with all oppressions and persecutions, while electing to be affiliated to one's natal community, comes from the artist R.B. Kitaj, in whose paintings Rosa Luxembourg and Walter Benjamin are emblematic figures of that particular and permanent condition of diaspora in which he is at home" (1994, 175). Parry, however, also wants to re-appropriate the critical role of anti-colonialism for its reversal of colonial hierarchy and divestment of definitions of the colonized. For her, to revisit the steps that lead to postcolonialism means to appreciate the revisionist value of the "anti" without dwelling on its tendency toward inverse ethnocentrism. Parry argues that postcolonialism tends to evacuate meaning from anti-colonialism by reducing it to the binarism between colonized/colonizer. Rather, she proposes a historical turn toward anti-colonialism and seeks to rehabilitate it through a postcolonial perspective that can veer away from excessive theorization and abstraction. Echoing Parry in her own way, Barbara Christian sounds the alarm bell about literary theory that becomes too abstracted from the political reality that it should, in the first instance, seek to elucidate.

Steven Slemon, for his part, calls into question the trans-historical dimensions of a postcolonialism like Bhabha's, which make it difficult to isolate and describe theoretical moves. Slemon likens Bhabha's theoretical gesture to a transposition of postcolonial power dynamics into the domain of writing itself. For Slemon, postcolonialism represents first and foremost the relationship between writing and power – and within this, its possibility of resistance. Here again, then, we encounter the poetic dimension of post-colonialism that Bhabha's oeuvre works so hard to put in place. Bhabha's model collapses nonetheless, at least for Slemon, when one tries to apply it to a multiplicity of different cultures because it ignores the ways in which colonial power takes on specific forms within each of these cultures. Slemon fears, among other things, the imposition of a sort of theory of "resistance" conceived by the West for the Third World: "A *theory* of literary resistance *must* recognize the inescapable partiality, the incompleteness, the untranscendable *ambiguity* of literary or indeed *any* contra/dictory or contestatory act which employs a First-World medium for the figuration of a Third-World resistance, and which predicates a semiotics of *refusal* on a gestural mechanism whose first act must always be an acknowledgment and a *recognition* of the reach of colonialist power" (1996, 74). Bhabha's postcolonialism is thus inherently linked to the American intellectual milieu, and to the very colonial gesture it ostensibly aims to deconstruct. Postcolonial theory is not free of the nefarious links between criticism and the colonial enterprise, no matter how abstract or disordered its internal musings become. Moreover, postcolonialism should never pretend to remove itself from the strident debates necessary for question-

ing its own theoretical status and its ability to subvert the dominant
forces within its functional paradigm. In this way, the theory itself must
be characterized by a sort of continual regeneration, itself inflamma-
tory and openly contradictory.

THE MIGRANT AS WESTERN INTELLECTUAL

Kwame Anthony Appiah, in his analysis of post-colonialism via post-
structuralism, points out two important "waves" in Francophone postcolonial thought. For Appiah, the second generation of this writing
adopts a trans-national aesthetic that holds universal ethics over and
above any nationalist sanctioning of tradition. He makes reference to
the cultural contamination that preceded the traditional, monolithic
division between Africa and the West. But he also remains suspicious of
a post-colonial project comprised of intellectuals, or what he calls *a
comprador* intelligentsia: "Postcoloniality is the condition of what we
might ungenerously call a *comprador* intelligentsia: a relatively small,
Western-style, Western-trained group of writers and thinkers, who me-
diate the trade in cultural commodities of world capitalism at the periphery" (1996, 62). Even though the most important thinkers of
post-colonialism are often from diverse origins in the Third World, their
writing is a specimen of Western education, where they participate in
a debate initiated and supported in Western bastions of knowledge. Appiah, borrowing the terminology of Immanuel Wallerstein, insists that
postcolonial intellectuals have a tendency to want to dictate rules for
the *periphery* from their privileged perches in the capitalist *centre*. To
the contrary, he maintains that Africa has never seen itself as Other and
that its cultural production merits consideration independent from a
postcolonial criticism that poses as an explanation for its conditions
of production.

Following Appiah's lead, Arif Dirlik responds to Ella Shohat's famous
question about the precise moment when post-colonialism intervenes
in world history. For Dirlik, the answer is the very moment when Appiah's *comprador* intelligentsia enters the picture in the Western world.
The advent of post-colonialism coincides, for Dirlik, with the arrival of
intellectuals from the Third World in the great institutions of the West
(1996, 294). Dirlik's work thereby highlights the shift between the
terms "Third World" and "postcolonial" as a replacement of a fixed geographic position (far too vague to help understand the heterogeneous
historical circumstances of the societies that make it up) to a consciousness of the global exchanges that encapsulate these very societies.

Post-colonial history thus exists more in relation to subject positioning than it does to national origin. Dirlik therefore accuses postcolonial intellectuals of having created a discursive identity for postcolonialism that reflects only themselves – a discourse that unfolds according to an epistemological universalist pretension that only characterizes the West (1996, 302).

Like Young, Dirlik perceives the great influence of post-structuralism in postcolonial language, and aligns it with a deconstructed, decentred Marxism. As a Marxist himself, Dirlik interprets postcolonial thought as a condition of world capitalism of which postcolonial intellectuals are the beneficiaries and not the victims. Through Eurocentrism, which resides at the heart of this new capitalism of global proportions, and transnationalism, which abstracts everything, the migrant intellectual finds a language and creates a theoretical field that confers a new form of power. Postcolonialism is thus yet another quest for power rooted in the West – power that profits from the dependence of the rest of the world. The question that Dirlik asks is an important one about the responsibility of postcolonial criticism toward what it represents and, moreover, about its realistic capacity to even call into question its own ideological moorings, much less to formulate a practical form of resistance against the system to which it owes its own existence.

THE MIGRANT IN SUBALTERN STUDIES

Opposition to a post-colonialism conceived and practised in the West was a founding tenet of the second strain we are isolating here, developed in the first instance by the *Subaltern Studies* group. Founded during the 1970s, the group made its goal a re-writing of the history of India from the point of view of subaltern classes. It later found an international audience thanks to the publication in Delhi of the series *Subaltern Studies: Writings on South Asian History and Society*. The first volume of five appeared in 1982 and included a foundational article by Ranajit Guha, editor-in-chief and a contributing historiographer. For Guha, the history of Indian nationalism has been dominated by an elitism, both colonial and bourgeois-nationalist, born from the English presence in the country. Even after independence and the transfer of powers, this elitism lives on in the neo-colonialist and neo-nationalist discourses of Great Britain and India, which Guha proposes should be countered with a study of nationalism in its more popular forms. "What clearly is left out of this un-historical historiography is the *politics of the people*" writes Guha, describing the autonomous domain that makes up working class India's contribution to anti-colonialist struggle (1988, 40). A new form of historiography, as proposed by Guha and his colleagues, gives a primary role to these subaltern classes for whom political mobilization happens in a horizontal fashion, contrary to the vertical processes favoured by the elite. The central problem arises from this historical blockage suffered by the Indian nation, specifically in its inability to assure a victory over colonialism. For Guha, this blockage contributes to the ongoing deficiencies of both the Indian bourgeoisie and the working class.

In an articled entitled "The Prose of Counter-Insurgency," Guha analyzes the discourse of counter-insurgence and examines documents written by British officers during the brief delays following or preceding an act of insurgency. His study focuses most often on memos or letters issued by military councils, usually with the goal of responding to popular insurrections and of preventing future outbreaks. Guha proceeds to examine the historiographic discourses of colonialism, and his interpretation emphasizes in particular the temporal lag between historical events and their narration. Foucauldian of inspiration, the task of the Subaltern Studies Group turns therefore toward an analysis of colonial and anti-colonial discourses in primary documents drawn from the post-colonial moment itself. Since imperialism can be said to infiltrate Marxism, they adopt the notion of the "subaltern" from Antonio Gramsci's *Prison Notebooks* in order to designate those classes dominated by a hegemonic situation. They therefore work to unveil the real exploitation and domination of Western capitalism, realities to which even Marxist critics – and their theoretical tools – have often been blind.

As a whole, the field of Subaltern Studies strives to add a politico-economic dimension to discussions about postcolonialism. It does so by revealing the material conditions that subtend the "hybridity" propagated by Bhabha and other American intellectuals. On this view, any study of post-colonial aesthetics should be doubted for the ways in which its own discourses mask the structures of power which allow certain social classes to be "hybrid" while others not. One need only think here of the distinction between immigrant intellectuals, so well-placed to draw from multiple cultures and cultivate hybrid sensibilities, and immigrant workers, who are often excluded completely from the majority cultures in their new locales. Certainly literary critics like Bhabha should be included in the ranks of the postcolonialist movement. But one must always consider the economic conditions of those authors who are both minorities and immigrants – that is to say, those individuals who will comprise later the focus of this study. In this way, *Subaltern Studies* contributes a vital caveat to our theoretical discussion of postcolonialism, insisting that we look behind theoretical abstractions of "hybridity" to the material conditions and livelihoods of migrant subjects. Without this added dimension, hybridity runs a risk of turning into a sort of apology for the inequalities endemic to the global economic order, themselves a crucial part of any study of transnationalism or globalization. Indeed, the frequency of these last two terms in recent years only reinforces the urgency of this argument as postcolonial debates continue today. For Guha and his colleagues, what is really at stake here is a new sort of historiography, one that calls for more vigilance about exploited populations and that is alert to how criticism itself can fall prey to the lithe machinations of hegemony.

It is within this context that we must now add the work of Gayatri Chakravorty Spivak, which redefines the postcolonial one more time. The translator of Derrida's *Grammatology* to English in 1976, Spivak made her own entrance on the postcolonial scene as a feminist and Marxist-deconstructionist, inspired by Derrida's methods of rethinking not only imperialism and colonialism, but also the intellectual presuppositions and institutional affiliations of those who had shaped postcolonial studies to that point. Spivak begins by recognizing her own engagement in the system she opposes, promoting a form of criticism that plays on the writer's own subjective status, and also on how that socio-political identity subtends all acts of writing. Even though she began as a member of the Subaltern Studies Group, Spivak is less interested in the reinterpretation of colonial history than she is in how imperialism infiltrates contemporary academia. A first article to this effect, published in 1981, discusses the imperialist presuppositions of French – and by extension Western – feminism in its relationship to the Third World. In her most influential essay, "Can the Subaltern Speak?" Spivak calls into question the representation of Third World subjects in discursive production of the West. Through a study of the epistemic violence inherent to the British codification of Hindu law, Spivak reveals the complicity between the international economic interests and the intellectual production of the West. Addressing her own place as a member of the North American intellectual community, Spivak insists on the need to unlearn the forms of ideology that she claims haunt a Freudian understanding of language. Rather than trying to give the "Third-World woman" a voice to speak, Spivak measures the discursive power of this subject's silence, arguing that this non-participation is the only true resistance to universal ideology. She also warns of a new orientalist tendency within postcolonial studies to fetishize difference by claiming "the world as immigrant" (1990, 228). Later, in her exhaustive analysis of post-colonial theory called *Postcolonial Reason: Towards a Theory of the Vanishing Present*, Spivak probes the fields of philosophy, history, literature, and cultural studies in search of an imperialist current that contaminates all texts through an omnipresent episteme of reason. Spivak signals here the foreclosure of the indigenous subject whom she terms the "native informant" in the foundational texts of the West, and particularly in the works of Kant and Hegel. She traces the vicissitudes of this native informant as a critical and literary figure (1999, 112). Her analyses are always aimed at the biases of philosophy, even though her work betrays its own parasitic debts to the contributions of Kant and Hegel. In this, she finds her main theoretical flaw in fact – for even as Spivak chides German philosophy for its oversights, she also criticizes contemporary theorists for reproducing their "principle of reason from within," which guides a perception of both the West and the Third World. In Spivak, the native confronts an inevitable, (im)possible impasse since she, as a pariah in Indian society, has no way of participating in language and in the discourses that are being formulated about her. Yet it is our consciousness of the native's presence and our acknowledgement of her silence that constitutes the sole escape to the paradox that is her life, especially as it is represented in postcolonial discourse. In the appendix to her celebrated book, Spivak offers a further refinement of her thought, this time in the guise of summary: "I have attempted to imagine or construct (im)possible practices, re-constelled classics into implausible and impertinent readings for the sake of disciplinary critique, applauded gestures that could not lead to a model for action, made an effort, indeed, to take a distance from the principle of reason from within, without inclining toward irrationalism: obtuse angling" (1999, 336). This "obtuse" Spivakian prose is thus also a philosophical and literary method for trying to preserve postcolonialism from its own ghost. Haunted by Western logic, molded from multiple centuries of European rationalism, postcolonialism as a current poetic-aesthetic or historiographic practice cannot hope to leave its own origins behind.

Spivak's critics have been great in number within the American academy and elsewhere, and they most often reproach her for embracing a discourse that verges many times on nonsense. Terry Eagleton, for instance, offers one of the most scathing attacks on Spivak in which he highlights her purposeful obscurantism, her arrogant dilettantism, and her aggressive (and very American) cult of personality. A resolute Marx-

ist, Eagleton cannot resist calling Spivak out for her own, ironic participation in a form of colonial auto-performance, wherein the "subject"
becomes the focal point of all analysis, even while it tries to excuse itself from that practice through excessive self-development. Eagleton's
critique, famous for both his virulence and for his clear appreciation
for Spivak's work, calls once again for a political denunciation of the
postcolonial movement, where he sees a focus on celebrity personalities
obscuring both the abject conditions of class struggle in the West and
the lack of organized, revolutionary nationalisms in the former
colonies. In other words, postcolonial studies go hand-in-hand with
world capitalism and the birth of the American empire, substituting
an interest for the most destitute populations of the world for a class
consciousness that should include both the domestic and foreign consequences of America's neo-liberal superstructure.

THE MIGRANT EXOTIC

As a whole, we might say that the most elemental part of postcolonial
studies has been a pervasive concern with trying to displace the subject
of analysis. All along, the figure of the migrant finds itself implicated
in the very centre of this discussion, whether as a point of poetic escape, as a rallying point for concerns about the writing of history, or as
a necessary obstacle for the path of intellectual inquiry itself. Here, we
propose a study that extracts the writer from this postcolonial theoretical context in order to analyze his or her contributions to a national
and international economy that makes writing the experience of migrancy into a commodity.[11] For this, Graham Huggan's *The Postcolonial
Exotic: Marketing the Margins* (2001) is a crucial theoretical move away
from a postcolonial aesthetic of resistance and on to analyses that place
the postcolonial writer at the centre of a global capitalist economy. Huggan points to the ways in which exoticism is *repoliticized* "to unsettle
metropolitan expectations of cultural otherness" (2001, ix), while it is
also a much sought-after consumer product of late capitalism. Huggan's
discussions of the exoticist production of otherness as both dialectical
and contingent (2001, 13) is especially useful for the types of analyses
we will pursue in the second half of this book because he places the
postcolonial text at the intersection of cultural assimilation and diversity. Sarah Brouillette takes Huggan's insights one step further in suggesting that the postcolonial author is an agent of his or her own
strategic exoticism and self-consciousness (2007). As an outgrowth of
postcolonialism and postcoloniality – as Huggan distinguishes one

from the other[12] – the migrant text is constantly caught in the lure of, and struggle against, exoticism and otherness. It is precisely this tension, however, that also ensures the viability of this literature and the strategic creativity of its authors for the global age.

THE MIGRANT IN POSTCOLONIAL THOUGHT FROM THE FRENCH-SPEAKING WORLD

As Achille Mbembe argues in "Provincializing France?" postcolonial studies in the Hexagon have lagged disturbingly behind much of the Anglo-saxon world despite efforts in recent times by the *Achac* research group of historians and literary scholars such as Jean-Marc Moura to introduce postcolonial thought into French academic inquiry and imagination.[13] Mbembe's essay is particularly accusatory in tone since France was the birthplace – and French the original language – of significant anticolonial writing exemplified in the work of Aimé Césaire, Frantz Fanon, Albert Memmi, Jean-Paul Sartre, and Jean Genet for example. While postcolonialism has met with virulent criticism in France over the last thirty years, theoretical contributions to postcolonial thought in French have mostly occurred back in the United States, insists Mbembe, thanks to the likes of Maryse Condé, Valentin Mudimbe, and Édouard Glissant.[14] On the other hand, Charles Forsdick and David Murphy's *Postcolonial Thought in the French-speaking World* (2009) makes a case for theoretical contributions to postcolonial thought not only by Mbembe's three aforementioned thinkers – to whom they also add Assia Djebar, Jacques Derrida, and Abdelkébir Khatibi – but by that earlier "anticolonial" generation as well (including Césaire, Fanon, Memmi, Senghor, Sartre, and Ho Chi Minh).[15] Forsdick and Murphy's edited volume reclaims these thinkers for the postcolonial project even though much of their work predates the coining of the term as it is deployed in critical circles today.

Discussions of the migrant in postcolonial theory, as thus more broadly defined by Forsdick and Murphy, have been remarkably absent in postcolonial French-language texts, however, unlike their counterpart in the English language.[16] Immigration, on the contrary, remains a crucial cornerstone of this critical discourse in French particularly in the work of Édouard Glissant and Maryse Condé whose Caribbean-birthed models for global belonging are based on a history of multiple migrations. Both Glissant and Condé have been called *post*-postcolonial thinkers in that their work has evolved past a concern with the colonial legacy and postcolonial struggles of the Caribbean to tackle the question of diversity as it applies to all world cultures today.[17] With migration as the marker of a globalizing world, Glissantian concepts such as "opacité" and "relation" are meant to cultivate a sensitivity for all that which is untranslatable between different systems of cultural representation and yet remain invariably linked, interdependent, and interlocking. In his *Traité du Tout-monde*, what we might call Glissant's epistemology of the global, he seeks to foster awareness for analogous phenomena taking place across different cultures and time zones in order to make better local citizens of us all. Thus conceived, it is the poeticized condition of migration, or perhaps a "migrant epistemology," that is at the heart of Glissant's new global imaginary. I need not rehearse here the varied accusations of utopian abstractionism that have been levered against Glissantian thought. One need only conclude that what Glissant perhaps imagined in less concrete terms, we are here endeavouring to anchor back in the material conditions of migration in order to truly extract what a poetics of migration may look like in literary terms.

GLISSANT'S MIGRATIONAL CONSCIOUSNESS

In his very first essay *Le Soleil de la conscience* (1956), Edouard Glissant uses a form akin to the prose poem to detail his experience of Paris from the perspective of the colonized Martiniquan. This essay, which not only sets the stage for his next major work *Le Discours Antillais* (1981), as Romuald Fonkoua's analysis of *Le Soleil de la conscience* as Antillean ethnography suggests (1995, 798), foregrounds much of Glissant's later thought as well, from *Poétique de la Relation* (1990) and *Introduction à une poétique du divers* (1996) to his *Traité du Tout-monde* (1997) and *La Cohée du Lamentin* (2005).[18] In this part poem, part philosophical treatise, the Glissantian narrator goes in search of a new consciousness of the self that draws on a knowledge born of two divergent environmental experiences: the Caribbean sun and European snow. Much like Aimé Césaire whose Martiniquan coming-to-awareness requires a momentary return to Paris in his *Cahier d'un retour au pays natal* (1939), Glissant's text alternates between the island tropics and the île de France. While Césaire's return to his island home will, however, be a definitive one in the end, Glissant's narrator continues to move back and forth in order to engage in long-desired dialogue: "Telle m'est la neige: une illumination ... une ouverture ... l'élargissement, la communication établie (la neige aussi : une, durable, définitive que le soleil), le pouvoir maintenant d'accélérer le dialogue, de serrer de près les raisons communes, comme au coin d'un feu" (1956, 18). [Such is the snow to me: an illumination ... an opening ... the enlarging, the establishment of communication (snow also: one, enduring, definitive like the sun), the power now to accelerate the dialogue, to hold close our common reasons, like kindled by the fireplace.] Migration thus opens up the possibility for understanding through this environmental encounter between the familiar and the unfamiliar. Yet for Glissant, as it will be always, the dialogic exchange can only take place through the poetic medium, that is postcolonial consciousness occurs in the literary meeting space between the here and elsewhere: "Le poème offre au lecteur un espace qui satisfait son désir de bouger, d'aller hors de lui-même, de voyager par une terre nouvelle, où pourtant il ne se sentira pas étranger" (1956, 33). [The poem offers the reader a space that satisfies his desire to move, to go outside himself, to travel to a new land, where he will nonetheless not feel estranged.] This then is precisely what Glissant enacts in *Le Soleil de la Conscience*, a poetic journey towards a "sun" that is only accessible through the weight of a snow flake: "Si tu subis sans faiblesse l'étoile de neige et sa pesée sur ton corps, alors tes yeux s'ouvrent à l'espace ensoleillé de la mémoire" (1956, 43). [If you suffer without weakness the snow star and its weight upon your body, then your eyes will open onto the sun-filled space of memory.] Paris, France, and its connotative snow is likened by Glissant to a vaccine (1956, 51) that inoculates against simple binaries and allows for more meaningful crossings of the Atlantic ocean, strong from the knowledge that one remains bound in solidarity to both lands, albeit for very different reasons: to Martinique "zone de plus grande aisance" [the greatest comfort zone] and to Paris "où j'ai su tant d'autres visages de la connaissance" [where I came to know so many other faces of knowledge] (1956, 54). Migration for Glissant is the eye-opening tool that literature must above all mobilize to knock down walls and continuously move people beyond their own land and toward new ones.

What I here interpret as a migrational consciousness in this first essay by Glissant, other scholars have read as an ethnographic interrogation of the Caribbean and his Martiniquan identity anchored in the poetics of exile and what Michael Dash calls "a phase of creative dislocation": "The orderliness of the European landscape, the rhythmic measure of changing seasons, create for Glissant a kind of psychic unease" (1995, 12). Such agitation will eventually lead to the need for Glissant's "chaos d'écriture" [chaos of writing] that is already set up in *Le Soleil de la conscience*. Indeed, if we can identify certain tropes of migration in Glissant here, its inevitable transcendence or collapse is also signaled from the moment when geography loses its absolute hold over the movement of peoples ("le moment où la géographie cesse d'être absolue" [1956, 69]). Confronting landscapes (mountains, seas, sands, and volcanoes), climates (sun, heat, cold, and snow), and architectures (stony rocks, cathedrals, train stations, etc.), rather than nation-states and ideologies, affords Glissant something of a way beyond migration, whereby the tool – once it has served its purpose – can be dissolved or surpassed in favour of the new-found consciousness or *co-naissance* as Dash calls it based on Glissant's summoning of other poetic influences (1995, 12). Glissant's poetics extend far into the reaches of abstraction, wherein migration is no longer sufficient to express movement because it is too wedded to territorial delimitations and delineations of land. It is, however, pivotal in bringing about new sensibilities: "non pas comme exaltation d'un Inconnu, mais comme manière enfin de se débarasser de son écorce pour connaître sa projection dans une autre lumière, l'ombre de ce que l'on sera" (1956, 69). [Not as exaltation of the Unknown, but as a way at last to rid oneself of one's shell in order to know one's projection in another light, the shadow of what one will be.] Glissant's philosophical turn via poetry leaves the physical realities of migration behind, privileging instead the self-awareness that it leaves in its wake.

CONDÉ'S CRÉOLITÉ

Maryse Condé advocates for a reimagining of créolité as originally defined by the famous writers of the *Éloge de la créolité* (1989), Jean Bernabé, Raphaël Confiant, and Patrick Chamoiseau, precisely because it remains inscribed in the struggles of a colonial legacy that she feels no longer applies to the reality of migrants today. Moving between countries and continents, Condé argues that Antilleans are mostly a population of migrants who must no longer be defined in relation to old colonial paradigms or racial, national, and territorial markers of authenticity. Aimé Césaire, she insists, came under weighty criticism for making such claims long before this reality became the norm, and yet today she sees no other real alternative (1995, 305). Condé is especially critical of Caribbean literature that is somehow stuck in a quest for ethnic authenticity that feeds the hunger for exoticism in metropolitan France (1995, 308). Furthermore, she rejects the dichotomous relationship between creole and French, arguing that each writer must forge his or her own literary language regardless of mother tongue. Quoting author Wilson Harris, she claims: "Language is the ground for an interi-

or and active expedition through and beyond what is already known"
(1995, 309). Condé thus embraces literary migrancy as a natural evolution out of colonial frameworks and onto new ways of defining texts.
As part of this new understanding of the literary venture, she also pushes towards a more individualized approach to the examination of literature, arguing that the writer must no longer be asked to speak for the
collective as in years past. No two writers from the Antillean region
share quite the same global itinerary; "N'y a-t-il pas des versions multi-
ples de l'antillanité ?" (1995, 310) [Are there not multiple versions of
Antillanity?] she asks.

Moving away from what she terms the "colonial obsession" (1995),
Condé is also largely indebted to Glissantian concepts that disturb not
only a monolithic understanding of culture and identity, but all dog-
matic uses of the postcolonial or, for that matter, any categorization
that limits the creativity and autonomy of individual writers and their
texts through reductive reading practices.[19] Migration – like historical
uncertainty as well as cultural and racial discord – are thus literary and
theoretical devices through which she disrupts the postcolonial when
its uses appear to replicate the very mechanisms it seeks to upset.[20] Although Condé's prolific body of work, including her debut novel *Here-
makhonon* (1976), *Désirada* (1979), *Traversée de la mangrove* (1985), and
many recent others, is full of migrant characters, they do not impose
any ideological reading upon the condition of migration other than
complicating identity, race, gender, language, and culture. Migrants are
then synonymous in her writing with plurality, complexity, and mystery. They are translated figures who – by virtue of their inherent movement between nations – become the untranslatable subjects of a global
consciousness. Condé in many ways echoes Spivak's concerns about
universal and generalized readings of varied experiences of migration.
She resists the postcolonial in a gesture that heeds Spivak's warnings
against the totalizing possibilities that inhere within all categorization
of texts. It is very much in light of this admonition of the postcolonial
that *The Migrant Text* seeks to mobilize migration as an open-ended
reading practice that looks for new ways to approach texts outside
the overarching and well-rehearsed frameworks of the national and the
postcolonial.

3

Creative Agency and Literary Markets

INTRODUCTION

No theory of the migrant text can exclude the market considerations that have made this type of literature especially viable today. This is a literature of otherness that falls prey to the fear of the market. It is a literature often written by immigrants themselves, one that deals in an exoticism that is exploited for the sake of the literary marketplace. These works are then packaged, distributed, and sold and when successful, reprinted, repackaged, and sold again. These are novels that capitalize on ethnic heritage, especially when it carries a seal of marked otherness, saddling writers with the expectations and hopes of their communities of origin as well as those of their new countries. The authors of migrant texts are then called upon as spokespeople, lauded as model citizens and simultaneously accused of betrayal and treachery. They walk the fine line between exploitation and resistance, navigating a tension that challenges the autonomy of their very creative enterprise.

The pages that follow are a defense of migrant texts written by immigrant writers and the economic impetus that shapes their work. This chapter pursues several different lines of inquiry in order to unearth the institutional biases, sociological underpinnings, and individual stories that make up the complex and often contradictory relationship of literature to economics and of money to the migrant mode of writing. As countries of mass immigration in the French-speaking world, the French and Canadian examples are indicative of a global phenomenon brought about by the uncomfortable beauty of a partnership between immigrants, literature, and economics. Graham Huggan (2001) and Sara Brouillette (2007) have both paved the way for this type of enquiry in their respective work on Anglophone postcolonial writers and their studies of how writers deal in exoticism and consciously negotiate authorial positioning within global literary markets. The following pages propose to do the same for migrant texts, first by staking out a theoretical space for market-driven analysis and then by offering empirical evidence of this reality in order to demonstrate how best-selling migrant texts are always entangled in the market ambitions of their authors.

The chapter concludes with five accounts of how individual authors in Montreal and Paris negotiated their work for the reading public, working with their editors to ensure sales, secure revenue, and permit themselves to continue pursuing a vocation in literature. Each of these writers wrestles with the otherness that his or her work betrays and is painfully aware of its role in cementing success in the literary marketplace. In mapping out five authorial journeys through the economic reality of the publishing industry, these case studies make an argument not only for the authenticity and brilliance of creative endeavours, but also for the singular wisdom and agency that each of these authors showed in carving his or her own destiny as an artist in an adopted country and an unfamiliar culture.

LITERATURE AS TRADE: A HISTORICAL OVERVIEW

To study the economics behind a literary object is to somehow begin with the premise that pricing a work of art is a problematic if not impossible task. Yet to deny the function of a literary work as a commodity circulating in a marketplace – not just of ideas, but of goods to be bought and sold – is to disavow the historical relationship that writers have always had to money.[1] As a number of recent studies suggest, the delineation between literature as a picture of social life and a product to be consumed is one of many sweeping changes that occurred in symbolic practices of the nineteenth century.[2] When editorial and publishing practices as we know them began to take shape, an economy of literature developed, blurring the lines between so-called "industrial fiction" and literature, even for those authors who would later become France's canonical names (Balzac, Zola, Damas, etc.). Thus began the ideological legacy of a struggle for literary legitimacy that would persist well into the next century, perpetuated by literary critics.

Following the separation drawn by Romanticism between artistic autonomy and consumer-oriented production came Marxist inflected criticism that perceives the writer as a victim of a system of production and consumption, and whose art is exiled to the sidelines of a capital-driven economy. Literature-as-trade here succumbs to fetishism and alienation because any literary work made first for market consumption is thought not to involve much reflection, let alone critique. Marxism and its offshoots (cultural materialism and new historicism) celebrate writing that challenges dominant cultural paradigms and admonish works that play too easily into hegemonic ideologies. This mode of literary thinking, initiated by the Russian formalist response to Romantic idealism[3] and then propelled to new heights by the Frankfurt School (Max Horkheimer, Theodor Adorno), the advent of Critical Theory (Jürgen Habermas), and the work of a number of other prominent theorists (György Lukács and Frederic Jameson in the US; Louis Pierre Althusser in France; Terry Eagleton in the UK), consolidated the stronghold of class-consciousness as a crucial determinant of literary interpretation.

In other words, most any discussion of economics in literature proceeds with modes of reading that filter through a Marxian master narrative. This tendency becomes even more prevalent in critical analyses of literature that springs "from the margins"; theorists mobilize the ideology to describe the political impetus of writing by society's disenfranchised others – those who are reputedly alienated by oppressive socio-economic forces but who are in turn working to resist them. Literary works deemed worthy of academic study thus tend to favour a Marxist sensibility, awakening class-consciousness and pointing out societal inequalities that pit those in power against their dispossessed others. Marx's economic system has thus been adapted for the study of literature almost exclusively over other economic models. Literary critics have been eager to align migrant writing with a postcolonial aesthetic – whether through an abstraction of the material realities of the migrant as we saw in chapter 2 or via a Marxist bent that critiques postcolonial readings for prioritizing the point of view of an intellectual and literary elite. Such a reading of the literature of immigration is most often validated with Deleuze and Guattari, whose Kafkan model of minor literature works in opposition to the "desiring-production" machine, articulating how a literature of migration can undermine capitalism's exploitation of difference.

Paul Cantor and Stephen Fox's recent anthology *Literature and the Economics of Liberty* stakes a claim against the preponderance of such readings. Cantor and Fox privilege the "methodological individualism" of Austrian economics as a way to promote the freedom of the author over the socio-economic forces that conspire to stifle his or her creativity. It is not the purpose of this chapter to espouse a pro-capitalist model, as do Cantor and Fox, but rather to glean insights from their analytical approach into the ways in which human agency can be an

empowering alternative to structurally enforced modes of literary production. Cantor's study of the Victorian-era serial novel looks at how
the actions of individual authors, publishers, and readers shape a given
work of literature. Crucial to this interpretation of literary production
is the active role that consumers play in the creative lives of authors.
Cantor points out that "the market operates as a feedback mechanism,
allowing consumers to send signals to producers that guide their busi-
ness plans" (2010, 68). Arguing against the complacency of a naïve exploited consumer body that falls prey to advertising and the dictates of
an all-powerful marketplace, he instead highlights the ways in which
author and reader collaborate and conspire together to bring about a
work of art. Capital – both intellectual and financial – is generated at
the nexus of creativity between artist and art-lover, author and reader,
filmmaker and audience. Moreover, other actors work to facilitate and
negotiate the sometimes fraught relationship between the sovereign
consumer and the hegemonic producer, thus implicating a veritable
network of subjectivities in the creative process. The Austrian economic
model, unlike the Marxist one, emphasizes the intentionality of all these
actors even while attributing a mediating role to the market. Cantor
writes, "Austrian economics shares with Marxism the possibility of understanding literature as the product of a social process, but because
Austrian economics understands social processes in individualistic
terms, it shares with traditional literary criticism an emphasis on the
intentionality of authors as individuals" (2010, 75). To inform our analysis of the migrant text from the perspective of Austrian economics is to
consider the creative impetus of the market itself as well as the individual agency of writers.

THE USES OF CAPITAL:
A SOCIOLOGICAL APPROACH

The French intellectual tradition has not been completely devoid of
consideration of creative agency and the literary market. Sociologist
Pierre Bourdieu made valuable inroads into the study of how literary
texts are tied to the economic survival of their writers, editors, and publishers. In an essay entitled "Mais qui a créé les créateurs?" Bourdieu signals the importance of intermediaries who, together with the artist,
produce a work of art:

> Bref, il s'agit de montrer comment s'est constitué historiquement le
> champ de production artistique qui, en tant que tel, produit la

croyance dans la valeur de l'art et dans le pouvoir créateur de valeur de l'artiste. Et l'on aura ainsi fondé ... que le "sujet" de la production artistique et de son produit n'est pas l'artiste mais l'ensemble des agents qui ont partie liée avec l'art, qui sont intéressés par l'art, qui ont intérêt à l'art et à l'existence de l'art, qui vivent de l'art et pour l'art, producteurs d'oeuvres considérées comme artistiques (grands ou petits, célèbres, c'est-à-dire célébrés, ou inconnus), critiques, collectionneurs, intermédiaires, conservateurs, historiens de l'art, etc. (1981, 221)

[In a word, the aim would be to describe the historical constitution of the field of artistic production, which as such, produces belief in the value of art and in the value-creating power of the artist. And that would give a basis for what I posited ... namely that the "subject" of artistic production and its product is not the artist but the whole set of agents who are involved in art, are interested in art, have an interest in art and the existence of art, who live on and for art, the producers of works regarded as artistic (great and small, famous – i.e. "celebrated" – and unknown), critics, collectors, go-betweens, curators, art historians, and so on. (1993a, 148)]

Bourdieu's seminal work on literature, *Les règles de l'art*, is a collection of pieces he began writing from the late 1960s that study the point at which literature and commerce converge and diverge in the publishing house as institution. His discussions of economics are always accompanied by a value judgment since he perceives the effects and influence of commerce as something that should be resisted in order to protect the autonomy of the work of art.

And yet, Bourdieu's theories also offer a willingness to engage with the economic side of literature, which alone is helpful for our current purposes. Through his three notions of capital (social, cultural, and symbolic), Bourdieu suggests more complex ways of evaluating the value of a writer and his or her work. More specifically, he maps out the relationships that these types of capital entertain to questions of economics. The literary field, according to Bourdieu, sectors off into symbolic and economic capital according to two different logics – the first is unconcerned with financial profit and in search of "pure art," while the latter bows to the whims and fancy of mass consumption and market dictates (1992, 202). This second logic does not share in the autonomy that Bourdieu ascribes to symbolic capital. On the other hand, this autonomy is also exempt of political affiliations, refusing all complicity with existing power structures. The best-selling author and literary work, on the other hand, subscribes to the opposite logic according to Bourdieu. Catering as it were to a pre-existing demand, their success is carefully orchestrated by editorial forces driven by a desire for the immediate – albeit furtive – nature of economic capital.

To study this dichotomous reality, Bourdieu opposes Parisian publishers Robert Laffont and the Éditions de Minuit. In 1976, the larger Laffont publishing house produced seven novels with copies printed in excess of 100,000, while fourteen others met the 50,000-copy benchmark. Bourdieu argues that Laffont's exceptional literary output inevitably relied on the help of a marketing division, involved large advertising and public relations budgets, and appealed to a selective literary politics ("une politique du choix") favouring works in translation with a guaranteed track-record abroad. Though their lists of bestsellers were extensive, Laffont's obviously commercial slant puts the literary quality of its production into question for Bourdieu. The Éditions de Minuit, on the other hand, a small, traditional, artisanal publisher with only a handful of novels exceeding the 3,000-copy threshold, is described as investing in the symbolic – and therefore long-term – value of literary works. Éditions de Minuit only remained afloat in the midseventies because of the slow but steady success of Samuel Beckett's canonical work from 1952 *En attendant Godot*. Of course, Bourdieu's analysis does not exclude the complexity of publishing houses like Gallimard which over the years devised a two-pronged approach to ensure both sales and literary consecration through its now famous collections.[4] Bourdieu's work, spanning some 30 years, studies the role of the editor in the field of literary production as both banker and purveyor of art, investing as it were for short-term financial gain and longer-term cultural equity. The author's complicated complicity with this editorial hand is a reality Bourdieu returns to time and time again because of what he calls the "repression of personal interest" – meaning economic interest – that informs the relationship:

> Adversaires complices, ceux qui fabriquent les œuvres d'art et ceux qui en font commerce se réfèrent, on le voit, à la même loi qui impose la répression de toutes les manifestations directes de l'intérêt personnel, au moins en sa forme ouvertement « économique », et qui a toutes les apparences de la transcendance bien qu'elle ne soit que le produit de la censure croisée qui pèse à peu près également à chacun de ceux qui la font peser sur tous les autres (1977, 8).

[The makers and marketers of works of art are adversaries in collusion, who each abide by the same law which demands the repression of direct manifestations of personal interest, at least in its overly "economic" form, and which has every appearance of transcendence although it is only the product of the cross-censorship weighing more or less equally on each of those who impose it on all the others. (1993b, 79–80)]

Here Bourdieu suggests that the acknowledgement of financial interest is censured in the name of cultural production and artistic integrity, rendering discussion of the subject taboo in the literary world. Despite his clear criticisms of money-driven literary production, Bourdieu's commentary sets an important precedent, because he not only acknowledges the author and publishing industry's struggle for economic survival in a capital-oriented marketplace, but also explains the inherent censorship that has always afflicted a cultural industry.

Drawing on Bourdieu, Roger Chartier and Henri Martin do for the nineteenth-century French publishing industry what we propose to extend to migrant texts of the twentieth and twenty-first centuries. Their four volumes of *Histoire de l'édition française*, published between 1983 and 1987, survey the larger literary mechanisms at work in the nineteenth century: the increasing number of novels printed, the expansion of readership to include women and children, the inclusion of photography and engravings, the influence of advertising, and the fierce competition between editors, among other elements. Chartier and Martin's sociological look into the publishing world centres on the creation of the bestseller and the editorial forces leveraging literary success against great financial risk. *Histoire de l'édition française* sketches the beginnings of a capital-driven literary market wherein more and more writers began living off their trade. The third tome of their history focuses on the role of editorial houses in securing the literary and financial success of their respective authors.

Likewise, the five case studies that follow trace the itineraries of five bestselling migrant texts from inception to publication and distribution, exploring the marketing strategies and oft-untold stories that account for their tremendous success on the French, Canadian, and global marketplaces. Pieced together from interviews with authors, editors, agents, and publishing executives, as well as with sales records obtained from publishers and data collection sources, the pages that follow are a testimony to the individual agency of writers and publishers in ensuring literary success. Each of the resulting stories is emblematic of how economic success is as much a result of literary production as are the poetic strategies that we will examine in the second half of this book. To consider the poetics of writing without acknowledging the brilliant maneuvering that brings a text to its intended audience would be to ignore the survival tactics of writers who navigate the perils of global capitalism and, more importantly, to neglect the singular status of the migrant text as both a work of art and an object lesson in the negotiation between market and cultural value.

NAÏM KATTAN'S *ADIEU BABYLONE*

Quebec author Naïm Kattan, who immigrated to Canada from Iraq in 1954, figures among the very first wave of immigrants in Quebec to take up the pen.[5] Kattan's debut novel *Adieu Babylone* (1975), which came on the heels of an influential essay on Eastern versus Western ways of apprehending reality, *Le Réel et le théâtral* (1970), confirmed the author's status among Quebec's literary elite. From Baghdad to Paris and then to Montreal, Kattan was never a stranger to the exclusive world of literary production. As a member of the Jewish upper class of Baghdad, Kattan attended one of the prestigious elementary schools of the Alliance Israelite Universelle, and then one of Iraq's most prominent Muslim high schools. He was the editor of two Arabic literary journals before the age of 19, when he left for Paris on a government scholarship to the Sorbonne. It was 1947 and Kattan was the first Iraqi ever to earn such an honour.

If Kattan's choice education, impressive multilingualism, and general literary wherewithal did not grant him sufficient cultural capital to earn his way into the French literary world, then his exotic origins certainly did. It was not long before he frequented Paris's select circles made up of that year's Nobel Prize winner André Gide, the surrealist André Breton, and the Dadaist Benjamin Péret among others. "J'étais le plus jeune, l'exotique et le jeune" [I was the youngest, the exotic one and the young one] says Kattan of the Surrealist meetings at the Café des Deux Magots in Paris, lead by Breton (Jama 2005, 58). While in France, multilingual Kattan continued writing essays in Arabic for Iraqi newspapers, while translating articles from Arabic to English for the American Jewish Committee in New York and composing pieces in French for *La Tribune*. Working as a guide for American tourists in Paris, he finally made his way across the Atlantic on a cruise ship, lecturing to American students about life in Paris (Jama 2005). In Canada, he quickly became one of Quebec's elite voices on the airwaves of Radio Canada as a Francophone expert on the Jewish and Arab world. As he admits of his early days in Montreal, "Et là aussi, comme j'avais l'air exotique, on voulait m'interviewer" [And there too, because I looked exotic, they wanted to interview me]" (Jama 85). Founder of the *Bulletin du cercle juif*, the first non-Catholic French-language periodical published in Montreal, Kattan always turned social and professional opportunities into a forum for reflections on ethnic, linguistic, and religious tolerance, whether this involved Arabs and Jews or French and English Canadians. When he became head of the publishing division of the Canada Council on the Arts in 1967, he was the first immigrant to occupy such a position within the Canadian government, promoting the arts on a national scale.

When Kattan began to seek a publisher for his debut novel *Adieu Babylone* in 1975, he was well positioned to find a Canadian publisher, and did so rather easily through a personal friend and former editor, Claude Hurtubise. Since Kattan was a known quantity on the Quebec cultural scene, the first edition of his novel, from Montreal-based publishing house La Presse, received significant press in Quebec. Explicitly marketed as the work of an Iraqi Jew who writes in French, the novel sold remarkably well, suggesting that the same exoticist tendencies that helped Kattan land his first literary opportunities had once again come to his aid. As he sought a Paris publisher for a French edition, however, he was met with resistance. As he says about those first Parisian responses to his manuscript, "Bagdad n'intéresse personne, et encore moins sa communauté juive" [Baghdad interests no one, and its Jewish community even less so] (Jama 142). French publisher Gallimard asked the writer for a book on Iraq instead, while editor Monique Nathan at Seuil told him to add something about the Shoah; it was not until 1976 that the smaller Julliard publishing house finally picked up the book. All told, between 1975 and 2003, La Presse and Julliard sold a total of approximately 10,000 copies of the novel, with a majority of sales falling between 1975–1985. Although McClelland and Stewart in Toronto also came out with an English translation in 1976, printing was stopped within a year due to poor sales, suggesting that the novelty of Kattan's ethno-cultural heritage did not suffice to sell books to an Anglophone public. Though Kattan has since written and published another thirty-five books in French, none has elicited the readership of his debut novel.

When the second Gulf War irrupted in 2003, *Adieu Babylone* experienced a sudden rebirth, this time extending its influence to English-speaking circles. That year, Kattan received an urgent phone call from

Albin Michel editor Jean Mouttapa requesting the rights to a new French edition of the novel. Due to a change in marketing strategy, the novel underwent a transformation in literary genre, as Mouttapa modified the novel's title to *Adieu, Babylone: Mémoires d'un Juif d'Irak*. Promoted as the true story of a young Iraqi Jew in a forgotten Baghdad where harmony once reigned between Shia and Sunni Muslims, Jews, Christians, and Bedouins, the novel has sold over 3,000 copies since. Two years later, it sparked another French-language re-edition with the Bibliothèque Québécoise and Raincoast Books resurrected the original English translation with a new English re-edition entitled *Farewell, Babylon: Coming of Age in Jewish Baghdad* that included photographs of the author as a boy and young man in Iraq along with a very personal foreword by Kattan. British and American editions by Souvenir Press and David R. Godine Publishers followed only a couple of years later with an even further expanded foreword in which Kattan makes links to the Holocaust, the Gulf War, and Saddam Hussein's regime. With total sales of the novel over its lifespan now exceeding 20,000 copies – not including recent translations into Arabic (Camel 2007), Italian (Manni 2010), and unofficial ones into Chinese – the combined efforts of the French, Canadian, and American publishing industries have breathed new life into the book multiple times. Since its first re-edition in 2003, sales of Kattan's first work doubled in less than a decade. While the literary poignancy of Kattan's debut novel has now stood the test of time on its own merits, I would be remiss not to also emphasize the manner in which a collaborative publishing enterprise helped foster its status as one of the first successful migrant texts in Canada.

DANY LAFERRIÈRE'S *COMMENT FAIRE L'AMOUR AVEC UN NÈGRE SANS SE FATIGUER*

When Dany Laferrière's most recent poem-novel *L'Énigme du retour* was published in September 2009, it sold 20,000 copies in Quebec and 15,000 copies in France within two months, even before the novel was awarded the prestigious French Prix Médicis and the Grand Prix du Livre de Montréal in November of that year. Laferrière's eleventh and latest novel was launched simultaneously by Éditions du Boréal in Montreal and Éditions Grasset in Paris and by January 2010 it had already made the bestseller lists in both countries. What has made Laferrière such a recognizable literary figure that no sooner is his novel released than it becomes a bestseller within a few short months? *L'Énigme du retour* is a novel about Haiti and migration completely rendered in haikus. It is also the product of a formally innovative author

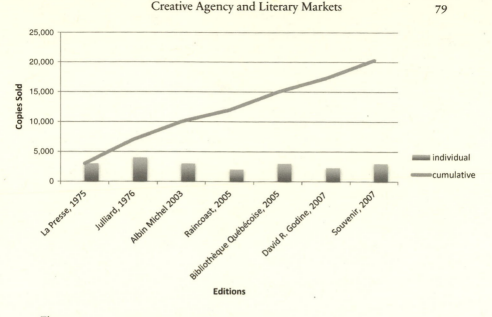

Figure 3.1
Adieu Babylone / Farewell, Babylon by Naïm Kattan
Copies sold by edition and total copies sold since publication

who burst onto the Quebecois literary scene fourteen years earlier with the internationally acclaimed bestseller *Comment faire l'amour avec un Nègre sans se fatiguer*. A sardonically titillating title that sold over 10,000 copies in its first year of publication in Quebec, Lafferière's first novel continues to rake in revenues worldwide with total sales across the globe well beyond one million copies. The 1990 film adaptation directed by Jacques Benoît was also a box-office hit, earning $130,000 Cdn in its first week in theaters. Hailed as one of the representative works of "migrant literature" in 1980s Quebec, Laferrière's first novel tells the autobiographically inspired story of a young black writer in Montreal. Literary critics agree that what first secured the novel's place on bestseller lists across North-America and Europe was a provocative title that sparked the curiosity of its potential readers (Vassal 30), a title that spurred Caribbean literary specialist Valérie Loichot to classify the novel in the genre of "fake pornography" (2013, 104).

Laferrière was both creative and strategic in his choice of title and his methods of diffusion in order to propagate the novel within this rather ambiguous genre. One week before the novel's launch in Montreal, Laferrière made 500 large posters advertising his debut work. The poster image was that of the author himself, seated on a bench at Montreal's illustrious Square Saint-Louis, barefoot with a typewriter on his lap and a beer bottle at his side with the bustling Saint-Denis street behind him. The novel's title figured prominently in bold, following the model of a film poster, and Laferrière placed the posters all over Montreal, especially targeting the city's richest neighbourhoods, most famous restaurants, and cafés. The title of course is aimed at a white female audience – or a tried and true literary-fiction-reading demographic – and suggests an instructional manual rife with secrets from the bedroom, as the word "nègre" is found in the object rather than subject position. Loichot points out that the word "nègre," however, troubles the self-help category that the novel's title might suggest upon first glance as the racial slur destabilizes the quiet heterodoxy of the proposed genre (2013, 114). Rather, it reads as an erotic invitation to white women, shamelessly luring them to act on racialized sexual fantasies based on stereotypes of black male hypersexuality. Yet because the novel is written by a black author and recounted by a black narrator, the disturbing dimensions of the title are somewhat alleviated and humour is injected into the tense racial equation that underlies it. As the "nègre" becomes the narrating subject, the racial power dynamic is reversed without compromising the voyeuristic promise of the title.

Laferrière even wrote an ironic essay on the power of his first novel's title, which he credits for his immense literary success. The essay begins, "J'ai connu le succès à cause du titre de mon premier roman" (CGM, 23) [The title of my first novel made me famous (WMB, 17)] and is made up of anecdotal reactions to his infamous title as well as his own responses to them. To a young woman in Leeds who wants to know why he chose his title after a screening of his film, he wittily answers: "Chère mademoiselle, sans ce titre, vous ne seriez peut-être pas ici" (CGM, 25) [Young lady, if it weren't for that title, you probably wouldn't be here tonight (WMB, 19).] Laferrière's disarming candor both in person – he has appeared and continues to appear on countless radio and television shows in Quebec – and in writing is no doubt responsible for the tremendous attractiveness of his work and the fact that his debut novel continues to sell remarkably well even twenty years after its publication.[6]

Comment faire l'amour avec un Nègre sans se fatiguer is an excellent example of how migrant texts position themselves at the nexus of commercial and cultural capital. Laferrière has never shied away from acknowledging the role of economics in literature or the moneymaking potential in exploiting certain themes over others. In a discussion with a young woman about an article on him entitled "Why do Black Writers prefer Blonds?" Laferrière writes, "C'est le titre de l'article qu'on m'a consacré. Toujours les questions raciales et sexuelles. Et leur mélange explosif. L'Amérique aime manger de ce plat. Et je suis prêt à lui en donner pour son argent" (CGM, 140) [That was the title of the article. Racial and sexual issues, as always. Their explosive combination. America can't get enough of it, and I'm ready to meet the demand" (WMB, 83)]. During the American launch of the novel's film adaptation, Laferrière was especially adept at this game, playing the *Washington Post* against the *New York Times* in a debate surrounding the censorship of his title, and even accusing the NAACP of ahistoricism when they protested at the film's opening. Not only that, but when *Comment faire l'amour avec un Nègre sans se fatiguer* was translated as the less threatening *How to Make Love to a Negro* for American audiences, Laferrière was not upset, accepting a change that Loichot calls "literary castration" (2013, 114) as a necessary vicissitude of his craft. As for the contested relationship between literature and economics, Laferrière waxes both playful and despondent at a reality few authors today are willing to admit out loud, much less in writing. As always, he uses irony to jab at the heart of a repressed truth:

> Faut éviter surtout de mêler l'argent à la littérature. Quel est le poids de l'argent dans l'œuvre de Proust ? Sans argent, aurait-il pu mener à terme cette interminable et asthmatique recherche du temps perdu ? Le temps, c'est de l'argent. Le temps perdu, c'est de l'argent perdu. Sauf le temps proustien, qui a aidé à enrichir les Gallimard. Quant à moi, je bénis l'argent et recherche sa compagnie. (CGM, 183)
> [I must avoid mixing literature and money. Look at Proust's work; where does money enter into it? Without money do you think he would have been able to complete his interminable, asthmatic search for time lost? Time is money. Time past is money past.[7] Except for Proust's time that helped the Gallimards in Paris get rich. I bless money and seek out its company. (WMB, 116)]

Laferrière's stance is thus reflected not only in the title of his first novel and a few subsequent ones (*Éroshima, Le goût des jeunes filles, Cette grenade dans la main du jeune Nègre est-elle une arme ou un fruit?*) but also in its content, which flirts with sexual decadence just enough to keep readers entertained while he delves into the darker, tragic side of Afro-American racial history.

In the complex workings from production to consumption, Laferrière's Haitian background and his decision to integrate the Quebec literary scene also affected the way his first novel was received. While readers and critics immediately hailed its brilliance – albeit with a few vociferous cries of misogyny – the novel's reception was mixed in the African and Haitian communities of Montreal and later Canada and the US. Some denounced the book as an exploitation of racial propaganda for economic purposes. In an essay entitled "Why Must a Negro Writer Always Be Political?" Laferrière cites one such accusation, reproducing his conversation with a Nigerian taxi cab driver in New York:

> – Des fois, je me dis que je te comprends d'avoir écrit cette merde pour faire de l'argent. C'est dur. Je le sais. C'est même très dur. On ne fait pas de cadeau, sauf si on accepte de vendre son âme. Pour ça, il y a toujours un acheteur.
> – Tous les écrivains sont des traîtres, d'une manière ou d'une autre ... La compétition est féroce ... Quand on n'est pas un génie, seul le strip-tease peut attirer le client. (CGM, 120–1)
> [– Sometimes I know why you wrote that shit. For the money. It is tough out there. I know. Real tough. You get nothing for free, unless you sell your soul. There'll always be a buyer for that.
> – All writers are traitors on some level ... I mean its tough for everybody ... Competition is fierce ... When you can't woo them with your know-how, a good strip tease will sometimes do the trick. (WMN, 347–8)]

In the above-mentioned essay, Laferrière angrily condemns what he perceives as the false *négritude* of the Afro-American community, arguing for literary and economic freedom for the black writer in a capitalist market. He defends his creative agency as a writer who does not – as a function of his race, gender, or ethnicity – speak for any one community or person other than himself. At the same time, he assumes his blackness both by using it as a marketing tool and by creating a work of irony that veils a wounded beauty inspired by the literary and musical genius of Chester Himes, Frantz Fanon, James Baldwin, Richard Wright, Derek Walcott, Miles Davis, Billie Holiday, and others. If *Comment faire l'amour avec un Nègre sans se fatiguer* can be classified as a migrant text, it is because it remains autonomous of any one national or ethnic affiliation, navigating 600 years of Afro-American and Afro-Caribbean history, and a few centuries of Quebecois literature and politics through the eyes and the body of a black immigrant in Montreal.

AZOUZ BEGAG'S *LE GONE DU CHAÂBA*

In 1986, Azouz Begag, the youngest son of a working class Algerian immigrant couple in France, published *Le Gone du Chaâba* with the illustrious Éditions du Seuil. This autobiographical novel recounts Begag's childhood in the destitute bidonvilles and suburbs of Lyon in the 1960s. It won the Prix Sorcières for youth literature the year following its publication and the first edition alone sold over 100,000 copies. Begag's debut novel was known as one of the founding works of Beur literature – a moniker of literature written by the children of North African immigrants to France that has today been abandoned in most scholarly work – although it was not the first novel of its kind. Published concurrently with novels by Farida Belghoul, Mehdi Lallaoui, Kamal Zemouri, and others, it came on the heels of an earlier wave of Beur novels by Mehdi Charef, Akli Tadjer, and Nacer Kettane that preceded it by only a couple of years.[8] It was Begag's novel, however, that by far retained the most public attention. It was made into one of the first films about this so-called Beur generation by French director Christophe Ruggia and added to the syllabi of most French high-school programs by 1990. Marketed from the outset for young readers in Seuil's pocket collection "Point Virgule," it was republished in Seuil's prestigious "Cadre rouge" collection only in 1997, the year Ruggia's filmic adaptation came out.[9] By 2007, the pocket edition had reached the 500,000 mark in copies sold, with annual sales averaging between 15,000 and 20,000 copies to this day.[10] The "Cadre rouge" edition, however, remains in circulation despite dismal sales figures – suggesting that the novel's impressive shelf-life is still due to the younger generation of school-age readers – and signaling Seuil's need to emphasize the novel's achievement of genuine literary status. It is no small feat for a migrant text, from the late twentieth century written by a Franco-Algerian author, to make the list of literary works studied in French schools since this list is heavily weighted toward French canonical writers from the last four centuries.

The reasons for *Le Gone du Chaâba*'s impressive commercial and cultural success lie in the way the novel showcases Begag's underprivileged, immigrant background alongside his decision to become a writer and participate in the great bastion of French literature. The triumph of Begag's work was heavily steeped in the integrationist politics of the time. In this 1986 novel, Azouz emerges as a model immigrant among a generation of delinquent youth wreaking havoc on French city suburbs. The early eighties saw the beginnings of what has today become

a familiar scene of violence among disobliged immigrant youth looking to make their voices heard in the ongoing struggle for equality and
fair treatment. While other Beur novels of the time are not devoid of
hope, none present a character as resolutely ambitious or unabashedly
naïve in his desire to integrate French society:

> J'ai honte de mon ignorance. Depuis quelques mois, j'ai décidé de
> changer de peau. Je n'aime pas être avec les pauvres, les faibles de la
> classe. Je veux être dans les premières places du classement, comme
> les Français ... À partir d'aujourd'hui, terminé l'Arabe de la classe. Il
> faut que je traite d'égal à égal avec les Français. (GC, 50–2)
> [I was ashamed of my ignorance. For a few months now I had been
> resolved on changing sides. I did not like being with the poor and
> the weak pupils in class. I wanted to be among the top of the class
> alongside the French children ... Starting from today I was not
> going to be the Arab boy in the class any more. I was determined
> to be on an equal footing with the French kids. (SK, 46–7)]

And when his fellow immigrant friends accuse him of being a "Gaouri"
and a traitor, Azouz retorts as an exemplary immigrant model: "Non, je
suis un Arabe. Je travaille bien, c'est pour ça que j'ai un bon classement.
Tout le monde peut être comme moi" (GC, 88) [No, I am an Arab. I work
hard; that's why I did well. Everyone can be like me (SK, 85)]. Such integration, is what would later earn Begag a political appointment in
Chirac's right-wing government as the "Ministre de l'égalité des chances"
in 2005. Begag's case was a perfect illustration of what CNRS sociologists
Rémy Leveau and Catherine Withol de Wenden termed the "third stage
of immigration" or the "beur-geoisie" in their 2001 analysis of the three
stages of associative immigration in France. Begag was indeed an exemplary Beur whom French reporter Bernard Philippe would cite as a
model of success in his 2004 book entitled La Crème des Beurs – an un-
fortunate title that clearly betrayed the author's racial bias – detailing
cases of second-generation Algerian immigrants who had "made it"
("réussi") in French society.[11]

In Mireille Rosello's effort to make sense of Azouz Begag's apparently divergent literary and political careers, the former deemed highly successful and the latter an utter failure, she argues that it was
precisely a lack of equal opportunity that lead immigrants like Begag to
find ways to succeed in France. In other words and in Bourdieu's terms,
Begag's story is one of overcoming a system in which he was disadvan-
taged from the perspective of cultural capital. He thus rose, in spite of

the odds against him, to integrate an elite of French writers and politicians. Rosello hence concludes, "The government is in bad faith to conclude that, as a result of this exceptional and unique trajectory, he is therefore the best spokesperson for those who have not succeeded. If we consider that his individual destiny is exemplary, and then, what he does represent is the possibility of the exception to the rule, the ability to engage in limited 'coups,' of transgressive maneuvers that the system precisely does not recognize as 'égalité des chances'" (2007, 241).

What Rosello's analysis points to is that Begags's literary work was never intended for his fellow immigrant population even though *Le Gone du Chaâba* became mandatory reading for many immigrant youth in French schools.[12] The novel pandered instead to the political leanings of French parents, teachers, and critics just as his short-lived political career catered to Republican ideals of integration, rather than the hopes of disenfranchised youth looking for a break. Despite all of Begag's best efforts to reinvent himself during his tenure as France's very first "Ministre de l'égalité des chances," he could not escape the *post* that he had worked so hard to attain, and to this day his national and even international appeal as a Beur writer depends on it. The political identity of dissident immigrant youth in France, on the contrary, lies precisely in a kind of resistance to the system that the example of Azouz Begag rallies against.

Today Azouz Begag has risen to international prominence as an actor on the global scene. When he was retained for questioning in the green room at the Atlanta Airport in October 2005, the incident sparked diplomatic controversy pertaining to racial profiling in the US. Since then, Begag has become a vehement spokesperson for the rights of Arabs and was a strong voice of opposition to Nicolas Sarkozy's policies on immigration. In 2007, he published a political memoir entitled *Un mouton dans la baignoire: Dans les coulisses du pouvoir* condemning Sarkozy's political treatment of Arab immigrants in France. The book is his most successful one since *Le Gone du Chaâba* and has sold over 60,000 copies to date. Begag also makes frequent trips to the US to teach and speak about the realities of immigration in France. As Laura Reeck argues in her analysis of Begag's now thirty-year career in French public culture, he has struggled to undo his reputation over the last decade as the "token Beur" of the eighties and nineties (2011). His livelihood as a writer is still ensured by a French national readership whose support, along with that of France's immigrant populations, he is once more soliciting to carefully reconstruct a political career, this time with France's centrist *Mouvement démocratique* party, perhaps entertaining hopes, like his character in *Le Gone du Chaâba*, of one day being France's first Beur president.

DAI SIJIE'S *BALZAC ET LA PETITE TAILLEUSE CHINOISE*

It was the year of the massacre at Tiananmen Square when Chinese filmmaker Dai Sijie, then living in France, wrote and directed his first feature-length film *Chine, ma douleur* (*China, My Sorrow*). With a title that captured the harrowing mood of a Chinese population in exile, Dai's 1989 film told the tragic story of Tian Ben, a thirteen year-old Chinese boy sent to a remote village in rural Sichuan for "re-education" during Mao's cultural revolution. The film – shot mostly in Cantonese and produced jointly by France and Germany – was met with much critical acclaim in France, earning Dai the Jean Vigo Prize awarded to a young director for his independent spirit. Though lauded by critics for its subtle portrayal of Maoist China, replete with a poignant political commentary, the film received very limited distribution in France. And yet the appeal of Dai's first film with wider French audiences was hindered it seemed by its language of production. Since it was denied entry into the Chinese market for its overtly political stance, Dai's career as a filmmaker quickly dwindled into oblivion with two more box office failures in *Le Mangeur de lune* (1993) and *Tang le onzième* (1998).

That was until he turned his attention to fiction writing. In 2000, Dai Sijie's bestselling first novel *Balzac et la petite tailleuse chinoise* seduced French readers the world over. A semi-autobiographical work that recounts the adventures of two young Chinese men in a rural reeducation camp in Sichuan, the plot closely resembled his earlier work with two significant changes. Firstly, the novel was written entirely in French, and later translated into over twenty-five other languages. The second was the introduction of Balzac, Dumas, Flaubert, Hugo, and a host of other canonical Western writers into the story line. Far from the heartbreaking reality of his earlier protagonist, Dai's novel now enacted a playful love affair between East and West that provided for a light-hearted escape from the dreary conditions of Communist China. Exploring a different kind of cosmopolitan sensibility that brings the salutary power of French literature to a simple-minded peasant girl in China, the novel was quickly adapted into a screenplay and restored Dai's ailing film career with a 2002 film that went by the same name as his bestseller. The novel sold over 300,000 copies in France within the first year of publication and has now sold approximately 1.3 million copies in its country of publication. By 2003, it had already sold

350,000 in the United States with thirty-five other countries in tow. *Balzac et la petite tailleuse chinoise*'s resounding success in France was made possible by a combination of factors, the most important of which was of course the tremendous attractiveness of the novel for its designated audience. Not surprisingly, soon after its launch, the book earned the Académie Française's *Edmée de la Rochefoucauld* Prize for best first novel as well as the *Relay du Roman d'Évasion* Prize that en-sured the book's widest distribution in all major cities in the country. Even before all this, however, came Dai Sijie's famous appearance on iconic Bernard Pivot's television show *Bouillon de culture* in January 2000. At the end of a round-table-style interview which included lit-erary heavy-weights Max Gallo, Daniel Pennac, Jacques Tardi, and Marc Levy, Pivot excitedly proclaimed, "Si ce livre ne devient pas un best-seller, alors cette émission ne sert à rien!" [If this novel does not be-come a bestseller, then this show is of no use!]. By the next morning, the 4,000 available copies of the novel were flying off the shelves and Gallimard had to reprint more and more again to meet the novel's unanticipated demand (Payot, 2003).

With the success of the novel secured, work on a film adaptation fol-lowed naturally afterwards since film had been Dai's art form of choice until then. China even opened its doors for an onsite production, some-thing that Dai had been denied since his initial exile to France. Though the film registered only mediocre revenues with no more than 250,000 tickets purchased throughout its run in French theatres, the stage was set for Dai's international acclaim as twenty-five other countries bought the rights to the film. China of course censored the film no sooner it was released, but Dai's career was by now assured. In 2003, he came out with a second novel *Le Complexe de Di* whose rights were purchased by an American publisher for $225,000 immediately after its initial launch in France. Other countries followed suit and Dai began production on a controversial film that he had been planning for years, *Les filles du botaniste* (2006), with funding from EuropaCorp.

The turn in fortune that Dai experienced in France through his best-selling debut novel thus allowed him to return to his former career as a filmmaker and opened doors for his continued success as an author. As we shall see in the next chapter, the novel was very astutely com-posed for French and Western audiences, so much so that when it was finally translated into Chinese in 2003, the translator expressed his own disagreement with the prominence given to French literature in his preface to the Chinese version. Reviews of the novel in China were less than laudatory, some even confused as to why the work had earned such accolades in France.[13] While Dai's French editors at Gallimard had grossly underestimated sales of *Balzac et la petite tailleuse chinoise* in France, his Chinese editors overestimated sales in mainland China and beyond. The 20,000 printed copies in Chinese sold very poorly among what is quite possibility the world's largest reading public (Hull 2009).

Dai's novel underwent a great many changes during its editorial process, one of which was of course the addition of Balzac to the title, but others included downplaying the influence of Chinese literature on the title character in favour of French literature. The end result of course, not only earned him a spot on one of France's elite literary television shows *Bouillon de culture* but has made him somewhat of a cultural ambassador for Francophonie abroad. In both instances, a humble soft-spoken Dai appears shy, almost overcome by the media attention as well as the cultural and national implications of his work. When Bernard Pivot asked him why he opted to write his novel in French, the unfailing sincerity of his response was lost on the magnanimous talk-show host. Dai's answer "Parce que maintenant j'habite en France et je dois manger" [Because now I live in France and I must eat] only elicited unease and a quick change of subject by Pivot.[14] The famous talk-show host – who has since been named chair of the prestigious French literary society *L'Académie Goncourt* that is responsible for France's renowned annual awards for literature – refused to even acknowledge the financial reality of his immigrant guest. Since then, Dai has published three other novels, the second of which earned him the illustrious Prix Femina in 2003. Instead of Balzac, Dumas, and France's canonical writers, it is the works of Sigmund Freud that Dai's protagonist Luo now takes to his native China in *Le Complexe de Di*. Exploring various genres in each of the works subsequent to his debut novel – comedy (*Le Complexe de Di*, 2003), history (*Par une nuit où la lune ne s'est pas levée*, 2007), and folklore (*L'acrobatie aérienne de Confucius*, 2008) – Dai has begun honing his craft in different directions since his auspicious start. Yet the further he moves from the "East meets West" model that brought him so much success, the less he appears to sell both in France and abroad. Of course, it remains to be seen whether his later novels will in fact have the afterlife in Chinese translation that his early novels could not enjoy.

MEHDI CHAREF'S
LE THÉ AU HAREM D'ARCHI AHMED

In 1983, Mehdi Charef published his debut novel while he was still sharpening tools at a factory in the suburbs of Paris. Charef immigrated to France from his native Algeria at the age of ten and, like many other Algerian families, lived in *bidonvilles* and *cités de transit* – an agglomeration of government subsidized buildings on the periphery of Paris. His semi-autobiographical novel *Le Thé au harem d'Archi Ahmed* was the very first literary work by France's Beur generation of authors and quickly lead to Charef's debut as a film director. As Kathryn Kleppinger's analysis of the novel's cover image and summary on the back cover point out, Charef's publishers privileged an "immigrant-framing" of the novel by spotlighting the immigrant character Madjid over his French counterpart Pat who is equally important to the plot (2015, 50). The popular success of Charef's novel was also ensured by the marketing strategies of his editor Isabelle Gallimard, who targeted France's North African immigrant populations with pointed distribution to book stores in the suburbs of Lyon, Paris, and especially Marseille (Xavier 2006a), The novel sold 25,000 copies during its first two years (Hargreaves 1997, 34). Unlike Begag's *Gone du Chaâba*, Charef's novel did not benefit from widespread national marketing and distribution, nor did it make the bestseller list or even the list of novels taught in French high schools. French journalists and critics, however, were most moved by Charef's poignant portrayal of young immigrant life at a time when uprising by and shootings of Maghrebi youth were becoming rampant. The famous "Marche pour l'égalité" baptized as "Marche des Beurs" by the French media took place during the fall of 1983 only months after the novel's launch in February of that same year. In many ways, Charef's novel was seen as a beacon of hope in difficult political times as François Mitterrand's left-wing government was trying to implement policies to integrate its insubordinate immigrant youth. As Kleppinger shows in her study of Beur writers and their media presence in France, Charef negotiated the French mediatic stage like no other Beur writer of his time, with a marked political sensitivity and humility that was enough to raise consciousness around the question of immigrant youth by emphasizing his personal involvement in the story he told (2015).

If Charef's book provided a counter-model to the violence of the time, it was because he took a different approach to political rebellion. In his own words, he confessed that he chose to take up the pen instead of lighting cars on fire, insisting that burning vehicles in the French suburbs were not a result of delinquency but a symptom of political frustration and helplessness.[15] *Le Thé au harem d'Archi Ahmed* was based on the life experiences of Charef, who even spent some time in prison for petty theft before he finally took a job in a factory. The reality of the *banlieue* as he depicts it in the novel was a considerably alleviated version of what Charef lived through in his youth. Conditions, he admitted, so dark and deplorable, no one would have wanted to keep reading had he faithfully portrayed them in his novel. "Les suicides, les drogues jusqu'à en mourir, il y en avait tant ... ça ne se comptait plus ... La famille ... c'était l'abandon, l'abus et la violence à ne plus en finir, c'était devenu la norme" (Xavier 2006d) [There were too many suicides and drug-related deaths to count ... The cases of neglect, abuse, and family violence so rampant, they were the norm], he said. Charef acknowledges his own participation in acts of political resistance that did not make it into the novel, and darker acts too he knew would upset the reader's sensibilities.

What is retained in the novel is just bleak enough to awaken consciousness, though it is the genius of Charef's unschooled prose that is most impressive. Charef's heart-breaking poetics is rife with colloquialisms and *banlieue* slang, replete with unsparing dialogue that expresses the injured sensibility of a generation. When Charef was given his directorial debut only months after the release of the novel, his self-taught skills behind the camera were equally remarkable. His storyboards betrayed the eye of a far more experienced cameraman and the film's formal composition from shot scale to lighting, sound, and mise-en scène exuded measure and nuance. Most surprising of all was how quickly this first-time author and filmmaker adapted his novel from page to screen. Shooting ended almost a year after the novel was released with Charef also doing most of the editing that ensued. The film was met with much critical acclaim, a *César de la première œuvre*, and substantial enough box office revenues to establish Charef's career as a filmmaker in France.

Before Azouz Begag, Charef was thus poised to become France's prime example of the model Beur, an inspiring example of how one can rise from the dreary conditions of immigrant life in the *banlieue* to gain and deploy cultural capital with such extraordinary proficiency. When Charef was approached by political authorities, however and unlike Begag, he refused to align himself with either the French right or left. Instead, he remained in the *banlieue* of Gennevilliers even when given an option to move to Paris after finally accepting the *Légion d'honneur* award from the French government in 2005 – a title he had refused on political grounds on several prior occasions. In the end, Charef relented, on his own account, for economic purposes; he rented a workspace in Genevilliers and hired people to assist him in his ongoing artistic pursuits. His family needed a bigger apartment, but Charef channelled his earnings into more creative resistance. To this day, he has written four novels, one play, and eleven screenplays and directed all eleven feature-length films. Yet he defiantly claims only the Parisian *banlieue* for his national identity, "je suis un banlieusard, de parents algériens" [I am a *banlieusian*, born of Algerian parents] he asserts proudly, "et je suis beur!" [and I am Beur!]. Refusing the social capital that comes with artistic fame, Charef thus enacts a continued political resistance even while taking advantage of some of the financial perks of his current status: "L'intégration, c'est se mettre dans la rue, se battre contre les injustices en manifestant son mécontentement, sa colère devant tant de souffrance ... c'est s'exprimer ... Les jeunes qui brûlent les voitures, c'est de l'intégration aussi ... mais moi, j'ai choisi la plume." [Integration is taking to the streets, fighting against injustice by demonstrating one's discontent, one's anger at the sight of so much suffering ... it is to express oneself ... Burning cars is also a form of integration ... but I chose the pen.] Charef navigates the tumultuous waters of French politics by remaining an outsider to its factions but a voice of protest through his art. His way of conceiving integration in rather adversarial terms has in many ways kept him away from the spotlight as either spokesperson for the *banlieue* or ambassador for Beur culture. As he continues to publish however, *Le Thé au harem d'Archi Ahmed* remains his bestselling novel to date, just as the film adaptation is still his most successful and best-known film. As we will see in the following chapter, Charef strikes at the core of the young immigrant experience in 1970s France in his debut novel and film. His portrayal of the socio-economic forces that conspired against immigrant and especially Beur youth of the time was a powerful historical perspective on the violent events of the early eighties and a tragic lesson in how little has changed in France even some thirty years later.

CONCLUSION

In the age of global capitalism, financial success in the literary marketplace can no longer be conceived as the accidental after-effect of artistic genius. As the examples in this chapter illustrate, writers, editors, and their respective livelihoods are imbricated in the accessibility, readability, and likability of books as much as they are earned by inspired poetic musings. Though we have limited our case studies to five novels by five male writers, many other migrant texts tell similar stories of consciously navigated success for literary markets. Not all writers, however, are forthcoming about this oft repressed reality of artistic production and many fear losing the cultural legitimacy of their creative work to candid actions taken to secure financial viability.

As we will see in the next two chapters, each of the works discussed above also negotiates culture and language through creative textual techniques, but these strategies alone cannot account for the novels' presence on the global literary stage. As migrant texts, all of these works exploit a variety of national, political, racial, ethnic, and linguistic factors, making their economic success a result of conscious decision making about how the experience of immigration can be woven into the craft of fiction writing. In the second half of this book, we will delve into the practice of the migrant text, moving away from its theoretical underpinnings and its market-driven shelf life to its cultural, linguistic, and political viability as a literary object.

PART TWO

Poetics

4

Negotiating Culture

INTRODUCTION

The migrant text seeks a place in one culture while using it to speak about another. This is not a question of simply straddling two or more cultures at once but is rather the defining feature of a text that assures its readers of its complete participation in, knowledge of, and commitment to the culture in which it is published. Only from this well anchored position can a song of otherness arise, inviting readers on a journey to lands, peoples, and cultures beyond. The migrant mode is therefore always negotiating culture because its textual practices are geared toward those for whom much of the work's cultural content will be foreign. Though the goal is certainly not to exclude more cosmopolitan or globally minded readers, this approach makes no apology for its call to the sensibilities of a still largely homogeneous cultural body of bibliophiles. And while this Janus-faced appeal is what leads many migrant novels to popular success in their countries of publication, it can be the cause of critical failure in the very cultures that the content of their pages purports to express.[1] Few works succeed at walking the invisible line between conceding to the demands of one culture while maintaining the integrity of the other. Defined by the textual discomfort of selling culture while resisting its hegemonic and reified expressions, the migrant text engages in both cultural flattery and critique, often with the latter carefully couched in the terms of the former.

Moving away from postcolonial notions of "hybridity" and interstitial readings of the "in-between," the analyses that follow focus not on cultural negotiations of liminality between nations and ethnic identities, but on the way that these works are complicit with various national projects. These texts are entangled less in the ambivalent spaces of identity formation than in the material reality of cultural production through literary creation. In the previous chapter, we traced the stories of five migrant texts from creation to publication, highlighting the ways in which authors, editors, and publishers found marketing strategies for selling their respective novels first in France and Quebec and then within the Western hemisphere more globally, particularly Europe and North America. In the cases discussed in that chapter, we noted different levels of implication, collaboration, and consciousness by the authors themselves, some more comfortable than others with the exoticizing of their persona as well as their work.

In the pages that follow, we will now return to the text itself and to the literary strategies mobilized by four writers to negotiate their cultural positioning. Our readings of Naïm Kattan's *Adieu Babylone*, Dany Laferrière's *Comment faire l'amour avec un Nègre sans se fatiguer*, Mehdi Charef's *Le Thé au harem d'Archi Ahmed*, and Dai Sijie's *Balzac et la petite tailleuse chinoise* each centre on a crucial association with French or Quebecois culture and a fraught relationship with the "foreign" culture at the heart of their novels.[2] Since all four of our textual examples derive from the work of immigrants, there is a wounded silence that also mars the cultural ties that are forged in each text, one that lies behind each author's decision to exploit his native culture for profit while at the same time refusing to conform to a cultural exotic that is not of his own making.

COSMOPOLITAN QUANDARIES IN *ADIEU BABYLONE*

It was in 1975 that Naïm Kattan's first novel *Adieu Babylone* was published by the Éditions La Presse in Montreal recounting the youth of an Iraqi Jew in Baghdad during the Second World War. The novel would be published a year later in Paris by the Éditions Julliard with a preface by celebrated French writer Michel Tournier and translated into English that same year by Sheila Fischman.[3] Though the English translation would go out of print right after it was published, the French-language editions sold remarkably well and launched Kattan's literary career. Having immigrated to Canada in 1954 after studying law in Baghdad and literature at the Sorbonne in Paris, the novel is a squarely autobiographical look at Kattan's final years in Iraq as well as those of a thriving Jewish community that would be forcefully relocated to Israel at the end of the war. The novel opens to a lively scene at the café Yassine in Baghdad where a group of young Iraqi boys are engaged in a passionate discussion about literature. Among the group are adolescents from every ethnicity and religion; the narrator points out that apart from himself and his friend Nessim who are Jews, one boy is Chaldean, another Armenian, and all the others Muslims (*AB*,10). Writing about his home country before the irruption of Arab nationalism and the creation of the Israeli State, which would lead to the expulsion of some 145,000 Jews from their ancestral land, Kattan's first novel is a return to the idyllic though precarious ethno-religious balance of pre-war Iraq. "Dans notre groupe, nous n'étions ni Juifs ni Musulmans. Nous étions Irakiens, soucieux de l'avenir de notre pays" [In our group we were neither Jew nor Muslim. We were Iraqis, concerned about the future of our country (*FB*, 11)], writes Kattan about a group of friends that included Jews, Sunni and Shiite Muslims, Bedouins, and Christians; "Nous étions les deux seuls Juifs du groupe, à part un Chaldéen et un Arménien, tous les autres étaient musulmans" (*AB*, 12) [We were the only Jews in the group. All the other, except for a Chaldean and an Armenian, were Muslim (*FB*, 8)] he concludes, revealing a cosmopolitan sensibility that rings rather unfamiliar to anyone acquainted with the political tensions that defined that part of the world at the time of the novel's publication in 1975, and certainly today. The narrator goes to great lengths to defend his ethnic and religious tolerance despite the nascent anti-Semitism that inevitably creeps into the narrative: "Sauf que les Musulmans se sentaient plus irakiens que les autres. Nous avions beau leur dire : 'Voici notre terre et nous sommes là depuis vingt-cinq siècles'. Nous les avions précédés. Nous ne les convainquions pas. Nous étions différents ... Notre identité était entachée" (*AB*, 13). [Except that the Muslims felt more Iraqi than the others. It was no use for us to say to them, "This is our land and we have been here for twenty-five centuries." We had been there first but they were not convinced. We were different ... Our identity was tainted (*FB*, 11).] Nostalgia for the old country colours the narration and hints at the regret that is alluded to in the novel's title.

"Adieu Babylone" is an expression of forced and irrevocable exile that haunts Kattan's tale from beginning to end. In an article devoted to Kattan's writing, critic Sylvain Simard explains the significance of Babylon to Jewish history and mysticism, a reality that the above quotation from the novel makes reference to in no uncertain ways. Simard thus explains:

Babylone n'est pas seulement le champ de ruines qui rappelle la gloire passée de Nabuchodonosor II, non plus que le souvenir d'un lieu d'excursion, c'est celui où cinq siècles avant notre ère les Juifs

de la tribu de Juda, après la destruction du temple, ont été amenés
en esclavage ; moment de l'existence d'un peuple qui a non
seulement donné certaines des pages les plus belles de la Bible,
mais lieu de rédaction du Talmud qui a fondé une partie de la
mystique juive. (1985, 36)
[Babylon is not just a field of ruins that recalls the past glory of
Nabuchodonosor II, or the memory of a site of excursion, it is the
place where, five centuries before our era, the Jews of the tribe of
Juda were taken as slaves, after the destruction of the temple; it is
the moment in time that recalls the existence of a people that not
only resulted in hundreds of the most beautiful pages of the Bible,
but the place where the Talmud that shaped a part of the Jewish
mystique was written.]

Judaism's endangered plight in Iraq surfaces time and time again as a
leitmotif, while the narrator strives to maintain a relentless sense of optimism ["optimisme imperturbable" (AB, 15)] in the name of his cosmopolitan values. The narrator insists, "Nous avions affaire à des
libéraux affranchis et à des révolutionnaires qui œuvraient à la gigan-
tesque démolition de tous les murs édifiés par les préjugés et l'incom-
préhension" (AB, 15) [We were dealing with emancipated liberals and
revolutionaries who were working to demolish the walls put up by prejudice and misunderstanding (FB, 13)]. The horrifying memories of the
Farhud – the 1941 pogrom against the Jewish people of Baghdad where
over 300 Jews were killed, another 2,000 wounded, and some 900 Jewish homes burned to the ground or destroyed – serve as a troubling call
to order. Kattan recreates the scenes of pillage, massacre, and rape in an
almost frigid detail as the violence overcomes the text and the narrative succumbs to the inevitable horrors of history:

Ils avançaient. Munis de pics, de poignards, parfois de fusils. Ils
déferlaient par vagues, cernaient la ville, l'investissaient. Des cris de
ralliement fusaient de toutes parts ... Ils ne pourchassaient que les
Juifs ... Ils défoncent les portes ... On démolit ce qu'on ne peut pas
transporter. Puis une deuxième vague fait son entrée dans les lieux
dévastés. Plus de butin. On éloigne les hommes. Ceux qui opposent
la moindre résistance sont égorgés sur le champ. Et on soumet les
femmes à la volonté des mâles. Malgré leurs cris, les juives sont
belles ... Ce sont de bonnes bêtes. (AB, 20)
[They advanced. Armed with picks, daggers, sometimes with rifles,
they unfurled in waves, surrounded the city, beleaguered it. Rally-

ing cries crackled on all sides ... Only the Jews were being pursued ... They pushed down the gates and moved in. What could not be carried away was demolished. Then a second wave entered the devastated site. The men were sent away. Those who put up the slightest resistance had their throats cut on the spot. And the women were made to submit to the will of the men. Despite their cries, the Jewish women were beautiful ... They were good animals. (*FB*, 18–19)]

These were scenes that Kattan witnessed as a boy and ones that appear in shocking tonal contrast to the young protagonist's naiveté and cosmopolitan idealism. The boy narrator is shaken not only by the tenor of these events but by the very fact that he survives them. Yet the narrative voice refuses to yield to the devastating reality that encroaches upon it so early in the novel. Though the protagonist's friend Nessim – traumatized by a pogrom witnessed so young – loses all hope in a political resolution to the country's ethnic strife, the narrator continues to persevere in his ambition to unite Jew and Arab. Even as a child he claims to "franchir des frontières que les adultes n'auraient pas l'audace d'enfreindre" (*AB*, 41) [[cross] boundaries that adults would not have the audacity to transgress (*FB*, 35)]. Thanks to his multilingualism, he earns a position in the civil service of the occupying British government and strives to create a political climate that is ripe for ethnic and religious cohabitation in Iraq. The stylistic contrast that Kattan enacts between his adolescent narrator's unfailing hopefulness – expressed in the flourish of his prose and at times inflated rhetoric – and the tragic destiny that awaits the Jewish community in Iraq – recounted in a rather elliptical simplicity – is a crucial marker of Iraq's true cultural hybridity. His choice conveys a refusal to cast judgment on his Bedouin compatriots right to the bitter end. As our cosmopolitan narrator, now heading to France to pursue his education on a French government scholarship, bids goodbye to his family and friends, his "au revoir" turns into "adieu," and his homeland turns from multi-ethnic "Iraq" to the Judaic ancestral grounds of "Babylon." Still, he chooses to take with him only a slice of the Iraq he so desperately believed in: "Ainsi mon enfance sera préservée, je ferai mon entrée dans le monde nouveau sans m'amputer d'une part privilégiée, sans disperser en pure perte ce monceau de rêves et de souvenirs (*AB*, 237). [In that way my childhood would be preserved. I would enter the new world without cutting off a privileged part of it, without dispersing my dreams and memories (*FB*, 198–9).] And that is what 87-year-old Kattan's most successful novel to date continues to portray: a bittersweet glimpse into a forgotten slice of Iraqi history and the death of his cosmopolitan dream.

As we saw in the last chapter, *Adieu Babylone*'s initial success in Quebec and France, selling some 10,000 copies in its multiple French editions between 1975 and 1985, was largely due to the complicated identity politics of Kattan himself. Marketed both as the work of a Jew and an Arab, the novel clearly walks the dangerous line of political affiliations in a conflict-ridden zone with remarkable aptitude. Furthermore, the novelty of a Jewish-Iraqi author writing not only in French but in a prose that pays homage to the language of Proust was noteworthy in any Francophone literary circle. Kattan's ode to the French-speaking world does not stop there, however, as the novel is truly engaged in a cosmopolitan quest to earn recognition in what critic Sylvain Simard calls "the West":

> *Adieu Babylone* est aussi le lieu d'une contradiction fondamentale, l'aspiration à l'enracinement dans un lieu, une nation, une langue et l'appel quasi irrésistible de l'Occident, de sa civilisation, de sa culture. Aucune autre œuvre, contemporaine, n'associe avec autant de force et de vérité ces quêtes contradictoires et leurs manifestations linguistiques ; entre les dialectes arabes juif et musulman, la langue du Coran et celle de Gide et d'Aragon se joue une partie serrée parce que chacune exprime des choix culturels et politiques mutuellement exclusifs. (1985, 35–6)
>
> [*Farewell Babylone* is also the site of a fundamental contradiction, the aspiration for rootedness in a place, a nation, a language and the quasi irresistible call of the West, of its civilization, of its culture. No other contemporary literary work associates with as much force and truth these contradictory quests and their linguistic manifestations; between the Arab Jewish and Muslim dialects, the language of the Coran and that of Gide and Aragon, a tense rivalry unravels because each expresses mutually exclusive cultural and political choices.]

Simard is particularly disturbed by what he terms the contradictory aspirations of *Adieu Babylone*, which is at once engaged in telling the difficult story of Iraq's Jewish community and pre-war history and consumed by a love affair with the French language and its literature.

Kattan devotes several chapters to the protagonist's discovery and infatuation with French, its literature, and culture. This aspect of the novel betrays an exaggerated, even exotic fascination with all things French that both rouses the laughter of French-speaking readers and flatters their cultural sensibility by attributing such pre-eminence to their language and literature. The narrator's description of his French examiner, the very first Frenchman he meets, is a revealing first taste of this obvious favoritism: "Je regardais avec mes yeux avides mon examinateur : c'était le premier Français authentique que je voyais en chair et en os. Cet homme appartenait à la race de Molière et de Baudelaire. Je le dotais d'un pouvoir magique. Il n'était sûrement pas notre semblable" (*AB*, 133). [I looked avidly at my examiner. He was the first Frenchman I had ever seen. This man was of the race of Molière and Baudelaire. I endowed him with magical powers. He certainly was not our equal (*FB*, 116).[4]] A page later, the narrator is once again beside himself upon learning that his examiner is a friend of celebrated French poet Louis Aragon. Suddenly, the French teacher is elevated into a quasi divinity: "Il appartenait à la race des élus qui vivent dans l'entourage des dieux et des mages ... J'étais en présence vivant de ce royaume privilégié auquel appartiennent les porteurs des noms qui figurent à la première page des livres français" (*AB*, 134). [He belonged to the chosen race that lives among gods and magi[5] ... I was in the presence of a living representative of the kingdom inhabited by people whose names appeared on the first page of French books (*FB*, 117).] The city of Paris also holds tremendous power over our child narrator for whom it embodies the very notions of cultural capital and political freedom. Yet the reality of wartime France cannot be ignored by this young Jew who, when asking his French examiner if it would be safe to go to a Nazi occupied country, is met with a confident allusion to French universalism: "Les Allemands n'y seront pas toujours. La France, une fois libérée, offrira sa culture à tous les hommes" (*AB*, 135). [The Germans won't be there forever. When France is liberated, she'll offer her culture to everyone (*FB*, 127).] This colonial-type response is sufficient it seems to appease the very legitimate concerns of the narrator who is reassured enough to make plans for his departure.

Such pandering to French culture – something we will see again in the work of Dai Sijie later in this chapter – is common to the migrant text and often constitutes one of its characteristic features. Rather than a subtle inter-textual reference to the canonical writers of French literature, Kattan engages in blatant veneration. Asked about these passages in an interview, Kattan confirms his boyish impressionability, his own exotic adoration of France, and the pride of writing in the language of his great literary heroes.[6] Kattan's editor, critic, and long-time friend Jacques Allard admits that in those early years, he and others were held completely captive by this young Iraqi's mastery of French. Such gushing over France was not only expected but endeared him first to his teachers and later to his readers.[7] The contradiction that Simard attributes to Kattan's text is thus a direct result of strategic cultural positioning on the author's part as he embraces a multifaceted cosmopolitanism that is not without its paradoxes.

Recent theorists of cosmopolitanism like Kwame Anthony Appiah and Pheng Cheah have been concerned with the ethical quandaries posed by intercultural relationships. When authors such as Kattan play into the egos of their French readership, flattering one culture's sense of self-importance over that of the very culture the novel is supposed to promote, it is a crisis of cosmopolitan morals, a crisis that Simard's work signals under the guise of contradiction. Critics Allard and Nasrin Rahimieh, who have both come to the defense of Kattan, argue for the complexity of the writer's cultural stance from different vantage points. Allard invokes the writer's transcultural outlook, arguing that he is impossible to pin down within any traditional framework of belonging:

> Un voyageur du transculturel, soucieux de comprendre les rapports de l'Orient et de l'Occident ... Juif d'Arabie, Arabe de la judéité, oriental d'Occident, occidental d'Orient, l'homme de Baghad est inépinglable, ce francophone québécois est toujours ailleurs que là où on le fixe. (1985, 7)
> [A transcultural traveller, concerned with understanding the relationship between the Orient and the Occident ... Jew from Arabia, Arab from Judah, Easterner from the West, Westerner from the East, the man from Baghdad is impossible to pin down, this Francophone Quebecois is always somewhere other than where we fix him.]

Of course, Allard does not hesitate to claim him as Francophone and Quebecois, although Kattan is a native speaker of Arabic and perfectly fluent in English. What is at stake for Allard are Kattan's joint allegiances to the Arab world and the Jewish one, the East and the West. Meanwhile Rahimieh suggests a reading of *Adieu Babylone* through the opening scene of the novel when the protagonist chooses classical Arabic over the dialectical Arabic of Iraqi Jews or that of Iraqi Muslims when discussing world literature with a group of friends: "Le voilà qui me pose une question directe. Inutile de me dérober. Il ne me lâchera pas. Je choisis un moyen terme. Mes mots n'étaient ni ceux des Juifs ni ceux des Musulmans. Je m'exprimai en arabe littéraire, coranique" (*AB*, 12). [Finally he asked me a question directly. It was useless for me to escape. He would persist. I chose a middle course. My words were neither those of the Jews nor the Muslims. I spoke in literary Arabic, the Arabic of the Koran (*FB*, 10).] His choice of the Coranic language is thus highlighted as the middle ground since "the compromise reached by the protagonist, and by extension Kattan, is one which avoids simple polarities and insists upon complex inter-relationships," argues Rahimieh (1990, 34). Though the novel is written in French and grants significant ascendency to French literature and culture, it is the unwritten presence of the Coranic language in the mouth of a young Iraqi Jew that is Kattan's cosmopolitan plea to the Western world: "I could have written in Arabic, but it was to the French, to the West that I wanted to speak" says Kattan.[8] In this light, Kattan's novel may be interpreted in light of his many failed efforts while in Paris to draw attention to the urgent plight of his fellow Iraqi Jews. The novel may be read as an accusation against the dispossession and forced airlifting of 120,000 Iraqi Jews to Israel between 1951 and 1952 and the Allied complacency that facilitated the process. Even his refusal to write in English – the language of Iraq's colonizers – can be construed as an overt strategic alignment with the French over the British, who disapprovingly stood by as the expulsion took place.

The initial failure of the English translation of *Adieu Babylone* in the mid-seventies – when the novel was as yet a fiction inflected with strokes of autobiography – was perhaps due to its lack of historical engagement, something that was rectified by Kattan's foreword in the later re-editions. In 1977, Critic D.O. Spettigue was especially aggravated at Kattan's elliptical description of the Farhud and blamed it on the author's privileged background and the lack of any real traumatic encounter with the horrifying events of 1941. As we saw in chapter 3, Kattan belonged to the upper classes of Iraqi society and, much like his narrator, lived in the wealthier Jewish neighbourhood of Battawiyeen in Baghdad. Whereas the narrator's friend Nessim lives in the poorer Jewish quarter and experiences the worst of the Bedouin mob's wrath, order is restored just as the mob approaches the richer area. "Nous étions l'appât supreme" (*AB*, 23) [We were the supreme target (*FB*, 21)], writes Kattan of the Battawiyeen quarter. Spettigue thus takes issue with Kattan's recreation of the pogrom as a direct reflection of the author's complicity with the dominant classes: "One does not question the authenticity of the representation; but the result is to deepen the shadow-effect. All seems disembodied, unreal, except in moments of commonplace reality ... Socially and politically we are filled in on the current movements, journalistically ... but at the same time it reinforces the feeling that with the protagonist we inhabit a world of shadows ... It is not that *Farewell Babylon* is unconvincing, but that it is exile literature, essentially colonial, recording marginal people for whom everything important happens somewhere else" (1977, 510). To an Anglophone audience, who was perhaps not as touched by the protagonist's love for all things French, the reframing of the novel through memoir was then a crucial means of eliminating this "shadow-effect" and bringing the narrator closer to the reader. The personal tone of Kattan's foreword to the Canadian edition connects with the Anglophone reader by appealing to a political culture he now shares with them: "Today when I visit the Babylonian or Assyrian galleries in the Louvre, the British Museum, the Pergamon Museum in Berlin or the Royal Ontario Museum in Toronto, I relive my childhood excursions to Babylon and Nineveh. So many civilizations blossomed in that country! The traces they left are richer and more meaningful than all the oil wells. And I think to myself: what a waste! A country that cannot hold on to all of its citizens!" (*FB* 2005, 8). The critical response to Kattan's 2005 translation was overwhelmingly positive as most reviews cited the timeliness of its human perspective on Iraq.[9] In the foreword to his American edition, Kattan even specifies what became of each of the characters in the novel, from his brothers and sisters to his Jewish and Muslim schoolmates whose real names he reveals. He tells his life story in abridged form, explaining his difficult itinerary across nations and continents, detailing his professional vocation and achievements. In a candid presentation of himself to his American readers, an octogenarian Kattan sets the stage for the naïve idealism and distance of his adolescent narrator. By situating the novel within the political realities of post-Gulf War Iraq and detailing the current status of resettled Iraqi Jews in Israel, Kattan's book tells the story of his native country as it did not before. Kattan's cosmopolitan dream is perhaps finally actualized in the various lives and afterlives of his debut work, which through the combined vision of editors and publishers, as well as Kattan's own creative complicity in the process, yielded a literary object of global reach.

CULTURAL SEDUCTION IN *COMMENT FAIRE L'AMOUR AVEC UN NÈGRE SANS SE FATIGUER*

The staggering commercial success of Dany Laferrière's debut novel, as we saw in the earlier chapter, was carefully orchestrated by none other than the author himself. Laferrière was not only strategic in selecting a provocative title for his novel, but also in constructing a powerful social critique through the suggestive combination of sex and race relations.

Yet the novel was very much written for a Quebecois market as it reaches out to this specific literary audience in deliberate ways. While taking aim at the racial question at the heart of its stereotypical representations and taboo, Laferrière manages to speak to the nationalist sensibilities of his Francophone Quebecois audience, aligning himself with a discourse that has historically excluded Quebec's immigrant populations. It is less the critical triumph of the book that is remarkable here than its popular success with a mainly white Quebecois readership because the novel viciously attacks the clichéd portrait of the Black man as it is constructed by white culture. In a satirical reversal of slavery, Laferrière arms his black protagonist with an irresistible erotic appeal that leaves white women at his sexual mercy. Yet, what amounts to a stark, even offensive critique of white racist attitudes is nonetheless negotiated for a Quebecois audience in such a way as to link the political fate of the Black man with that of the Quebecois, both subject to dominant forces of oppression.

First the story of the black Muslim narrator and protagonist, fondly referred to as "Vieux (Os)" [Old Bones] by his roommate Bouba, is deeply anchored in the realities of urban life in Montreal. The city figures prominently as the backdrop to the indolent lifestyles of the two Black characters who live in a dingy apartment on rue St-Denis, pick up girls from the rich neighbourhoods of Outremont, Westmount, and Notre-Dame de Grâce, and spend their time reading, debating philosophy, listening to and discussing jazz music, sleeping, or fornicating. Laferrière's portrait of Montreal goes into painstaking detail in his description of the city to emphasize the narrator's intimacy with his new found home. He gives us the exact address of Vieux and Bouba's apartment, mentions the names of streets, bars, restaurants, bookstores, metro stations, and even bus numbers in recounting daily events in the idle lives of the two men. The two men's apartment also gives onto Montreal's golden Square Saint Louis where the likes of Quebec's national poet Émile Nelligan, famous poet and orchestrator of Quebec's Quiet Revolution Gaston Miron, and internationally renowned playwright Michel Tremblay also lived. Pascale De Souza argues that the precision of toponymic information serves to bring author and narrator closer to one another (CFA, 63). This is undoubtedly true since the narrator is also writing his first novel *Paradis du drageur nègre* or *Black Cruiser's Paradise*, the catchy title of which cleverly resembles Laferrière's. Moreover, the autobiographical elements that permeate the novel create an illusion of intimacy between author and reader, something that Laferrière confirms in a later essay where he cites a conver-

sation he once had with a young female reader who recognized him
on the street and wanted him to confirm the novel's veracity:

> – Pourquoi est-ce si important de savoir que l'histoire s'est
> réellement passée ?
> Un temps bref.
> – On veut savoir si tout ça est vraiment arrivé à l'auteur.
> – Oui... Pourquoi ?
> – Je ne sais pas, répond-elle, avec ce sourire douloureux... On se sent
> plus proche de lui. (CGM, 31–2)
> [– Why is it so important if the story really happened to the author?
> She thought about that one.
> – You just want to know.
> – I see... Why?
> – I don't know, she said with a pained smile. You feel closer to him
> that way. (WMB, 30)]

This closeness is fostered in other ways throughout the novel as well, by
reinforcing popular Quebecois opinion, as in various episodes involv-
ing the famous cross that stands on Mount Royal in Montreal. The cross
is repeatedly described with the irreverence in tone of someone who no
longer subscribes to the cultural nostalgia of this historic and religious
symbol. It is derided as "cette saloperie" (CFA, 74) or "cette saleté de
Croix" (CFA, 111, 124) [this lousy Cross (HML, 65, 101, 112)]. What may
appear sacrilegious to the uninitiated reader, however, sets Laferrière's
novel in a long tradition of anticlerical Quebecois literature. The cross
that adorns the top of the Mount Royal holds little emblematic value
in contemporary secular Quebecois society and signifies even less to
the immigrant, who looks on it with disdain as the exalted sign of false
religiosity. Laferrière thus reduces the cross to its material reality, metal-
lic in the daytime, phosphorescent at night, puncturing the skyline of
urban Montreal life that Black immigrants, even Muslim ones, now
claim as their own: "Je n'ai pas vu la nuit venir. Un croissant de lune, en
chapeau, derrière la Croix" (CFA, 76). [I did not see the night close in. A
crescent moon, like a hat behind the Cross (HML, 66).] Yet, satire remains
the driving force of the novel and Laferrière will even go to the extent
of placing the cross in the background of a scene in which his protagonist engages in sexual acts, perversely told by the narrator: "Je l'entraîne jusqu'au lit sans vraiment arrêter de la baiser ... Comme une fleur
au bout de ma pine nègre. La fenêtre encore ouverte sur la Croix du
mont Royal" (CFA, 80). [I carry her to the bed with no let-up in the

rhythm, holding her at the end of my cock. Like a flower blossoming at the end of my black rod. The window still open on the Cross of Mount Royal (HML, 70).] The monument is sarcastically mocked standing as it were a witness to the sexual debauchery of the black immigrant and arousing the laughter of the knowing Quebecois reader.

As for Vieux's and Bouba's numerous sexual conquests, they are always Anglo-Saxon Protestant women who hail from Montreal's richest and, for the most part, Anglophone neighbourhoods. These women remain nameless except for the English designation "Miz" followed by a nickname that the novel's protagonists give each one (Miz Littérature, Miz Suicide, Miz Sundae, etc.). Miz Littérature studies at McGill University and the narrator never fails to take jabs at the bourgeois hypocrisy of the prestigious Anglophone institution: "Tu t'imagines, elle étudie à McGill (une vénérable institution où la bourgeoisie place ses enfants pour leur apprendre la clarté, l'analyse et le doute scientifique) et le premier Nègre qui lui raconte la première histoire à dormir debout la baise" (CFA, 31). [Imagine: she's studying at McGill (venerable institution to which the bourgeoisie sends its children to learn clarity, analysis and scientific doubt) and the first Negro to tell her some kind of fancy tale, takes her to bed (HML, 25).] Pascale De Souza's study entitled "Stratégies perlocutoires d'un best-seller chez Dany Laferrière" insists that the narrator's quest for identity through sex must necessarily involve the most powerful women in Quebec: white, bourgeois, and Anglophone (1999, 65). What De Souza overlooks, however, are the political implications of the narrator's decision to "screw" those in power, allying himself by default with the nationalist lower classes of Quebec. Indeed, Laferrière's work even mentions Pierre Vaillères, a former member of the Front de Libération du Québec, whose political autobiography *Nègres blancs d'Amérique* (1968) [*White Negroes of America*] is implicitly referenced by Laferrière's title. Vaillères's book compares the plight of the Quebecois to that of African Americans. It is then not surprising that Vaillères also makes an appearance in *Comment faire l'amour avec un Nègre sans se fatiguer*, lauding Vieux's recently published novel with "Voici, enfin, les Nègres Noirs d'Amérique !" (CFA, 157) [Finally, the true Black Niggers of America! (HML, 142)]. The reference is once again especially meaningful and humorous to the Quebecois reader, but no footnote or explicative clue is furnished by the text to illuminate this historic allusion to the non-Quebecois reader.

Just as Laferrière inscribes his work within Quebecois literary history and politics, it is also a stark critique of race relations in North America. Beneath its vulgar hilarity lies a painful portrait of black masculinity in crisis. The novel links the plight of the black immigrant in Quebec

to that of the African-American slave and the colonized African subject, in a poignant rewriting of Chester Himes, Frantz Fanon, James
Baldwin, Richard Wright, Derek Walcott, and many others. Interwoven
through suras from the Koran – Vieux Os's roommate Bouba is a lapsed
Muslim philosopher – and the sexual exploits of the two out-of-work
immigrants, is the recurrent motif of black racial stereotypes. Since he
is unable to escape it, Vieux Os gives in to cliché and vengeance fuelled
by an inferiority complex based on the sexual objectification of the
black male subject. The African Bouba, for his part, embodies the mys-
tification of African wisdom, cabalistic, misunderstood, and exotic to
his naïve sexual partners in Montreal. By reinforcing stereotype to the
point of hyperbole through repetition, word plays, and double entendre, Laferrière takes control of the stereotype's ideological power: "On
dirait la période de Négritude née, *has been, caput, finito,* rayée. Nègre,
out. Go home Nigger. La Grande Passe Nègre, finie ! *Hasta la vista, Negro.*
Last call, colored. Retourne à la brousse, p'tit Nègre. Faites-vous hara-kiri
là où vous savez" (*CFA*, 17). [The black period is over, has-been, kaput,
finito, whited out. Nigger go home. *Va-t-en, Nègre.* The Black Bottom's
off the Top 20. *Hasta la vista*, Negro. Last call, colored man. Go back to
the bush, man. Do yourself a hari-kiri you-know-where (*HML*, 13).] Laferrière accomplishes what Mireille Rosello calls a "politics of grammar" where refusing a stereotype involves "paying attention to the
formal characteristics of the stereotype so as to control its devastating
ideological power ... Declining a stereotype is a way of depriving it of
its harmful potential by high-lighting its very nature" (1998, 11). Laferrière negotiates his text through a racial and sexual economy that emphasizes the linguistic mechanisms that subtend stereotype. In this way,
the novel conjures up Frantz Fanon's *Black Skin, White Masks* as Jana
Evans Braziel's analysis of black masculinity in the works of Dany Laferrière brilliantly points out. The repetitive use of the word "nègre" is
directly borrowed from Fanon who only in this way can spell out the
dehumanization enacted by a word. By the interpellation of Black man
in the expression "Tiens, un nègre !" [Look! A Negro!] – tragically articulated through the wonder and horror of a White child – Fanon describes the fragmentation of the Black psyche that Laferrière
exacerbates to sexual heights: "Regarde, maman, dit la jeune Blanche, regarde le Nègre coupé. Un bon Nègre, lui répond le père, est un Nègre
sans couilles" (*CFA*, 17). [Look, Mamma, says the Young White Girl, look
at the Cut Negro. A good Negro, her father answers, is a Negro with no
balls (*HML*, 13).] Just as Fanon imitates the racist voices that propagate
myths about Black hypersexuality, so Laferrière returns to the theme of

castration in the disaffected voices of his Black male protagonists. Giving in to the faulty logic of racism, Vieux Os in the chapter entitled "Le pénis nègre et la démoralisation de l'Occident" [The Black Penis and the Demoralization of the Western World] concocts a ploy to avenge Black oppression through the sexual murder of the White man. The narrator discusses his theory with a woman who is henceforth known as "Miz Mythe":

> – ... le Nègre et la Blanche sont complices.
> – Complices ! Où est le meurtre ?
> – Le meurtre du Blanc. Sexuellement, le Blanc est mort. Complètement démoralisé ...
> – Tu reprends tout simplement le mythe du Nègre Grand Baiseur. Je ne crois pas à ça, moi.
> – Et c'est quoi, ton idée à toi ?
> – Pour moi, Nègre et Blanc, c'est pareil.
> – On parle sexualité, pas mathématique. (*CFA*, 133–4)
> [– Black [man] and White [woman] are accomplices.
> – Accomplices? Where's the murder?
> – The murder of the White man. Sexually, the White man is dead. Completely demoralized.
> – You're just reworking the Myth of the Black Stud. I don't believe in it.
> – What do you believe in?
> – Black and white are the same to me.
> – We're talking sexuality, not arithmetic. (*HTM*, 121–2)

This exchange is of course a rewriting of Fanon but with a sardonic touch, since the narrator's overturning of the stereotype involves a concession that is completely misconstrued by the young woman. Laferrière's character summons Fanon's parodying assault on racial stereotypes – "Les nègres, eux, ont la puissance sexuelle. Pensez donc ! Avec la liberté qu'ils ont, en pleine brousse ! Il paraît qu'ils couchent partout, et à tout moment. Ce sont des génitaux" (1965, 148). [As for the Negroes, they have tremendous sexual powers. What do you expect, with all the freedom they have in their jungles! They copulate at all times and in all places. They are really genital (2008, 121)] – but his interlocutor misses this inter-text, interpreting his assertions at face value. Likewise, Laferrière goes to great pains to obfuscate his novel with intertextual references to works by thinkers, writers, musicians, and artists of all races, as if to further signal the cultural alienation of his protagonist who, for all his knowledge of the world, is only best known for his sexual prowess. As Vieux Os and Bouba thus get off on sexual stereotype, pleasure turns to bitterness in some of the novel's most anguish-filled moments. In a chapter entitled "Et voilà Miz Littérature qui me fait une de ces pipes," during the very act of fellatio that symbolically overturns a history of racial oppression according to the narrator, the protagonist's mind cannot help but wander to the words of a Motown song about lynching and castration:

> Ça parlait d'un lynchage. Du lynchage, à Saint-Louis, d'un jeune
> Noir. On l'avait pendu et ensuite châtré. Pourquoi châtré ? Cette
> interrogation me poursuivra toute ma vie. Pourquoi châtré ? Hein !
> Pouvez-vous me le dire ? Naturellement, personne ne voudra se
> mouiller sur un pareil sujet. Bon dieu ! J'aimerais bien savoir, être
> tout à fait sûr que le mythe du Nègre animal, primitif, barbare, qui
> ne pense qu'à baiser, être sûr que tout ça est vrai ou faux. (CFA, 49)
> [The song was about a lynching. The lynching in St. Louis of a
> young black man. He was hanged then castrated. Why castrated? I'll
> never stop wondering about that. Why castrated? Can you tell me?
> Of course no one wants to get involved with a question like that.
> I'd love to know. I'd like to be one hundred percent sure whether
> the myth of the animalistic, primitive, barbarous black who thinks
> only of fucking is true or not. (HML, 41–2)]

The comedic distance between the narrative action and the narrative discourse turns almost aberrant here as Laferrière injects a macabre humour into his text. As Braziel's analysis shows, Laferrière clearly means to situate his novel among a long line of African American literary and artistic contributions, thereby retracing the history of Vieux Os and Bouba's immigration to Montreal back to the first forced immigration of their enslaved ancestry. A novel that hence promises sexual fantasy at the outset turns into a novel about sexual depravation and loneliness. A novel that suggests heterosexual pleasure in its title turns into a novel about homosocial camaraderie and friendship. A novel that implies inter-racial orgasms on the surface turns into a novel about inter-racial chasms and impasses.

The danger of sexual relations between blacks and whites as analyzed in the work of Fanon is of course heavily steeped in colonial history, something Laferrière deliberately sidesteps in this novel. It is indeed surprising that, in a debut work by a Haitian writer, no mention is made of Haiti. The recurrent character of Vieux Os in the sub-

sequent writings of Dany Laferrière will later make his Haitian ancestry well-known to the reader, but in *Comment faire l'amour avec un Nègre
sans se fatiguer*, the author goes to great lengths to leave his native country completely out of the narrative. While most writers of migrant texts
steep their novels in stories of homelands or nations abandoned, Laferrière strives to situate this work so categorically within his city of
adoption that the novel leaves us with an absence of "home" in any traditional sense. Indeed, we are told that both male characters are immigrants, that they are black, and that Bouba is African. Their racial
heritage is linked only to slavery and, much like slaves themselves, the
story of their origins amounts to a great abyss. Their Montreal apartment is described as old and dingy, small, messy, and hot. There is food
left on the table while flies hover above and Bouba sleeps on an old
tired couch. The men have little in the way of furniture, nothing that
makes their apartment comfortable or homey. The narrative is anchored
in the present, in the unrelenting heat of a Montreal summer in the
mid-eighties. The past is only conjured up through literary and musical intertext: Bouba reads Freud and cites the Quran, Vieux Os listens
to Billie Holliday and quotes André Gide. They listen to Charlie Park-
er and Miles Davis and the narrative borrows from the literary style of
Charles Bukowski and Henry Miller, even drawing on the colour palette
of Jean-Michel Basquiat. Indeed, the home that Laferrière creates for
the writer protagonist and his philosopher roommate is a literary one
steeped in cultural history. Laferrière stakes a claim to his share of the
literary market in Quebec and beyond with nothing less than his cultural and literary know-how; "C'est vrai, l'Occident a pillé l'Afrique
mais ce Nègre est en train de lire" (*CFA*, 43) [True, Europe did pillage
Africa but this Black is reading a book (*HML*, 35] the narrator tells us, as
though Laferrière were speaking about none other than himself. The
novel ends with the completion of Vieux Os's first manuscript, an autobiography by all appearances, signaling his entry, like that of Laferrière, onto the cultural scene as a creative force to be reckoned with
henceforth.

CULTURAL SCHIZOPHRENIA IN
LE THÉ AU HAREM D'ARCHI AHMED

Charef's debut novel in 1983 and the first literary work from the Beur
generation stood in for a model of integration, as we saw in the last
chapter, because of the author's incredible ascension out of the
harrowing conditions of the Parisian housing projects and into the

cultural spotlight as a writer and filmmaker in France. While the example of Charef tells one story however, *Le Thé au harem d'Archi Ahmed* tells quite another, painting a stark portrait of life in the *banlieue* among the French lower classes. Charef's novel was a timely commentary on the experience of immigrant youth and the uphill battle they wage against a conglomerate of social forces that condemn them to the sidelines of society. Though the film adaptation of the book reached a wide and international audience – even to the point of becoming a cult film among lovers of French art cinema – the novel continues to sell best among France's North African populations, perhaps because it depicts the painful reality of inhabiting two cultures that are often at odds.

Though Charef's film would indeed cater to some of the Republican political aspirations of the time, his novel far from endorses integration, pointing instead to the cultural schisms that hinder its realization in French society and especially among the underprivileged classes.[10] With its clever title that plays on Archimedes's theory, *Le Thé au harem d'Archi Ahmed* is a novel about institutional racism and poverty. Much like Laferrière's title, Charef also capitalizes on racial stereotypes, only here with an Orientalist twist. Through its suggestive invitation to voyeurism – by way of the sensually mysterious world of polygamy – Charef's title hints both at a long history of Orientalist French art and the anti-Islamic political discourse of its time. As the first novel from a generation of North African children who grew up in France – and an author of Algerian descent no less – *Le Thé au harem d'Archi Ahmed* gestures almost in parody to an exotic image of the Arab world that is quickly effaced by the dark narrative that follows. Indeed, the meeting of the two worlds takes place not in a harem, but in the cold concrete structures that Charef ironically names *Cité des Fleurs* and which house the Algerian immigrant protagonist Madjid and his family, as well as a host of other French and non-French characters.[11] Charef paints a desolate picture of life in the Parisian *banlieue* rife with poverty and hopelessness. Plagued by neglect, physical abuse, alcoholism, drug addiction, theft, and prostitution, the immigrant children have integrated only the poorest, most downtrodden class of French society to become what Charef calls "les enfants du béton" [children of the concrete]:

> Ça chante pas le béton, ça hurle au désespoir comme les loups dans la forêt, les pattes dans la neige, et qui n'ont même plus la force de creuser un trou pour y mourir. Ils attendent comme des cons, voir si quelqu'un viendrait pas leur donner un coup de main. Ils attendent comme les mômes du béton. (THA, 63–4)

[The concrete doesn't sing, it screams – howls despair, like wolves in the forest, in the snow, without the strength to dig a hole to die in. They wait there like idiots, waiting to see if someone will get them out. They wait like the children of the concrete. (*TH*, 52)]

When cultures in contact are met only with hard concrete, rendered in a poetics of despair, it is impossible to read Charef's novel as anything other than a critique of French integration policy. In fact the title of his novel comes from a passage mid-way through the novel when Madjid's fellow Algerian schoolmate Balou mistakenly spells out "le théorème d'Archimède" as "le thé au harem d'Archi Ahmed" (*THA*, 102).[12] The error in understanding betrays the sociocultural gap that separates Balou from his teacher – the odious Monsieur Raffin – and ultimately from the educational system in which the adolescent finds himself. Eventually Raffin's failed efforts at rehabilitating such children lead to fatal illness in the teacher, while Balou opts for a life of crime. The novel not only refuses to deliver on the promise of exoticism suggested in its title, but the text's only reference to the title comes in a quick homophonic undoing of its alluring significance.

At the same time, Charef enacts a perverse reversal in meaning through the harem of prostitutes – so to speak – that Balou later creates around himself as a pimp: "Le bruit courait qu'il était maquereau à Barbès ... c'était gratuit pour les copains. Il faisait des fleurs, on pouvait même choisir sa pute" (*THA*, 90). [There was a rumour that he was pimping in Barbes, and even a rumour that if anyone wanted a screw they should go and see him, because it was free for his pals (*TH*, 73).] Charef's novel is full of such uses of sex as a way in which the forlorn, young, mostly immigrant boys take back power in a society that has made them completely ineffectual. Madjid and his friends sleep with, prostitute, rape, and fantasize about women and girls from the dominant group, that is those who are ethnically French, racially white, and ideally rich. Sex functions in the novel much as it does in the lives of the young boys: a momentary relief from the dreariness around them that is nonetheless painfully devoid of any solace or meaning.[13] Charef writes these scenes in crude, matter-of-fact terms, making sure to leave all emotional responses aside. Along with alcohol and drugs, sex is one of the diversions Madjid resorts to after every failed attempt to integrate, be it at home, at school, in his efforts to find work, and finally even with his friends. Toward the end of the novel, Madjid solicits a prostitute only to discover that she is Chantal, the older sister of his French friend Pat. The discovery leads to binge drinking and drugs as

Madjid swears to keep her secret from Pat. In the novel's grim ending
a few pages later, a resigned Madjid sleeps in the back of a police van
after he is arrested for riding in a stolen BMW. Though his friends flee the
scene upon sight of the approaching police, abandoning the stolen vehicle behind them, Madjid is described in only resigned terms: "Il re-
gardait droit devant lui, les yeux mi-clos, las, dégoûté, fatigué" (THA,
183–4). [He just stared straight in front of him, his eyes half-closed, fed
up and tired (TH, 156).] With Madjid refusing to fight or to escape a system in which he is already condemned, Charef closes his novel on a
note of ultimate despair. The sweet, seductive Orientalist heaven of the
novel's title is now nothing more than the barren prison cell that awaits
Madjid and his friends.

Madjid's disaffected response to his plight is developed throughout
the novel as a disconnectedness that results in cultural schizophrenia,
a phenomenon that Penny Kaganoff points to in her review of *Tea in the
Harem*. Though Kaganoff's use of the term is rather cursory, the expression – or the equivalent psychological condition of "cultural jet lag"
– is useful to understand how Charef muddles his protagonist's sense
of cultural belonging.[14] Madjid is described by the narrative voice as
disassociated from both French and Algerian culture alike right from
the beginning: "Convaincu qu'il n'est ni arabe, ni français, depuis bien
longtemps. Il est fils d'immigrés, paumé entre deux cultures, deux
histoires, deux langues, deux couleurs de peau, ni blanc, ni noir" (THA,
17). [For a long time he's been neither French nor Arab. He's the son of
immigrants – caught between two cultures, two histories, two languages, and two colours of skin. He's neither black nor white (TH, 13).]
Charef carefully builds upon this reality by developing a character with
fraught ties to everyone around him. He gets in constant fights with
his mother over his lack of diligence and duty where the family is concerned. Since his disabled father can no longer work, she expects Madjid to take up the mantle as the eldest son. Her continuous rebukes of
his indolent and delinquent lifestyle – she calls him "finiant" and
"foyou," the Arab-inflected pronunciation for the French "fainéant" and
"voyou" [layabout and hooligan (TH, 12)] – and her despairing pleas for
action punctuate the novel. Madjid obeys his mother Malika only re-
luctantly, waiting for a way out of an angst-ridden existence: "Pour l'instant il attend ... il attend. Il ne veut pas y penser, il ne supporte pas
l'angoisse" (THA, 17). [For the moment he's waiting ... waiting ... He does-
n't want to have to think about it (TH, 13).] This relationship remains
central to the novel in spite of the misunderstanding and distance that
belie it. Charef defines Madjid's character in relation and opposition to

his mother from whom he is so culturally estranged. He is unable to communicate with her, nor relate to her mournful complaints. Despite their shared story of immigration from Algeria, the numerous instances of collapsed dialogues between mother and son emphasize the difference between their individual experiences of cultural displacement.

The protagonist's friendship with Pat, though partners in mischief and crime, is no less fraught with tension. While there is very little confrontation between the two, Charef depicts Pat as brutish and obtuse where Madjid is shown to be sensitive and bright. After all, it is Madjid who carries his doped up friend home, brings his mentally challenged father home from the bar each day, stops his drunken French neighbour from beating his wife and kids, and even prevents the suicide of Josette – a young, single, out of work mother. If Madjid remains jobless throughout the novel, it is because he is discriminated against or reduced to tasks that are well beneath his skill level. Pat, on the other hand, is described as having difficulty with simple factory work and Madjid taunts him about his inability to read. *Le Thé au harem d'Archi Ahmed* is certainly a novel about friendship, but in this central camaraderie, Charef once again singles out the immigrant boy's plight from that of his French counterpart to ultimately explain Madjid's loss of hope at the end of the novel. While everyone else strives to survive, Madjid it appears is too intelligent to simply accept the status quo and yet too depressed to do anything about it. Charef thus enacts a disassociation between the character and his cultural surroundings within the home and without. The boy leaves his sex-obsessed friend for a sad home front at times and flees his anguish-filled mother for the desolate streets of the *banlieue* at others. Madjid partakes of both Franco-Algerian immigrant culture and French *banlieue* culture liberally. Yet Charef's subtle use of words describing the character's weariness – first at home with his mother, later in a stolen vehicle with his friends – open and close the novel: "résigné" (*THA*, 9) [resigned], "impuissant" (*THA*, 9) [powerless], "fatigué" (*THA*, 16, 184) [tired], "lassitude" (*THA*, 120) [weariness], "las" (*THA*, 184) [fed up]. Madjid lives within both cultures schismatically and simultaneously but disaffectedly, as though he cannot fully participate in the reality either one has constructed for itself.

Critic Mireille Rosello proposes the term "départenance" to challenge national and cultural paradigms of belonging that are imposed on the immigrant subject. In her study of Farida Belghoul's novel *Georgette!* Rosello defines her neologism as follows: "'Départenance,' a refusal to define one's identity, not because it is "lost" between two continents, but because it is inexpressible with the context of existing discourses that weave a net of contradictions ... 'Départenance' would thus be a way of acknowledging that one had been called upon to 'belong,' while fully recognizing what would be lost if one remained satisfied with a national or cultural identity fashioned by others" (1993, 23). On the one hand, Madjid's dysfunctional relationship with his mother points to the obsolescence of one discourse of belonging that is defined by an earlier generation of North African immigrants and based on the knowledge of Arabic and the observance of tradition. On the other hand, Charef filters the "appartenance/départenance" question through issues of class to further complicate his protagonist's cultural positioning. Madjid's failure to integrate into anything other than delinquent youth culture in France is a direct result of the poverty-stricken immigrant masses that were completely ignored by French government policy in the 1970s when the novel takes place. Little by little, the narrative voice dismantles the discourses of belonging that are of little use to the disenfranchised populations of the *banlieue*:

Ils se retrouvèrent dehors ... comme un étranger débarquant dans un pays neuf où tout va très vite. Cet étranger, il lui faut s'adapter au mode de vie, aux exigences, au tempérament des autres pour survivre. Faire semblant de suivre le mouvement, ou alors refuser de suivre le système et se mettre à dos la société. Parce que c'est épuisant de courir après une carotte quand, de surcroît, on la sait pourrie depuis lurette. (*THA*, 59)
[They joined each other outside ... They felt like they were foreigners newly arrived in a country where everything moves very fast, newcomers who have to adapt to the demands, the style of life and the temperament of others in order to survive. You either pretend to follow the crowd, or you reject the system and turn your back on society. Because it wears you out when you go running after a carrot – especially when you know that the carrot's been rotten for a long time anyway. (*TH*, 48)]

The experience of immigration is here compared to that of underprivileged youth who are kicked out of school and left to fend for themselves in a society in which they remain outsiders. Immigrant youth like Madjid, are then doubly marginalized, something Charef makes painstakingly evident in the novel through the plight of his character. Indeed, his is a rejection of all normative French discourses of belonging and integration, occupying as it were a space of cultural rebellion that claims a place especially for delinquent immigrant youth who have been relegated to the metaphorical and literal outskirts of society.

The difficult dynamic of "départenance" as rendered for the first time in a French migrant novel, coupled with the parlance of French adolescents in the 1970s, was hence understandably most successful with France's young immigrants. *Le Thé au harem d'Archi Ahmed* captures the cultural schizophrenia of an entire generation of immigrants and their subsequent politicization in France. Madjid's inability to break out of his class is a reality that would hold true for many immigrant youth even two decades later (Hargreaves 2010, 664). Though Charef's work also caught the eye of others such as duo Michèle Ray-Gavras and Constantin Costa-Gavras who financed the film adaptation, the novel carves a literary and political space for a forgotten part of French society who no doubt felt empowered by their literary representation. The film rendition of the novel *Le thé au harem d'Archimède*, transformed from its very title to make the word play less obtuse, had its sights on wider French audiences and was successful in appealing to other demographics than simply those to whom the novel was primarily marketed in Marseille.

TRADING CULTURES IN DAI SIJIE'S
BALZAC ET LA PETITE TAILLEUSE CHINOISE

With a title that evokes the revered name of Balzac alongside that of a Chinese character, Dai Sijie's debut novel is intriguing at first glance; on various French internet pages dedicated to Dai's novel, readers consistently mention the title's allure as piquing their interest from the outset.[15] The addition of Balzac's name was an editorial decision that would prove especially rewarding for Dai who had never intended to include the canonical literary name in the title of his novel. In fact, an earlier rendition of the novel gave as prominent a place to Chinese literature as it did to French literature, but his editors warned that readers would better identify with the influential role of a literature they knew rather than one that they did not. The resulting cultural trade-off was most beneficial to Dai himself, whose cosmopolitan mastery of French and Chinese literature alike seduced many a reader.

It is thus the novels of Alexandre Dumas, Honoré de Balzac, Gustave Flaubert, and Romain Rolland that have a transformative effect on the young title character in whom it awakens an urban, even cosmopolitan sensibility. Through her contact with French literature, the Little Seam-

stress comes of age and acquires a worldly quality about her. She is at
first essentially illiterate and must be read to by one of her suitors. The
impenetrability of the translated Chinese text, however, sparks a fond-
ness in her for its very materiality. In one instance, Ma, one of Dai's two
male protagonists, writes down a passage from Balzac's *Ursule Mirouët*
on the sheepskin lining of his jacket. When his friend Luo reads the
passage out loud to the Little Seamstress, she is described as entering an
almost trance-like state as she dons the jacket with childlike reverence.
Luo recounts the scene in sheer disbelief:

> Ce vieux Balzac ... est un véritable sorcier qui a posé une main
> invisible sur la tête de cette fille ; elle était métamorphosée, rêveuse
> ... Elle a fini par mettre ta foutue veste ... elle m'a dit que le contact
> des mots de Balzac sur sa peau lui apporterait bonheur et
> intelligence. (*BPT*, 78)
> [This fellow Balzac is a wizard ... He touched the head of this
> mountain girl with an invisible finger, and she was transformed,
> carried away in a dream ... She ended up putting your wretched
> coat on ... She said having Balzac's words next to her skin made her
> feel good, and also more intelligent. (*BLC*, 65)]

Such sensual savouring of Balzac's words by a character, who is described by the narrative voice as a true "montagnarde" (*BPT*, 135) [moun-
tain girl (*BLC*, 115)], beautiful yet "inculte" (135) [in need of culture (*BLC*,
115)], pays homage to Balzac's rousing prose. Other references to French
novels punctuate the text as well. The Little Seamstress is captivated by
drawings of a dress in Balzac's *Cousin Bette* and another illustration in
Flaubert's *Madame Bovary* that inspire the creation of a brazier. The
character goes through a Bovary-type metamorphosis that her two
proud suitors call a "rééducation balzacienne" (*BPT*, 223) [Balzacian re-
education (*BLC*, 192)]. After an unplanned pregnancy and ensuing abor-
tion, however, the Little Seamstress abruptly flees the village with
parting words that return to Balzac: "Elle m'a dit que Balzac lui a fait
comprendre une chose : la beauté d'une femme est un trésor qui n'a
pas de prix" (*BPT*, 229). [She said that she has learnt one thing from
Balzac: that a woman's beauty is a treasure beyond price (*BLC*, 197).] In
the name of a newly discovered sense of femininity and freedom, the
Little Seamstress abandons all – father, lover, and friend, not to mention
the village where she has spent all of her life. Her sudden and unexpected departure also echoes the narrator's earlier discovery of individualism in Rolland's *Jean-Christophe*: "*Jean-Christophe, avec son*

individualisme acharné ... fut pour moi une révélation salutaire" (*BPT*, 137). [Jean-Christophe with his fierce individualism ... was a salutary revelation (*BLC*, 116).] The literary revolution that undermines Mao's cultural one affects all three of Dai's main characters as they read and are read to in order to escape the dreary conditions of the reeducation camp.

After the discovery of forbidden literary texts by its two protagonists Ma and Luo, the novel turns into a somewhat romantic portrait of Maoist rural China augmented with French values derived from its literature. The novel bestows French literature with a redemptive power that is somehow able to silence the despair of characters in forced exile, subject to heavy labor and starvation as part of their cultural rehabilitation. Most critics were angered by Dai's use of French literature to lighten his burden to the history of oppression within which the novel is set, and some accused him of unabashedly catering to a French sense of cultural superiority.[16] *Balzac et la Petite Tailleuse chinoise* is certainly a mockery of Mao's reeducation camps, especially because the peasants who run them are easily duped by the silly antics of Dai's intelligent, well-educated duo. Though Luo intermittently alludes to a depression, it is only sparingly noted by Ma's narrative voice, which privileges the love story above all else. Critic Yvonne Hsieh is further perturbed by the intra-diegetic reading of French literature, which somehow elides the darker aspects of the novels that better fit the Chinese context of the time. Instead, the characters' reading favours concepts like freedom and individuality over "ambition, greed, betrayal, vengeance, envy, hate, wickedness," argues Hsieh (2002, 100). French literature functions merely as an escape and the social critique they comprise is completely lost on the naïve young Chinese readers. The cultural trade-off that results is an erasure of both the dismal sides of Mao's China and that of Balzac, Dumas, Flaubert, and Roland's France.

It is through the play of narrative voice, on the other hand, that Dai enacts a subtle critique of both cultures as they collide in his novel. Ma's narrative voice dominates much of the novel and it is this character's perspective that has been largely critiqued as Dai's failed obligation to history. Ma watches and reports as his friend alternately tricks, amuses, and educates the peasants, the Little Seamstress, and her father – the village tailor – with his cultural know-how. Though at times, this narration lends itself to a certain melancholy owing to the extreme conditions of the camps, Ma's perspective remains decidedly optimistic, even whimsical at times. It is his friend Luo who references a depression – forced as they are to work in the coal mines and paddy fields of Phoenix

Mountain: "j'ai l'impression que je vais mourir dans cette mine. Sa phrase me laissa sans voix ... je me sentis soudain trempé de sueur froide. À partir de cet instant, je fus contaminé par sa peur de mourir ici" (*BPT*, 43). [I've had this idea stuck in my head: that I am going to die in this mine. Hearing this my breath failed me ... I suddenly broke out in a cold sweat. I had become infected by the same idea as Luo: from that day on I shared his terror of not leaving the place alive (*BLC*, 32).] Since it is Luo who ultimately wins the girl, Ma's narration centres around the love story via the illicit literature, paying only credence to his friend's despair in short but poignant passages like the one above. When Luo briefly takes over as narrator, however, he is at pains to conceal his obvious distress. While recounting a love scene between himself and the Little Seamstress, he interrupts the story, remembering his former life in a fury:

> Soudain je me suis demandé :
> « Qui me relâchera un jour de cette montagne ? » Sur le coup, cette question, sûrement idiote, m'a fait beaucoup de peine. J'avais un cafard impossible ... en regardant les clés accrochées sur l'anneau, les clés de chez moi, à Chengdu, qui ne me serviraient plus jamais, je faillis me mettre à chialer ... Dans un élan de désespoir, je jetai mon porte-clés très loin dans l'eau profonde. (*BPT*, 175–6)
> [Suddenly I wondered:
> "Who will ever release me from this mountain?" This question, although pointless, plunged me into the depths of despair ... those Chengdu keys that I probably wouldn't ever use again, I had a lump in my throat ... With a heavy heart I flung my key ring into the pool. (*BLC*, 151)

Unlike Ma, Luo's narrative voice momentarily opens a window onto a darker side of the novel that is veiled by the dominant narration. Luo's words resonate with anguish in ways that Ma's do not, although here again it is the seductive love-games with the Little Seamstress that take over the narration as the young girl plunges naked into the water in search of her lover's keys.

In the following chapter, the Little Seamstress also provides an oblique insight into her own distress when exalting the virtues of literary role play: "Avant, je n'imaginais pas qu'on puisse jouer quelqu'un qu'on n'est pas tout en restant soi-même, par exemple jouer une femme riche et 'contente', alors que je ne le suis pas du tout" (*BPT*, 180). [Before, I had no idea that you could take on the role of a completely different person, actually become that person – a rich lady, for example – and still be your own self (*BLC*, 155).][17] The narrative voice's marked emphasis (in the French version) on happiness reveals her true emotional state, despite the literature and affection with which her two male suitors surround her. Like Luo, it is apparent in her narration that the love affair is not enough to erase her difficult plight as a peasant-women in rural Communist China. It is in this chapter that Dai carefully sets up the title character's sudden departure at the end of the novel. She is neither as naïve nor as carefree as the young boys imagine. "Luo m'a dit que je pourrais être une bonne comédienne" (*BPT*, 180) [Luo told me I'd make a good actress (*BLC*,155)], she says in her own narrative voice as though hinting at the role she has been playing since the beginning. The character's unexpected departure interpreted through this chapter points to Ma and Luo's complete misreading of their object of love and fantasy. More importantly, it signals the novel's subtextual critique of French literary artifice in Maoist rural China and the collision of worldviews that ensues. In the end, one cannot help but return to the novel's clunky title that pits Balzac against the Little Chinese Seamstress; theirs is not a happy meeting but one rife with cultural misunderstanding. The autodafé scene at the end of novel – that critic Yvonne Hsieh argues almost bolsters Maoist era sanctions on Western literature[18] – certainly reflects the cultural and literary misreadings at the heart of this novel. It is the educated boys who ultimately fall most prey to literary misinterpretation and the apparent cultural trade-off enacted by Dai goes up in flames, much like the French books his protagonists burn out of despair and frustration.

CONCLUSION

All four of the debut novels chosen for this chapter had remarkable initial success in their countries of publication as well as subsequent lives in translation. Spanning a quarter century from the launch of Kattan's novel in Quebec to Dai's novel in France, these works by authors from four different continents constitute both a sampling of the global reach of migrant textuality and evidence for its lasting scope as a mode of writing. While critics like Hans-Jürgen Grief signal the death of "migrant literature,"[19] its new and expanded iteration that is here proposed as a mode tailored for the global literary market is both necessary and very much alive. The tension that all of these novels face between exploitation and resistance figures in the two-sided reality of this type of writing, one that each of the texts analyzed in this chapter displays in its own way (a "quandary" for Kattan, "schizophrenia" for Charef, a "seduction" for Laferrière, and a "trade-off" for Dai). While other critics, as we have seen, often favour one reading over the other, we have sought to situate these migrant texts between its constitutive polarities – never only "selling out" or "opting in," never critiquing without also pleasing. Thus is the paradox of the migrant text, which concedes dominant paradigms and discourses while slowly undoing them from within.

5

Linguistic Interference

INTRODUCTION

Since migrant texts are always the product of cultural exchange, they carry the imprint of language encounters. The linguistic "meetings" in these works may be more or less concealed, often to ensure broad readability while maintaining an ounce of exotic untranslatability. An important linguistic politics is at play here, since integration into French-speaking national communities first requires mastery of the dominant language. Much like the cultural content of migrant texts, which anchors in France or Quebec before voyaging into uncharted worlds, the linguistic peregrinations of these works are firmly rooted in the dominant French medium. At first glance then, native languages appear much like interference on the narrative airwaves of migrant fiction, intermittent signals of an engagement with the language politics of immigration.

When studying languages brought into contact through literary form, extant conceptual models vacillate between two poles, with some conjuring notions of irreducible diversity (heteroglossia, heterophony, heterology)[1] and others calling for unity to combat against linguistic purity (multilingualism, plurilingualism, polyphony). Yet none of these concepts offers a completely satisfactory working space for the language of the migrant text, where the pull of the monolingual continually distorts the writing of the multilingual author, who is forced to contain, negotiate, and sometimes quarantine his or her native language(s).

Whenever we think we have found the perfect example of multilingual brilliance and linguistic hybridity, we might do better to view it not only with a dose of skepticism, but also with an openness to the strategies employed by the text in every respect. This is a literature often accused of ethnographic mimicry and exoticism. Then again, that is precisely the point. For these criticisms derive from the naturally variable qualities of texts that come to us from authors who have travelled from far-off horizons and whose journeys are fraught with the dynamics of trying to express their experiences via the foreignness of the French language. Clément Moisan and Renate Hildebrand call them "ces étrangers du dedans," writers who appropriate the French language to tell a story that is in so many ways foreign to the vehicle of its own enunciation. As Jacques Derrida discusses in *Le Monolinguisme de l'autre*, this dynamic is both alienating and desirable at once, as it expresses the fundamental insufficiency of human communication in the face of all language. At the same time, as Ginette Michaud points out, there is a problem of language identification contained in the paradoxical writing of Derrida himself. Even though he is in some ways an outsider to the French language due to his Algerian birth, Derrida adopts a contradictory position toward his own accent. It is ultimately the hinge point for his distinction between a "private" and a "public" function of language: "Je n'en suis pas fier, je n'en fais pas une doctrine, mais c'est ainsi : l'accent, quelque accent français que ce soit, et avant tout le fort accent méridional, me paraît incompatible avec la dignité intellectuelle d'une parole publique" (1996, 77–8). [I am not proud of it, I make no doctrine of it, but so it is: an accent – any French accent, but above all a strong southern accent – seems incompatible to me with the intellectual dignity of public speech (1998, 46).] This is a startling confession from a philosopher known for deconstructing the very concept of linguistic purity – and his words are equally shocking and revelatory.

Derrida is here extending a tradition with a long history, to which any number of philosophers and migrant texts have succumbed before him. The French language, and most notably as it is spoken in France, has always been the object of a linguistic protectionism by the Académie Française, founded in 1635 by Cardinal Richelieu. Any immigrant writer who wants to publish in France must not only master the French language but also defend it against corruption or, worse still, a decline of influence. Derrida explores his own aversion to accented language, one that pervades his writing: "À travers l'histoire que je raconte et malgré tout ce que je semble parfois professer d'autre part, j'ai contracté, je l'avoue, une inavouable mais intraitable intolérance : je ne supporte ou n'admire, en français du moins, et seulement quant à la langue, que le français pur" (1996, 77–8). [Throughout the story I am relating, despite everything I sometimes appear to profess, I concede that I have contracted a shameful but intractable intolerance: at least in French, insofar as the language is concerned, I cannot bear or admire anything other than pure French (1998, 46).] The author of a migrant text must face up to this same kind of intolerance, negotiating the different linguistic influences that compose his or her French, which will always be impure. Although many critics have celebrated the "hybridity" and the "plurilingualism" of contemporary authors writing in France, these processes can also be analyzed from more close up – highlighting the diverse mechanisms by which this form of literary writing contains and even isolates linguistic difference at the behest of a language which, in order to be published, must evince a certain control and purity.

In the case of Quebec, the French accent has obviously been politicized for centuries now – but this does not mean that there is a greater openness to divergent accents. Marooned in a fierce battle to preserve linguistic difference amid an Anglophone Canadian dominant strongly influenced by the United States, Quebec has quite often intervened in terms of language.[2] Yet despite a Canadian politics of multiculturalism that was put in place in 1971, indigenous and immigrant populations in Quebec have never been free from threats. And if migrant texts have been welcomed and supported by the provincial government, and been the subject of many studies, it is because they represent the success of immigration policy as well as the dawn of a new "multicultural" Quebec – albeit a francophone one.

Immigrant writers therefore tell their stories with a certain distance from their own ethnic and linguistic roots, and the portrait they create for readers of their cultures of origin becomes inscribed in this linguistic self-awareness. It is a self-awareness that is different, however, from that proposed by Lise Gauvin in that it is strongly marked by the expectations of a French and/or Quebecois readership that would never be completely reachable without some form of exoticism. In other words, theirs is a "there" that must pass by "here" – expressed in the language of "here," in the codes of "here," and negotiated for readers from "here." This is also a literature with a clear connection to ethnographic mimicry as, despite a clear desire to minimize any constraint on individual expression, it ultimately requires a writer who can express him/herself in perfect French. I borrow again from Derrida to conclude: "Cette exigence [de pureté] n'est ni éthique, ni politique, ni sociale. Elle ne m'inspire aucun jugement. Elle m'expose seulement à la souffrance quand quelqu'un, et ce peut-être moi, vient à y manquer." (1996, 78–9) [This demand [for purity] is neither ethical, political, nor social. It does not inspire any judgment in me. It simply exposes me to suffering when someone, who can be myself, happens to fall short of it (1998, 46).]

AZOUZ BEGAG, *LE GONE DU CHAÂBA*:
FUNCTIONAL MONOLINGUALISM

When it was published in 1986, Azouz Begag's first novel *Le Gone du Chaâba* met with immediate success. It won the Sorcières prize a year after its publication and sold more than seventy thousand copies. It was also the first Beur novel – written that is by the second generation of Maghrebian immigrants to France – to be integrated into the scholarly canon. How exactly can we explain the fantastic success of this one novel with the French public, since it was not one of a kind, but in fact part of a larger eruption of Maghrebi novels by authors such as Mehdi Charef, Farida Belghoul, and Mehdi Lallaoui? In 1983, Charef had given this nascent corpus its start with *Le thé au harem d'Archi Ahmed* which, along with Begag's novel, have been the only titles to retain the interest of French readers and critics for nearly a decade. We examined Charef's case in the last chapter, however the success of *Le Gone du Chaâba* has far surpassed that of Charef's novel.

Le Gone du Chaâba dramatizes linguistic encounters on at least three different levels, as the colloquial parlance of a family in the *banlieue* of Lyon crisscrosses with a narrative voice couched in standard, correct French. This linguistic configuration is augmented as well by the language spoken by the parents of the protagonist, who mix their native Algerian Arabic dialect from El Ouricia with a French they have apparently learned phonetically. The young Azouz, as both narrator and protagonist of the novel, tells us the story of his life in a ghetto called *Chaâba*, where he follows two intertwined paths – one spatial, the other scholarly – which both lead to the desired integration into French society. From a marginalized shantytown to an HLM in the Lyon ghetto, Azouz and his family make a better life for themselves by moving to an F4 in Duchère after spending many years in huts without electricity or heating. At the same time, the little Azouz moves from his neighbourhood *collège* to the Lycée Saint-Exupéry and learns very young that mastering French is the only way he will guarantee hospitality in his new country, as the quality of an immigrant's treatment is invariably dependent on his or her ability to use the language.

Although it is sometimes imbued with a regional accent or encumbered by an Arabic accent, most of the text is written in a language that obeys French norms. The linguistic divergences, which manifest themselves in the spoken words of children or in the Arabic expressions of the community in the ghetto, are scrupulously relegated to specific characters or situations. In other words, linguistic difference, although present in the text, is subsumed by correct usage or even literary language, which pushes accents to the margins, figuring them as exceptions. The Lyonnaise pronunciation of the |o|, indicated by the use of a circumflex accent on the letter, and the typical expressions of young people in the region are communicated through dialogues that are clearly separated from the dominant narration of the novel:

À Hacène qui se tient à côté de moi, je lance :
– T'as vu le bonone qui s'est approché de moi ?
– Non.
– Eh ben, il voulait me choper. Je lui ai fait peur tout seul. J'lui ai balancé une bôche en plein dans la tête à ce hallouf. Il s'est sauvé.
(GC, 46)
[I shouted to Hacène, who was standing close to me:
"Did you see the guy who came up to me?"
"No."
"Well, he wanted to get me. I scared him all by myself. I gave the hallouf a crack on the head. He ran off." (SK, 42)]

Here Azouz uses the childish mispronunciation "bonone" to stand in for *bonhomme*, (guy) as well as several expressions common to his community – *bôche* for *caillou* (stone) – and a few Arabic words – *hallouf* for *cochon* (pig) – in speaking about his friend Hacène who is also of Algerian origins. Then, his narration continues its course by reporting the thoughts of a young boy in a normative French. For example, when Azouz speaks to his classmate in French, the best student in the class, he uses a sentence completely purged of both slang and of Arabic expressions:

– Bonjour Azouz ! ... Alors ? C'est aujourd'hui que le maître rend les compositions ?
–Tu le sais bien ...
– Moi j'ai une peur terrible...
– Pourquoi ?
Il me regarde droit dans les yeux, intrigué par ma relance.
–Et toi, t'as pas peur ?
– Non, lui dis-je. Pour moi, ça a bien marché. De quoi veux-tu que j'aie peur ? (GC, 69–70)
["Hello Azouz! ... Isn't the teacher due to give us our compositions back today?"
"You know he is ... "

"I'm really scared."
"Why?"
He looked me straight in the eyes, puzzled by my response.
"Aren't you scared too?"
"No," I said. "As far as I'm concerned it all went OK. Why should I
be scared?" (SK, 66)]

More surprising, Azouz also uses this same type of language, without
slang or dialect markings, when he speaks with his sister Zohra, of
whom he often asks advice, or even with his friend Moustafa, with
whom he is constantly fighting. Elsewhere, Azouz's brother and sister
also use a standard French grammar when they speak to one another.

Azouz's parents, and in particular his father Bouzid, use, on the other
hand, a French that Marc Sourdot describes as "[French structures
pronounced according to Arabic phonetics, words from an Arabic
lexicon combined with French vocabulary]" (1996, 112). In his study of
language in *Le Gone du Chaâba*, Sourdot emphasizes the numerous false
equivalences that exist between Arabic and French pronunciation,
hence leading to a phonic distortion of words. *Fainéant* become
"finiane," *bon à rien* becomes "bouariane," *professeur* turns into
"broufissour," etc. The statements made by Bouzid have to be quoted at
length here to make sense of them: "Tan a rizou, Louisa. Fou li fire
digage di là, zi zalouprix. Li bitaines zi ba bou bour li zafas !" (GC, 42).
[Tu as raison, Louise, faut les faire dégager de là, ces saloperies. Les
putains, c'est pas bon pour les enfants !³] [Y're right, Louisa. We gotta
get 'em outta here, the bitches. Bitaines (hookers) is no good for kids!
(SK, 37).] [You're right, Louise. Hookers are no good for children! (SK,
203).] As narrator, Azouz distances himself from this manner of speaking by using dashes or parentheses that show that our hero does not
share the words of his parents. He even expresses a certain exasperation
at the bad French that his mother uses when she asks for "li ziou" as opposed to *les oeufs*. The narrator follows with a reply that confirms his
embarrassment: "Emma, les zeux! La corrigeais-je sans cesse" (GC, 120).
["Yemma, *les zeux* [the eggs]," I corrected her each time (SK, 118).]

Azouz, like his sister Zohra and his brother Moustafa, plays the role
of linguistic "life preserver" for his parents. In fact, Zohra ends up act-
ing in this capacity for nearly all of the community in Chaaba. When
students receive their report cards from school, Zohra goes around the
neighbourhood translating the contents of the reports for the parents
of each student. For the Algerian fathers, most of them illiterate, she
even shows exactly where they need to sign the forms by marking them

with a cross. Following a police investigation and the discovery of an illicit beef trade in Chaaba, Bouzid asks his daughter to read a newspaper article to him. Frustrated by his lack of comprehension but
desperate to maintain his role as chief of the family, Bouzid accuses
Zohra of having left out information during her reading. When
Moustafa intervenes to defend his sister, Bouzid asks him to translate
the report into Arabic. The episode, which ends with the young girl in
tears, aligns the narrator, Zohra, and Moustafa with the sympathies of
the reader, as all of them share knowledge of French. Their father, an illiterate immigrant, is set aside as the reader is encouraged to identify
with his second-generation children, benefiting from the pleasure of
shared linguistic understanding.

Thanks to a "guide de phraséologie" and two glossaries included at
the back of the novel, Begag provides us with a key that allows us to de-
code the Franco-Arabic language of the first generation of immigrants
from Sétif, as well as the language of the youths of the Lyon *banlieue*.
The title of the novel itself puts the reader in contact with this het-
eroglossic aspect, as it mixes the two lexicons as if to warn about the
presence of multiple languages. These appendices are of little use in the
end, as Begag also makes sure the reader is following from page to page,
sprinkling clues throughout the text in parentheses – for example "Une
pompe manuelle qui tire de l'eau potable du Rhone, l'bomba (la
pompe)" (GC, 7) [the only source of water in the shantytown, *l'bomba*
[the hand pump], which drew drinking water from the Rhône (SK, 1)].
He also uses a form of reformulated translation for those words that
are borrowed directly from Arabic and inserted into the French flow, as
in the passage below:

– Va m'acheter deux boîtes de chemma chez le birou taba.
Il me tend quelques pièces. Je les prends et soudain une question
pratique me vient à l'esprit :
– Comment on dit le chemma en français Abboué ?
– Le tababrisi ! Demande de tababrisi.
Je suis descendu chez le buraliste ... Il n'avait pas du tababrisi ...
– Vous voulez du tabac à priser ?
J'ai dit :
– Oui. Deux boîtes. Et un paquet de Zig-Zag.
Le buraliste m'a servi en riant. (GC, 148)
["Go and get me two tins of chemma from the tobacconist."
He gave me some coins. I took them, and suddenly a practical ques-
tion came to my mind:

"How do you say *chemma* in French, Abboué?"
"*Tababrisi*! Ask for *tababrisi*."
I went down to the tobacconist ... He did not have any tababrisi ...
"You mean *tabac à priser* [chewing tobacco]?"
"Yes, two tins. And a packet of cigarette paper."
The tobacconist served me, laughing. (*SK*, 147–8)]

Begag thus goes to great pains to translate these words not once but twice; first, he does so in the text, which clearly illustrates the meaning of "chemma," and second in his meta-text, the "petit dictionnaire des mots bouzidiens" which closes the novel. In response to this redundancy, Sourdot asks:

N'a-t-il [Begag] pas fait confiance à l'intuition linguistique du lecteur potentiel ? Ne s'est-il pas plutôt amusé, à travers cet essai lexicologique, à ancrer l'œuvre romanesque dans le réel d'une table d'équivalence ? Ou, plus prosaïquement, n'est-ce pas son éditeur qui, craignant que le roman se coupe du plus grand nombre, l'aurait orienté vers cette activité dictionnairique ? (1996, 113) [Did Begag not have confidence in the linguistic intuition of his potential reader? Was he just amusing himself, through this lexico-logical essay, trying to anchor the novel in the reality of a table of equivalence? Or, more prosaically, was it not his editor who orient-ed him toward this dictionary-like activity, fearing that the novel would be inaccessible to most readers?]

Sourdot is right to point out these decentring strategies put in place by Begag who, in initiating his readership to a new terminology, preserves the narrative continuity and textual fluidity of his novel thanks to these multiple processes of equivalency.

All in all, what is evident here is a veritable linguistic meta-con-sciousness, in the sense that what appears in Begag's writing is a will to avoid any sort of misunderstanding or disorientation for the reader. As Sourdot notes many times, the pleasure of reading this novel lies in its accessibility. However, this lack of interruptions also protects the read-er from any experience of alterity, in that it circumscribes his or her ex-perience of linguistic disorientation. French remains the unquestioned dominant language, and its preponderance is never called into ques-tion by the other dialects that punctuate the text. Both the regional Lyon dialect and Arabic are present, but never for a moment do they undermine the quality of the normative French that guides the majority of the novel. The resolute goal of the protagonist is to perfect his French and ascend to the top of his class, hence doing away with the monolingualism of his parents:

> J'ai honte de mon ignorance. Depuis quelques mois, j'ai décidé de changer de peau. Je n'aime pas être avec les pauvres, les faibles de la classe. Je veux être dans les premières places du classement, comme les Français ... À partir d'aujourd'hui, terminé l'Arabe de la classe. Il faut que je traite d'égal à égal avec les Francais. (GC, 50–2)
> [I was ashamed of my ignorance. For a few months now I had been resolved on changing sides. I did not like being with the poor and the weak pupils in class. I wanted to be among the top of the class alongside the French children ... Starting from today I was not going to be the Arab boy in the class any more. I was determined to be on an equal footing with the French kids. (SK, 46–7)]

When his Algerian friends accuse him of betraying them and treat him like a "Gaouri" (Frenchman), Azouz responds by pleading innocent and claiming that his path is the one that should be obvious, as it leads to the advantages of integration: "Non, je suis un Arabe. Je travaille bien, c'est pour ça que j'ai un bon classement. Tout le monde peut être comme moi" (GC, 88). [No, I am an Arab. I work hard; that's why I did well. Everyone can be like me (SK, 85).] A bit later, he does a complete about-face, admitting that he feels a certain guilt: "J'ai terriblement honte des accusations que m'ont portées mes compatriotes parce qu'elles étaient vraies. Je joue toujours avec les Français pendant la récré. J'ai envie de leur ressembler" (GC, 88). [I was terribly ashamed by the accusations made against me by my fellow citizens because they were true. I was always playing with French kids during break (SK, 85).] This desire to become French is accelerated by Azouz's success in school. With a drive to work and a clear intelligence, he is rewarded for his French compositions, which demonstrate his high mastery of the language. Later, when a classmate treats their teacher in a racist manner, Azouz is the point of reference for good behavior. Finally, when our hero graduates to CM2, he is the only Maghrebi in his new class, and his teacher refers to him as the "petit génie" (GC, 151) [little genius (SK, 151)].

Bouzid's failure to master the French language contrasts sharply with his son's eloquence. Azouz's father's accent spurs laughter not only from his childrens' classmates, but arguably from the reader as well, since the exercise of pronouncing Bouzid's dialogue out-loud becomes one of the novel's sources of humour. The father's accent becomes so ridiculous in places that the novel's fascination with this character and his so-called "bouzidien" language can be said many times to verge on outright exoticism. The novel offers us an ethnographic look at an Arab community in a shantytown via the perspectival remove of Azouz, who as a narrator clearly prefers to associate with others, the French and later the Jews of the Lyon ghetto, rather than with Arabs. Bouzid's macho ethnicity is overtly critiqued in the newspaper episode described earlier, as well as in a scene where he fights with his sister in-law, Zidouma, after a police investigation. His son, on the other hand, shows a softer side, a sensitivity that awakens the sympathy of his teachers, his French friends, and the readers alike. The linguistic and cultural alienation of the father in France is thus worsened by the apparent integration of the son who succeeds, in most every way, at blending into the monolingual model required by his new culture.

Even though we know that Azouz must also speak Arabic, the language never so much as crosses his lips other than during an episode, taken up numerous times by critics, where his school master translates "chritte" and "kaissa" as *gant de crin* and *gant de toilette* (GC, 81–2) ["chritte" = loofah (SK, 79) and "kaissa" = washcloth (SK, 78)]. Azouz does intimate that he knows Arabic words are important to use for certain things, yet he seems to have difficulty finding any examples other than said *gant de toilette*: "Je me suis rendu compte aussi qu'il y a des mots que je ne savais dire qu'en arabe: le kaissa par exemple (gant de toilette)" (GC, 50). [I had also realized that there were some words that I knew only in Arabic, such as *kassa* [facecloth] (SK, 46).] It is clear, then, that Azouz's Arab side is completely relegated to the domestic sphere, whereas his father's overflows into public time and time again. Here Begag, as author, also made a choice – to reserve his own Arabic for the privacy of his own home, not to let it accent his text too much. The use of quotation marks, parentheses, and glossaries in the book is hence a stylistic attempt to quarantine the parlance of the older generation to the *banlieue*, and to privilege standardized French above all. Put another way, Begag echoes here the thoughts of Jacques Derrida on this subject, distinguishing between a "private" and "public" function of language, and most of all when it is a question of accent and proper usage. If letting jargon, slang, accents, and foreign words are the excesses of language that might contaminate a text, Begag writes carefully, never letting arise this veritable heteroglossia which nevertheless gives each language and accent a strict and authentic place. There is then a sort of monolinguistic sleight of hand that animates this text, in which the dominance of normative language is reinforced at most every turn. Nevertheless, the narration establishes a hierarchy that exploits the so-called "polyphony" of the novel, pushing the numerous alternative voices to the margins and characterizing them as exceptions. The linguistic economy that drives the novel is hence one that dovetails rather nicely with any call for integration.

School becomes, in this narrative economy, the hinge point for the linguistic itinerary of the Beur writer. School is the privileged place of integration, which in the 1980s was a main target of the Mitterrand government via its establishment of Zones d'Education Prioritaires (les ZEPs). The scholarly success of the protagonist and his exemplary performance at school becomes a motif that will return in Begag's later work as well.[4] In an article entitled "Voleur d'écriture: ironie textuelle, irone culturelle chez Azouz Begag," Michel Laronde examines the series of compositions written by young Azouz in *Le Gone du Chaâba*. He draws a helpful connection between a child's stages of writing and the specific positioning of a Beur student *vis à vis* French culture. For Laronde, Azouz's writing evolves from that of a plagiarist who brazenly imitates Maupassant, to the production of stereotypes where he regurgitates platitudes and clichés commonly learned in school like "les feuilles d'automne qui tourbillonnent" et "le manteau de neige de l'hiver." Eventually, the boy succeeds in detaching himself from canonical models and writes an essay about racism that his teacher judges original. Laronde interprets each of these literary phases of the narrator as tactics of resistance against institutionalized teaching methods. For him, Begag effects, little by little, a decentring of the French language that calls into question dominant French cultural discourse:

En se déplaçant vers un autre discours, celui du racisme, qu'il oppose à celui de la littérature, Azouz découvre à ses dépens, la réversibilité du stéréotype. Avec la rédaction sur le racisme, c'est-à-dire en introduisant un bruit dans le discours culturel français, Azouz vole la parole à « la Maîtresse » [qui l'avait autrefois accusé de plagiat]. (2000, 53)

[By moving toward another type of discourse, that of racism, that he opposes to the literary discourse, Azouz discovers the reversibility of the stereotype at his own cost. With his essay on racism, that is in introducing some noise in the French cultural discourse, Azouz's voice replaces that of the teacher (who initially accused him of plagiarism)].

In borrowing the metaphor of the "parasite" from Michel Serres, Laronde follows his analysis and attributes a parasitic role to the essay on racism where French culture is concerned. Following from this, then, is the claim that the intrusion of Arabic words in the French text (the famous *gant de toilette*) redoubles this cultural leeching at the level of language.

In his desire to make this novel subversive and post-colonial at any cost, Laronde ignores, it would seem, the strong mimetic tendency in Begag's novel. A first novel, after all, it seeks to assimilate Azouz to French culture via the mastery of the linguistic medium. The composition on racism, even though it may seem drawn from personal experience, is not really that. It tells in reality the inverse of the author's story – the return to school of a young Arab boy who had chosen to remain at home rather than to integrate into his host community. The teacher requires Azouz – first in his class – to read the text aloud in front of the class, as Azouz's own case effectively contradicts the story he has written. Via this clever *mise-en-abime*, Begag invites the reader to reflect on the role and status of Beur writers of course, but also on the irony of this episode, which features a distanciation between a narrator and his fictional character – even though Begag the writer is himself using the autobiographical form to tell his own story. As we saw in the first chapter, postcolonial discourse is slippery any time it is applied in an unexamined way to the real migrant condition, since it tends to idealize the resistant position of the subject, even though the sole desire of so many such subjects is only to integrate successfully.

LEÏLA SEBBAR,
JE NE PARLE PAS LA LANGUE DE MON PÈRE:
LATENT HETEROGLOSSIA

Leïla Sebbar is a prolific novelist whose literary corpus returns incessantly to her country of her childhood, Algeria. She is an immigrant writer of mixed lineage, born in 1951 in Hennaya, near Tlemcen, to a French mother and an Algerian father. She spent her childhood and part of her adolescence there before moving to France. Even though she spent seventeen years in Algeria, Sebbar claims to never have learned Arabic and to know nothing of her father's language. Her 2003 novel claims as much with its title, *Je ne parle pas la langue de mon père* [*I don't speak my father's tongue*]. In it, she tells the story of a youth spent without communicating in the language of not only her father but also of so many others in the Sebbar household – her grandmother, her pa-

ternal aunts, and countless servants. This lack of language is also one of
a repressed history, namely the trauma of the Algerian war, stories of
which her father never revealed to her while he was living. Written five
years after the death of her father, the novel is a poetic homage to his
memory as well as an evocation of the pain she endures having never
been able to share with him the complicity of language. Sebbar's text
is thus punctuated with allusions to the power of an absent language
that seems to actively deprive the narrator of the perspective that might
come with bilingualism – instead ensuring her alienated, monolingual
state throughout.

Each chapter of the novel opens with a sentence that reiterates in
some way the title of the work – but with important variation. The
narrator takes on various different grammatical positions, sometimes
that of subject and sometimes that of object, hence modifying subtly
her role in determining linguistic meaning as a whole: "Je ne parle pas
la langue de mon père"; "Mon père ne m'a pas appris la langue de sa
mère"; "Je n'ai pas parlé la langue d'Aïsha et de Fatima"; etc. [I don't
speak my father's tongue; My father never taught me his mother's language; I did not speak Aïsha and Fatima's language; etc.] Through repetition, each of these phrases reveals the gap created by Arabic in a
French text that tries mightily to retrace the steps of a missing Algerian
heritage. In other words, Sebbar's return to her childhood home can
only occur in the language of the oppressor. It is hence the writer's guilt
about narrating in the dominant language that both haunts and animates her creative evocations of a country colonized so long ago.[5]

In each of these opening phrases, the verb tense vacillates between
present and past until the final chapter, where the narrator espouses
the simple future: "Je n'apprendrai pas la langue de mon père" [I will
not learn my father's tongue]. This categorical refusal, which brings the
novel to a close, puts a definitive end to the reproaches that guide her
voice in other chapters, but it also perturbs us with a certain obstinate
tenacity. As such, it slams a sort of obtuse, linguistic finality onto the
plaintive regret and nostalgia that pervade earlier passages – she has set-
tled, at last, on the limitations of the monolingual.

Habiba Deming interprets all of Sebbar's work in light of this stub-
born declaration, which mimics, she argues, the colonial gesture. Deming reveals in Sebbar's work a sort of voluntary refusal of Arabic that
runs throughout the author's later novels as well. In *Lettres parisiennes;
Autopsie de l'exil*, Sebbar claims to have spent seven years studying classical Arabic (2005, 148). For Deming, it is impossible that Sebbar could
have acquired no understanding of the language after having spent

eighteen years in semi-rural Algeria. In *Je ne parle pas la langue de mon père* she even admits to being surrounded by the language at her French school – even though the administration forbids its Arab students to use their mother tongue:

> [L]a langue maternelle, prohibée dans l'enceinte de l'école, la cour de récréation ne réussit pas à l'interdire, et les maîtres, debout sous le caroubier qui donne la plus belle ombre au centre de la cour, ont renoncé à surveiller le verbe arabe qui revient en force, dans un bruit joyeux, si vif que rien ne l'arrête. Au sifflet, la langue défendue se tait, de murmure en murmure jusqu'au silence, les garçons entrent dans l'autre monde. (*JNP*, 43)
> [The maternal tongue was prohibited around the school, but the grounds at recess could not banish it, and the teachers, standing under the carob tree that gives the nicest shade in the middle of the playground, refused to monitor the use of the Arabic verb which returns in full force, in a joyful noise, so strong that nothing can stop it. At the whistle, the banished language is hushed, from whisper to whisper until complete silence, the boys enter into the other world.]

But this "other world," the French school where Sebbar's parents are both teachers, and also where they live, is the only space restricted to French. Arabic was hence always inevitably present: "tout autour de l'école c'était l'arabe ... Les murs n'étaient pas si épais" (*JNP*, 42). [All around the school was Arabic ... The walls were not so thick.] Yet the vernacular Arabic spoken by the school children as well as by the narrator's family – one in which almost all the women are illiterate – does not seem to affect the narrator, or at least according to what Sebbar acknowledges. Deming writes: "En dépit de cette longue cohabitation linguistique, elle a toujours insisté qu'elle ne comprenait ni ne parlait la langue de son père" (2005, 188). [Despite this long linguistic cohabitation, she has always insisted that she neither understands nor speaks her father's language.] Given that Arabic was spoken by her classmates, her playmates, her grandmother, her aunts, and of course her father, Deming wonders whether Sebbar's refusal to speak it was due to a deliberate choice or rather to a sort of linguistic repression. Her childhood resistance, transformed in her novels into a veritable form of obsession, reeks – at least for Deming – of a form of pathology, of a sort of "semi-conscious censure." Taken in a colonial context, Deming argues, this rejection of Arabic can be lined to the phantasm of colonial purification: "Enfant, elle ne voulait pas apprendre l'arabe, langue associée aux colonisés et qui aurait contaminé son univers linguistiquement pur" (2005, 188). [As a child, she did not want to learn Arabic, a language associated with the colonized and which could have contaminated her linguistically pure universe.]

Whereas Deming attributes Sebbar's repression of her paternal language to the author's semi-conscious desire to align herself with colonial power, I interpret the novel as an attempt to revisit the trauma of a childhood that has relegated Arabic to the domain of the subconscious. Yet the originality of Deming's analysis is the manner in which she distances Sebbar's writing from postcolonial readings, which tend to idealize a "hybrid" identity politics that privileges a literary perspective deriving from its "in-between-ness." It is true that the way in which Sebbar is haunted to the point of obsession by language is disturbing, especially when we consider the surprising number of her published works, all of them in French and all of them about Algeria. Her refusal to learn or re-learn Arabic is difficult to square with the content of her writings, let alone to figure out the reason for it. What is clear is that Arabic, for her, remains associated with a terrible past. Sebbar herself confirms this psychological dimension elsewhere: "Naïvement je crois qu'apprendre l'arabe maintenant aurait le même effet qu'une analyse ... M'allonger sur un divan et suivre des cours d'arabe, cela reviendrait au même" (1986, 149). [Naively speaking, I think that learning Arabic now would have the same effect as therapy ... Lying on a couch and taking classes in Arabic, would amount to the same thing.] In other words, Arabic for her – and for her readers perhaps – carries with it realities that will never and should never be known. French, for its part, eddies constantly around these aporia but never comes close to gaining access to its secrets.

The narrator's lack of comprehension of Arabic alienates her from her father's life and from the war, and she constantly feels the power of the things that will never be available to her in French:

Bientôt, ce serait l'heure des hommes, je les entendrais à peine, des murmures. Mon père m'appelle : Ne reste pas là, sur le balcon. – Pourquoi ? – C'est dangereux ! – Dangereux ? – Tu m'écoutes ? ne reste pas là. Il commence à faire nuit. – À cause de la nuit ? – Tu sais pourquoi, alors ne pose pas toujours des questions, je ne veux pas te voir là, c'est tout. (*JNP*, 20)
[Soon, it will be the men's hour, I will barely hear them, whispers. My father calls me: Don't stand there, on the balcony. – Why? – It's

dangerous! – Dangerous? – Are you listening to me? Don't stand
there. Night is starting to fall. – Because of the night then? –You
know why, so stop always asking questions, I don't want to see you
standing there, that is all.]

These murmurings by her father's friends, probably discussing the war
in Arabic, are untranslatable in French, and when young Leïla asks her
father for an explanation, he refuses her. His exasperated response – "tu
sais pourquoi" [you know why] – suggests even that his daughter does
understand Arabic, and that she's pretending not to. The girl seems to
give preference to French in this passage, demanding translation of him.
As an adult, the narrator feels estranged from her country of birth,
which now, as a free Algeria, refuses to translate for her in an official capacity: "Lorsque j'y reviendrai, je ne le saurai pas et je ne retiendrai pas
les mots de la langue étrangère. Je marcherai en aveugle, ne sachant lire
le sens des lettres arabes que ne redouble pas la langue coloniale, effacée
par la volonté officielle (*JNP*, 35). [When I return there, I will not know
them and I will not retain any of the words of the foreign tongue. I will
walk like the blind, unable to grasp the meaning of Arabic letters that
the colonial language no longer reproduces, erased by the official will.]
This linguistic exclusion felt by the narrator, according to Deming,
should be easy to cure with a little hard work, with an effort to learn the
father's language later in life. However, it is also clear that there is a
complex form of trauma at work here, one that can only be healed by
the obsessive return to language enacted by this novel and others.

In the influential *Unclaimed Experience: Trauma, Narrative and History*, Cathy Caruth proposes the study of what she calls a "wound" (*trauma* in Greek, *blessure* in French), related to the psychoanalytic term first
outlined by Freud in *Beyond the Pleasure Principle*. Freud was the first
thinker to pursue a definition of the word "trauma" beyond the sense
of a physical lesion to a psychological wound, as Caruth explains: "But
what seems to be suggested by Freud ... is that the wound of the mind
– the breach in the mind's experience of time, self, and the world – is
not, like the wound of the body, a simple and healable event, but rather
an event that ... is experienced too soon, too unexpectedly, to be fully
known, and is therefore not available to consciousness until it impos-
es itself again, repeatedly in the nightmares and repetitive actions of
the survivor (1996, 4). The trope of repetition is crucial for the traumatized subject to gain consciousness. It is only via narration and the repetitive usage of language that the source of trauma can be known and,
eventually, neutralized.

This type of repetition appears several times in Sebbar's narration of events in Algeria – most notably in her retelling of the events leading to the assassination of her father's friend and colleague Mouloud Feraoun and the subsequent incarceration of her father at Orleansville. There is also a scene from her childhood that recurs, where young Algerian boys yell insults at her while she is walking to school. In both cases, her ignorance of Arabic prevents her from understanding and reacting but not from feeling the effects of these incidents: "Ils nous guettaient, je le savais, et je crois que le tremblement intérieur qui se mêle à l'effroi était le signe de cette attente quotidienne des mêmes mots, appris par coeur, les seuls que je n'ai pas oubliés" (*JNP*, 40). [They preyed on us, I knew it, and I believe that the inner trembling mixed with fear was the signal of that daily expectation of the same words, memorized by heart, the only ones I have not forgotten.] Insults that are hurled at her everyday, and yet not understood, carry a violence that the narrator revisits even as an adult: "ces mots étrangers et familiers, je les entends encore, violents comme des pierres jetées, visant l'œil ou la tempe" (*JNP*, 37). [Those foreign and familiar words, I hear them still, violent like rocks thrown at the eye or the temple.] This verbal violence punctuates the narration like a sort of surging and uncontrollable subconscious that betrays the necessity of dealing with this trauma through the medium of language. However, in the novel, the words of these young boys are given neither in their phonetic translation nor in original Arabic. They are only mentioned in an indirect manner in French, given a sort of imagined aura: "je suis sûre que l'insulte est sexuelle" (*JNP*, 37). [I am sure that the insult is sexual.] She also returns with a similar obsession to the life of her father, from whom she demands details about the war on the telephone: "Je voudrais savoir ... Tu dis qu'il faut oublier et tu ne veux pas dire quoi ... Mais Papa, ce que tu sais toi, tu es peut-être le seul ... Et si tu ne racontes rien ... Tu crois que tout le monde sait ... Les livres ne disent rien et toi non plus (*JNP*, 12–13). [I would like to know ... You say that we must forget and you don't want to say what ... But Papa, you are perhaps the only one who knows what you know ... And if you don't say anything ... You think everyone knows ... The books say nothing and neither do you.] Her father refuses to respond, and Sebbar feels once again alienated by this language that carries her trauma. She assumes that her father refuses to tell her these stories because he prefers to relate them in his native language rather than that of the colonizer. The linguistic distance between father and daughter, exacerbated by her childhood assailants, becomes even more insurmountable when her father dies – ending forever the possibility that she will bridge this gap.

Sebbar's monolingualism is tinged with regret, melancholy, and guilt, and Arabic affects her text by its notable absence. Language serves thus a double function in Sebbar's writing, as French must fill the vacancy left by Arabic, all the while exposing even more the impossibility that any linguistic enterprise must face in the end. In another sense, French defaults in the face of Arabic and Arabic defaults when it encounters the Real. Here I refer, of course, to Lacan's concept which, in his reinterpretation of the Freudian unconscious, gives language a mediating function, one which is from the beginning doomed to fail. There is a double failure since the insufficiency of French in translating Arabic also reflects the more general deficit of all language – a lack that Arabic itself also suffers from. The absence that haunts Sebbar's text expresses then a linguistic anxiety in the face of trauma that she cannot express in a particular language but which is not curable in the end by any language anyway.

Sebbar's way of reconciling this impossible relationship is through a feminization of language that pushes her father and other aggressors of Algeria to one side and Algerian women to the other. Put differently, she rediscovers the gentle side of Arabic in the feminine figures of her childhood. In contrast to the ferocity of a language that she heard when she was very little – "des voix sonores, violentes" (*JNP*, 19) [loud voices, violent ones], "les mots de gorge, les sons roulés" (*JNP*, 21) [throaty words, rolled sounds] – she experiences its docility in her grandmother's house: "La langue de mon père, dans la maison de sa mère, n'est pas la langue des garçons qui nous guettent" (*JNP*, 106) [My father's tongue, in his mother's house, is not the language of the boys who prey on us]; "Le frère rit, un beau rire de gorge, le beau rire de sa langue, généreux et joyeux" (*JNP*, 122) [The brother laughs, a beautiful throaty laugh, a beautiful laugh in his language, generous and joyful]. She imagines conversations between Fatima, one of the Algerian maids, and her sons or between Aïsha, Fatima's sister, and her nephew. She invents fictional dialogues between her father and Fatima's son, and other ones between her father and her aunt. In these made-up interviews, the subject is still the civil war, kidnappings, insurrections, and death. At the same time, the conversations are retold with a sort of shared complicity between Arabic speakers. They oppose the narrator's feelings of cold exclusion with the warmth of inclusion. In this way, the French text works to depict for us an Arabic familiarity that the narrator knows exists but of which she has never felt a part.

As mentioned earlier, in the last chapter of the novel, Sebbar categorically refuses to learn Arabic. However, this declaration is followed by an explanation of the novel's *raison d'être*: "Je veux l'entendre [la langue arabe], au hasard de mes pérégrinations. Entendre la voix de l'étranger bien-aimé, la voix de la terre et du corps de mon père que j'écris dans la langue de ma mère" (*JNP*, 125). [I want to hear it [the Arabic language], randomly as I wander about. I want to hear the voice of the beloved foreigner, the voice of the earth and the body of my father that I write in the language of my mother.] Sebbar here searches for a way to write what she has heard, to reveal what has been lost, to capture the essential heteroglossia that her colonial existence in Algeria has denied for so many years. In this way, she overtly recognizes and accepts the illusory superiority of the French language, as well as of how it represses her memories of the civil war and the invectives of young boys. Rather than a form of resistance through French, as Deming would have it, Sebbar's is a usage of French as a form of therapy – a way to recapture those elusive sites of trauma that continue to haunt her. Her text in this way mediates the limits of colonial language and exposes the fragility of a language in the face of latent heteroglossia.

In these texts that return constantly to her country of birth, Sebbar reveals to an essentially French public her experience of immigration. Inherent to this act of writing is an ethical imperative to which Sebbar responds by recounting her trauma of living through the Algerian war. In her study, Caruth evokes Lacan's notion that all trauma brings with it the moral responsibility of speaking (1996, 100). It is in this light that we may read the insistence by the girl that her father tell his story, to inform the French public. Writing in French is a moral obligation, as it is through her heritage as a mixed French woman that Sebbar narrates Algeria, its people, and its language. In this way she counters, as notes Jane Hiddleston, the erasure of Algeria from French culture (2003, 61). It is by not learning Arabic that Sebbar thus fulfills her obligation. Elsewhere, she compares her own favoritism of French to the one she imagines in her father, who in French becomes a silent, troubling vessel of the war, of origins, of traditions: "Maintenant. Il se tait. Ce qu'il sait du vieux quartier de l'enfance, de la cour carrée au figuier ... de l'école coranique, du marabout ancestral, des fêtes et des deuils, du mouton égorgé et des garçons circoncis, de la révolte silencieuse qui s'organise, il ne dit rien (*JNP*, 21). [Now. He is silent. What he knows of the old quarters of my childhood, of the square courtyard under the fig tree ... of the Coranic school, of the ancestral marabou, of feasts and mourning, of slaughtered goats and circumcised boys, of the silent revolt that was being organized, he says nothing.] Sebbar's silence in Arabic and her father's

refusal to speak of the history and culture of Algeria in French are reflected in Sebbar's writing, which privileges in its own right the use of
a foreign language to revisit sites of trauma. In other words, Sebbar's refusal to speak Arabic is the ultimate gesture of complicity with a father
who, according to her, refused to speak of the Algerian war in the language of the enemy. Sebbar draws this parallel in explaining why she
does not want to tell her story in the language of those who aggressed
her: "Mon père n'aura jamais su que le silence de sa langue, dans la
maison de la Française, se muait en mots de l'enfer, la porte franchie, et
que ses filles seraient asphyxiées, étourdies par la violence répétée du
verbe arabe (*JNP*, 42). [My father will have never known that the silence
of his language, in the house of the French woman, was changed into
infernal words once we exited the door, and that his daughters would
be asphyxiated, stunned by the repeated violence of the Arabic word.]
These are then two characters that return to their maternal language
to accomplish a therapeutic goal of repetition and to a parallel condition – one of reconciling at last these events that they experienced too
suddenly and too horribly to completely process at the time they occurred. In her anaphoric title of the last chapter, Sebbar responds to her
young assailants at last, breaking the silence she held so many years ago.
At the same time, she confronts the wound of being unable to express
herself, the trauma of her father's language that has haunted her since
childhood. A highly personal journey that conflates the private sphere
with the political sphere, this is a novel that offers psychoanalytic in-
trospection as one way to work through the essential gaps that riddle
any language's attempt to capture its ephemeral literary object.

RÉGINE ROBIN, *LA QUÉBÉCOITE*: PLURILINGUAL IMPOSSIBILITY

One of the first novels to merit the term "migrant literature" in Quebec,
Régine Robin's *La Québécoite* was published in Montreal in 1983.
Among the very first wave of Canadian immigrant writers, along with
the Iraqi Naïm Kattan and the Haitian Émile Ollivier, Robin, a French-
born Jew, chose to immigrate to Quebec in 1977. *La Québécoite* is a work
of "bio-fiction" that narrates three hypothetical lives of a young French
immigrant of Jewish origins in Montreal. Each of the three storylines
in the novel recalls an amorous affair between the narrator and three
lovers, each with a different ethnic affiliation – first Jewish Anglophone,
then Quebecois, and then Latin American. All three of the stories end
unhappily and the novel ends with the narrator returning to France.

Just like the ethnic differences that determine the narrative, the text of the novel, which is primarily French, is interrupted multiple times by words, phrases, and utterances of Yiddish and English. The text is riddled with poems, history manuals, restaurant menus, journal entries, slogans from posters and billboards, all of which create a space where different languages are juxtaposed and interlaced, imposing themselves on one another. Each language is however used in a precise context relative to the space with which it is associated – signaling therein a sort of linguistic schizophrenia that imitates the cultural cleavages that separate different ethnic groupings in Montreal.

Yiddish is the narrator's mother tongue, but she feels exiled by it and no longer speaks it: "En exil dans sa propre langue" (*LQ*, 95). [In exile in one's own language (*TW*, 76).] It is her language of origin, but one that she lost with the death of her mother following the Vélodrome d'Hiver roundup in Paris on 16 July 1942. Her mother, a victim of the Holocaust, disappears during the German occupation and takes with her a language to which the narration of the novel seeks to return. As in Sebbar's case, the unknown language holds secrets and charms, all of which are inaccessible to the narrator:

> Sur les toits pentus des gros villages de Galicie, la lune dessine encore des א, des ב, des ג, des ד, dans les jardins d'Ukraine les tiges des tournesols dessinent encore des ש, des ק, des ל, mais plus personne pour les déchiffrer, pour en saisir la signification, la saveur, les sortilèges ... Toute une sagesse cachée ne s'y révèle plus. (*LQ*, 89)
> [On the sloping roofs of the towns of Galicia, the moon still traces א, ב, ג, and ד; in the gardens of Ukraine, the stems of the sunflowers still form ש, ק, and ל; but no longer is there anyone to decode them, to grasp their meaning, their savour, their magic ... An entire hidden wisdom is no longer revealed. (*TW*, 70–1)]

The narrator feels this loss of language in both its cultural and historical dimensions. Hebrew characters literally interrupt the French text, as if to point at another sort of interruption, a far more devastating one, that must be forgotten: "[Les lettres] Comme des feuilles d'automne envolées, accumulées, pourrissantes, abandonnées" (*LQ*, 89). [[Letters] Like autumn leaves blown away, piled up, rotting, abandoned (*TW*, 70).] These Hebrew characters thus betray the nostalgia of the narrator, who remembers her Yiddish, Jewish childhood. Memories of her mother mingle with those of a language, one that is brought to bear by Hebrew letters that are then associated with them: "Ta mère lisait ces livres à longueur de soirées, avec toutes ces petites taches brunes qui couraient sur les lignes" (*LQ*, 139). [Your mother spent whole evenings reading those books with the little brown marks running along in lines (*TW*, 113).]

The resurgence of the mother tongue in the narrator's experience is thus anchored in the trauma of losing her mother. The narrative proceeds as a series of structured memories, each eddying around the trajectory of a metro train that leads to Quai de Grenelle station, which is where the Vélodrome d'Hiver was situated until 1949.[6] In other words, the novel retraces the paths of Parisian Jews as they were borne toward execution in 1942:

APRÈS GRENELLE – JE NE SAIS PLUS
LA LIGNE SE PERD
                        DANS MA MÉMOIRE
          Les Juifs
          doivent
          prendre
           le
          dernier
          wagon ...
SA MÈRE – JAMAIS REVENUE (*LQ*, 73)

[AFTER GRENELLE – I DON'T KNOW ANY MORE
THE LINE GETS LOST
                        IN MY MEMORY
          Jews
          must
          use
          the
          last
          car ...
HER MOTHER – NEVER RETURNED (*TW*, 56)]

The disposition of words here imitates the narrator's memory blank as well as the positioning of the Jews in the last compartments of the train, while the capital letters emphasize death and genocide and the narrator's interrupted lineage. The play of language in French becomes a site of commemoration, a stele of sorts: "Un cimetière dans une petite bourgade juive. Cela aussi appartiendrait désormanis à la légende, à une saga muette qu'elle porterait au-dedans d'elle-même, impossible à communiquer" (*LQ*, 32). [The cemetery of a little Jewish town. That too would henceforth belong to legend, to a mute saga she would carry inside herself, impossible to communicate (*TW*, 20).] Yiddish becomes the language of the past, of trauma and death, while French expresses the present moment, lost as it is nonetheless in the haunting unrepresentability of the past. The novel's central preoccupation is indeed the narrator's inability to bear witness to the collective suffering of her people, and especially that of her own mother.

Robin's text wanders around the unspeakable horror that no language can express. "Irréprésentable" (*LQ*, 141) [Unrepresentable (*TW*, 114)], she says because even literary tropes are lacking: "Il n'y a pas de métaphore pour signifier Auschwitz pas de genre, pas d'écriture" (*LQ*, 141). [There is no metaphor to signify Auschwitz, no genre, no writing (*TW*, 114).] According to Caruth, rhetorical figures are often the preferred means of expressing trauma. While Sebbar, as we have seen, believes that the trauma can only be expressed in the mother tongue, Robin rejects the symbolic order altogether to speak trauma: "Le lieu entre le langage et l'Histoire s'est rompu. Les mots manquent. Le langage n'a plus d'origine, ni de direction" (*LQ*, 141). [The link between language and History has been broken. The words are lacking. Language no longer has a source or a direction (*TW*, 114).] This linguistic insufficiency is repeated and confronted in the French of her text while Yiddish seems to lie at the heart of all that is ineffable.

Sherry Simon describes the obstruction of language that is at the heart of *La Québécoite* as untranslatable. From its title that signals the narrator's silence, her quiet presence in Quebec, where she is incapable of voicing a pain immemorial. For Simon, Yiddish only enters the text through the memories that sustain it since the narrative voice inhabits this language even though she cannot speak it. Robin also uses the term "untranslatable" (*intraduisible*) to qualify her experiences that remain hidden in the Yiddish language, thus exposing her own inability to express them in her adoptive language:

> Tu as toujours habité un langage, une phonie qui tantôt sonne germanique, tantôt tinte hébraïque, tantôt slave aussi. Un langage carrefour, errant mobile comme toi, comme elle. Habiter un langage, une complicité intraduisible ... Un langage à l'envers, allant vers on ne sait quoi ... Un langage sang, mort, blessure, un langage pogrom et peur. (*LQ*, 139–40)
> [You've always lived in a language – in sounds that sometime ring Germanic, sometimes Hebraic, even Slavic. A crossroads language,

wandering, mobile, like you, like her. To live in a language, an un-translatable closeness ... A language in reverse, going towards who knows what ... A language of blood, death, wounds, of pogroms and fear. (*TW*, 113)]

It is in the French language that the scene of trauma repeats and re-plays itself, but always in an elliptic manner. The metro ride toward Grenelle is retraced several times without any mention of the journey's end in precise terms. Yiddish as language of trauma is articulated in the economy of the French text which points only to intimacy lost, mater-nal bonds destroyed, and a language forgotten.

Yiddish also conjures up the reality of a small ethnic community in bilingual Montreal, intent on preserving its culture and language away from the province's dominant languages: "Quartier d'immigrants à l'anglais malhabile ... où l'on entend parler yiddish, et où il est si facile de trouver des cornichons, du Râlé natté et du matze mail" (*LQ*, 23). [A neighborhood of immigrants with awkward English ... where you hear Yiddish spoken and it's easy to find pickles, braised challah, matzoh meal (*TW*, 13).] The Jewish neighbourhood of Snowdon in Montreal and the character of Mimi Yente – the narrator's Ukrainian aunt – as well as her husband Moshe belong to a world that maintains a few ties to the old country. "Le vieux ghetto," as the narrator calls it, the neigh-bourhood separates Eastern Europeans from the other inhabitants of Montreal. There, the narrator finds her own people but feels even more isolated from Quebec society:

L'Isolement   La coupure
Un vide de quelque chose ?
              Quelque chose d'autre ?
ON NE DEVIENDRAIT   JAMAIS VRAIMENT
              QUÉBÉCOIS.
De l'autre côté de la barrière linguistique ? ...
Un imaginaire yiddishophone ? Quel drôle de mot ! (*LQ*, 36–7)
[Isolation   Being cut off?
An emptiness of something?
              Something else?
WE WOULD NEVER BECOME   TRULY
              QUÉBÉCOIS.
On the other side of the linguistic barrier? ...
A Yiddishophone imagination? What a funny word! (*TW*, 24)]

Those who speak Yiddish are deprived of Quebecois nationality according to the narrator, hence the silence that cloaks the narrative voice as a
member of this community. Once again, the use of capital letters hollers
her exclusion while the exaggerated spacing between words arranged in
a calligram illustrates the sense of isolation, division, and emptiness experienced by the immigrant writer. The word "Québécois" is positioned
on the other side of the linguistic barrier, not on the same line as the immigrant "we" (*on*). The mockery of the word "Yiddishophone" – taking a
jab at the Quebecois mania of grouping people according to their native
tongues – is yet another way of exacerbating the ostracism felt by immigrants forced as they are onto the sidelines of society.

Finally, the dilemma caused by the narrator's maternal tongue results
not only from her inability to speak it, but also from the fact that it is
a language that is slowly disappearing. Yiddish is spoken less and less
in Canada, just as elsewhere in the world, and the narrator's identity
seems likewise condemned.

> La mort habite cette langue, une langue sans avenir avec ce passé
> trouble qui colle aux lettres fines, une langue sans présent, figé
> dans son Shtetl démembré, une langue à vau-l'eau, sans destin ... La
> langue est là avec son alphabet ... Mais plus personne pour y vivre
> la quotidienneté, pour y lover ses pensées secrètes, ses points
> d'impossible. (*LQ*, 153)
> [Death inhabits this language, a language with no future, with that
> turbulent past sticking to its delicate letters, a language with no
> present, frozen in its dismembered shtetl, a language swept away,
> with no destiny ... The language is there with its alphabet ... But no
> longer is there anyone to live in its everydayness, to wrap their se-
> cret thoughts or impossible points in it. (*TW*, 125)]

The narrator's anxiety surrounding the disappearing language is rav-
elled in a fear of forgetfulness, in memories that are in danger of extinction and a linguistic community facing dispersal. Hebrew, Judaic
culture and its religious heritage are even more at risk because their
link to the Yiddish language is broken in the younger generations.
Hence the story of the professor of Jewish history who is preparing a
class on the false messiahs of history, the first person narration of which
weaves its way around that of the protagonist. The professor complains
about the task set before him because the young Yiddish speakers in
his class know nothing of Jewish history nor are they very interested in

the subject. The fact that the language is spoken at home seems to exempt them from any real knowledge of history, at least that is how the
old professor makes sense of his student's disaffected attitudes.

English, Canada's dominant language, also interferes in Robin's text
although with no sense of nostalgia as in the case of Yiddish. The presence of this language spoken in Quebec, despite all the political protes-
tations within the province to curb its influence, occurs with as much
inevitability in the text as it does in political, social, and notably economic life:

Banque mercantile du Canada
Banque provinciale du Canada
La Toronto Dominion Bank
Banque – banque – le pays des banques – the big bank
Country – the big bank power
in God we bank. (LQ, 23)
[Mercantile Bank of Canada
Provincial Bank of Canada
Toronto Dominion Bank
Bank – bank – the land of banks – the big bank country – the big
bank power
In God we bank (TW, 12)]

Lists like this one frequently interrupt Robin's narrative, signaling the
omnipresence of English in Montreal. Other words that have been integrated into French vocabulary in Quebec are also summoned such as
in the following list of terms for roadways which typographically appear one below the other: "boulevards de ceinture, périphériques,
bretelles, highways, freeways, turnpikes, parkways, thruways" (LQ, 18)
[beltways, outer boulevards, ramps, highways, freeways, turnpikes, parkways, thruways (TW, 7)]. Robin's text suggests that no French description of Montreal is even possible without recourse to English words
because the names of stores, streets, banks, credit cards betray the city's
Anglo-Saxon past and the vestiges of British colonialism. And yet, the
words create a rather shocking effect within the text, pointing to the
inescapable need to know and understand English in order to decipher
public codes: signage, expressions, popular culture.

At other times, it is in the form of an English word placed in the middle of the French text that the foreignness of the language makes its
presence felt, interfering with the text in both a natural and awkward
way. In the line "Un milieu *quiet* et aveugle à tout ce qui ne le concerne

pas" (*LQ*, 69) [A quiet milieu, blind to anything that doesn't directly concern it (*TW*, 52)], the italics emphasize the foreign origins of the word and yet also justify its inevitable usage here to qualify the Jewish quarter in Montreal. Since the majority of the city's Jewish population is English-speaking rather than French-speaking, it is almost as though only the use of the English adjective could adequately describe their refusal to interfere with language politics in Quebec as well as the silent protest that weighs into their decision to snub French. Robin thus exchanges the linguistic unity of her text for the heterogeneous vividness that sometimes borders on the incomprehensible: "Si avec cinq langues je n'épuise pas le sujet, je guivappe" (*LQ*, 42). [If I can't cover the subject with five languages, I give up (*TW*, 28).] The neologic verb "guivappe" – a phonetic transcription into French of the English expression "to give up" – requires a pause on the part of the reader to decipher the unknown word, which is neither rendered in quotation marks nor in italics to signal its Anglophone source. Robin does not use a glossary of terms or footnotes to explain her linguistic additions, variations, and creations. One must pronounce the word in order to make sense of it or to understand its usage in context.

Robin refutes the idea of an unproblematic acceptance of linguistic pluralingualism in Montreal. The textual cohabitation of the three languages in her novel is rife with difficult encounters and insurmountable spaces:

N'y a-t-il rien d'universel ici ?
DES GHETTOS
    DES CLIVAGES
CHACUN SA LANGUE
    SA COMMUNAUTÉ ...
NOUS.   VOUS.   EUX. (*LQ*, 158)
[GHETTOS
SPLITS
TO EACH HIS LANGUAGE
    HER COMMUNITY ...
WE.   YOU.   THEY. (*TW*, 129)]

The separation between the different ethnic communities is reflected in each of the three love affairs that constitute the novel. Each relationship is cantoned into the specificities of a different Montreal neighbourhood: Snowdon, Outremont, Jean-Talon. As an immigrant, the narrator looks to situate herself between all the languages she speaks and all the cultures of which she partakes. Like a refrain in her text, she repeats her desire to transcend linguistic and cultural barriers through an impossible plurality of voices:

> Elle sentirait qu'elle ne pourrait jamais tout à fait habiter ce pays, qu'elle ne pourrait jamais tout à fait habiter aucun pays.
>   Pas de lieu, pas d'ordre
>   Mémoire divisée à la jointure des mots
>   Les couches muettes du langage, brisées
>   La parole immigrante en suspens
>   entre
>   deux HISTOIRES. (*LQ*, 152)

[She'd feel that she would never really be able to live in this country, that she would never really be able to live in any country.
                    No place, no order.
                    Memory divided at the connections between words
            The mute layers of language, broken
            Immigrant words in suspense
                    between
                        two HISTORIES. (*TW*, 124)]

The notion of an *hors-lieu*, which Robin developed in an earlier work (Robin 1989), appears here to offer as an alternative the possibility of a wandering immigrant identity that circles around questions of linguistic incommensurability.[7] Critic Pierre L'Hérault interprets this peregrination of sorts in light of Yiddish's complicated political history. "Attacked from all sides – the language it seemed equally hindered the nationalistic projects of Russification and Hebrewization – and was hence forced into an essentially oral status. Yiddish ensured its survival, nonetheless, through an unusual openness to the languages around it, borrowing signifiers and remodeling them for its purposes," notes L'Hérault (1991, 69).[8] As a language of exchange, it embraced linguistic equivocation, taking on a flavour of "otherness" when needed and where necessary, infiltrating itself everywhere despite the absence of any real institutional legitimacy. Janet Paterson calls this the "otherness" of the Yiddish language in Robin's novel whereby all identity construction and deconstruction is over-determined by the weight of history (2004, 157).

The missing linguistic centre to Robin's novel thus serves as a metaphor for the migrant text that often hides a textually repressed language at its core. Robin describes the immigrant voice as "une voix plurielle" [a plural voice] and "une voix carrefour" [a crossroads voice (*TW*, 137)], but at the same time the text moves in the opposite direction, reinforcing the protagonist's silence, an impossible reconciliation between tongues and the alienating heterogeneity of immigrant life in Quebec. Between these two poles resides "une voix de l'autre au brisant du texte" (*LQ*, 167) [a voice of the other where an underwater rock breaks / the flow of the text (*TW*, 137) [9]], which cleverly describes the narrative structure of *La Québécoite*. The text endeavours to translate the sense of strangeness and alterity experienced by the narrator through a poetics of rupture and the formal disruption that characterizes it.

Robin negotiates the different languages in her novel according to an economy that ascribes each tongue a metaphoric function within the text. French is constantly compromised, interfered with, and destabilized by the other languages that infiltrate the text – whether it be through the recurrence of English words, the resurgence of Hebraic characters, or constant allusions to Yiddish. French – though it may be the dominant language of the narrative voice – is inflected with an awareness of its own limitations in the Quebecois context, brought about by the realities of immigration and Anglicization. By refusing to claim Quebecois or even French national identity as her own, the narrator assigns an extra-national vocation to the French of her text that closely parallels that of Yiddish as detailed above by Pierre L'Hérault. The wordplay of Robin's French title even undermines the very possibility of Quebec nationalism from the onset. Claudine Potvin, for example, likens the cackling of chickens "coi-coi-coi" both to the incessant chattering of the Quebecois people and to coitus or *coite/coït*, in particular to the desired coupling of cultures embodied by each of the romantic relationships pursued by the narrator (1996, 265). In both cases, the narrator is banished by her silence and failed love affairs, only to be ultimately exiled from Quebec.

Even while anchoring her text within Quebecois culture and the French language as it is lived and practised in Montreal, Robin takes a jab at the nationalist project – so very much alive in Quebec of the early eighties and again even today. Through her writing, she participates in a French-speaking community speckled with the multilingualism of its immigrant interlocutors, all the while emphasizing her character's impossible integration into Quebecois society. Critic Simon Harel in fact argues that the migrancy of Robin's novel is best captured in the ways in which it opposes Quebecois national commemoration and identity through its spatial wandering within the cosmopolitan urban centre that is Montreal (2005, 148).

The linguistic flexibility, slippages, and displacements that define this text contest a rigid view of the French language by introducing as much variation as possible. For Robin, it is only in the language's malleability and changing contours that the migrant text can take form, allowing for the vacillations in identity of those who appropriate the French language to speak the intricacies of immigrant life.

Robin refuses the typical narrative structure of the novel to describe her experience as a new immigrant in Quebec. Madeleine Frédéric's study of Robin's use of the enumerative style to reproduce lists, inventories, programs, collections, menus, catalogues, metro lines, scoreboards, etc. serves to contrast two types of interruptions in the novel (1991). The first is caused by the Holocaust and the traumatic lapse in memory that results from the disappearance of the narrator's mother, while the second is caused by the fragmented nature of the modern cosmopolitan city.[10] Hence the narrator is temporally and spatially alienated from her past, just as she is from her present life, unable as it were to atone for the historical trauma of betrayal and loss through her disjointed immigrant life in Montreal and equally unable to attend to another form of betrayal and loss she experiences there.

YING CHEN, *LES LETTRES CHINOISES*: POETICALLY UNTRANSLATABLE

Ten years after Régine Robin, Ying Chen published her second and best known novel to date *Les Lettres chinoises* in 1993, following her debut novel *La Mémoire de l'eau* by only a year. *Les Lettres chinoises* tells the story of two young lovers, Yuan – a recent immigrant to Montreal from Shanghai – and Sassa his fiancée back in China. Written in the epistolary form, the novel is a reflection on immigration and identity where the linguistic question appears to play but an auxiliary role. For this reason, most literary analyses of this work sidestep the issue of language to favour the novel's rich themes as they are rendered through its unrivaled poetics.[11] The letters that are exchanged throughout the novel between Yuan and Sassa and at times between Da Li – another young Chinese woman and close friend of the couple who also elects to immigrate to Montreal – and Sassa, constitute an eloquent game of hide and seek. Each letter reveals and conceals, as the characters appear and disappear in the novel, struggling with issues of exile and national belonging, loyalty, and betrayal. Between Montreal and Shanghai and back, each letter is written in French, a language that Yuan claims he is only just learning while Sassa, a translator by trade, expresses an academic knowledge of the language. Da Li, for her part, admits that her French is better than her English, but to infer from there that all three characters would privilege French as a medium of communication seems highly implausible when they share a common native tongue. The text thus presupposes a translating mediator that remains unacknowledged throughout the novel. Chen carefully erases any overt references to the Chinese language, so much so that at first many critics took the author's Chinese-sounding name for a pseudonym.[12] Compared to *La Mémoire de l'eau* however, *Les Lettres chinoises* introduces words and expressions from Chen's mother tongue, which disappear once again in her subsequent works. Chen allots a very strategic place to the Chinese characters and expressions that punctuate her second novel, lauded for its poetic voice and the evocative simplicity of its prose.

The double connotation of the novel's title is reinforced from first contact with this work due to the Chinese calligraphy that adorns the Babel edition's cover. The sinogram that most francophone readers would not be able to decipher without help is the Mandarin character for poem, which only obliquely alludes to the poem by Tang dynasty poet Chen Zi-Ang, written around the seventh century, that was briefly on the 1993 Leméac edition cover of the novel. The poem describes the sense of desolation experienced by those who are uprooted. François Cheng translates the poem into French as follows:

Du haut de la terrasse du You-Zhou
[Devant], je ne vois pas l'homme passé
[Derrière], je ne vois pas l'homme futur
Songeant au ciel-terre vaste et sans fin
Solitaire, amer, je fonds en larmes [13]

Chen offers no explicit French translation of this poem and Cheng's is the only one that exists to date, although critic Betty McLane-Isles provides an English one as well (see note 14). Though no explicatory note provides the meaning of her cover page poem, Chen's character Yuan does quote a certain French rendition of the poem in a melancholy love letter to Sassa:

Du haut de la terrasse du You-Zhou
Nos larmes coulent dans la solitude
Le ciel est loin et la terre immense
Inutile de chercher ici et là
Nous n'aurons plus d'ancêtres ni d'enfants. (*LC*, 57–8)

YING CHEN
LES LETTRES CHINOISES

BABEL

ROMAN

Figure 5.1
Cover illustration to 1993 Babel edition of *Les Lettres chinoises* by Ying Chen, depicting the Mandarin character for "poetry"

> [*Climbing the Terrace of Yu-chou*
> Before, I cannot see the men of old.
> Beyond, can't see the men to come.
> Ponder the infinite, Heaven-and-Earth.
> Alone, confused, I melt to tears. (Cheng 1982, 99)][14]

The stark contrasts between the four versions of the translated poem signal both the complexity of rendering its Chinese message as well as the linguistic distance that separates the cultures that accompany each language. In the Chinese, notions of space and time fuse together, a reality that Cheng can only express using the parenthetical addi-

CHEN

LES LETTRES CHINOISES

Figure 5.2
Cover illustration to 1993 Leméac edition of *Les Lettres chinoises* by Ying Chen, depicting a poem by Chen Zi-Ang

tion of spatial qualifiers of time in order to stay true to the original text. McLane-Isles, on the other hand, simply blends the temporal and spatial markers as they are intended in Chinese without necessarily drawing attention to the untranslatability that Cheng's and Seaton's translated texts lay bare. Chen's version of the poem, however, most francizes its form, removing all references to its space-time conundrum, inverting the verses to stand the poem on its head of sorts. The causal relationship that explains the sadness of the uprooted diasporic subject here becomes the uprooted desolation of lovers torn apart by distance in a telling muddling of the poem's meaning. Indeed, Chen's translation of the poem is given to us through the fiction of her novel and in the voice of her character Yuan, who is struggling to save his relationship to Sassa while enamoured with his new-found home in Canada. As I have argued elsewhere, Yuan's love affair with Sassa stands in for his loyalty to the Chinese nation, which clearly wavers once he immigrates to Montreal (Xavier 2005). In a spinning of Chen Zi-Ang's verse through the metaphor of love, Chen both reveals and conceals the elaborate web of her novel where love and national belonging intertwine and intersect. Yet it is in the interstices of the translation from Chinese to French – where "I" becomes "we" and space-time is reduced to something more palpably romantic ("le ciel est loin et la terre immense") – that the key to the novel's interpretation resides. The untranslated Chinese intertext interferes with its romanticized French version, undermining Yuan's vain effort to reignite his love for Sassa through ancient Mandarin poetry. Zi-Ang's Chinese verse betrays Yuan's true feelings and elucidates the strangeness of the poem in the French love letter.

Similarly, the poem, once deciphered, reads as a warning against the Francophone reader's thirst for the exotic, since what are merely "Chinese letters" to one, is a beautifully sorrowful poem to another. The juxtaposition of the two languages on the novel's cover page thus serves as an introduction to the reader and a visual reminder of the linguistic gap that holds together the entire novel. The poetics of the migrant text emerge from this paradoxical meeting of languages where meaning does not always cross over from one to the other. Apart from a brief salutation in Chinese in one of Da Li's letters to Sassa, Chen's native tongue never interrupts the French of the novel, where words when referenced in Chinese are immediately followed by French translations or explanations. Émile Talbot argues that Chen chose to de-Asianize her work as much as possible in her search for a poetics of universality over ethnography. Still, the novel's title, when interpreted through the poem on its cover page, creates a haunting space between the language of the novel and the absent Chinese one.

All three characters, at various points in the novel, discuss the difficulty of navigating between French and their native tongue. French, as a language of the West, embodies Americanized values for Yuan who struggles to capture the nuances of his own culture in the language of his adopted land: "Mais il arrive souvent que nous ne trouvions pas, dans la langue française, un concept équivalent qui exprimerait ce qui nous paraît évident en chinois" (LC, 122). [But it often happens that we cannot find, in the French language, an equivalent concept to express that which seems evident in Chinese.] In a discussion between Yuan and Sassa about the valence of the words *droit* and *devoir* in French versus Chinese, both express a sense of resignation toward the inevitable cultural betrayal at stake. Veiled in this discussion is Yuan's unfaithfulness to Sassa in love. Once again, the language serves as a metaphor for love and vice versa. "Pour parler français ... il faut réfléchir en français. De même en amour" (LC, 129) [To speak French ... one must think in French], writes Sassa to Yuan, willing to see their relationship die. Like Régine Robin, Ying Chen's linguistic poetics refuses any notion of a third space where languages and cultures meet. Rather, there is only absence and the painful loss of one in the space occupied by the other. In one of her last letters to Yuan, Sassa asks that they end their love affair, burying it in the place and the language in which it was born: "Quand un amour est trop malade, on ne le transporte pas, afin d'éviter les complications. On attend tranquillement sa fin, on l'enterre dans son lieu de naissance et on inscrit des poèmes sur sa tombe, dans sa propre langue" (LC, 131). [When a love [affair] is too sick, we do not transport it in order to avoid complication. We await its end quietly, we bury it in its place of birth and we write poems on its tomb, in its own language.] Sassa's words once more remind the reader of the Chinese letters on the book's cover page, the poem inscribed on what is ultimately a memorial to a lost love, to a language that no longer has its rightful place in the land of immigration and whose meanings are forever buried with the untranslatable beauty of the Chinese text.

CONCLUSION

The four textual examples that constitute this chapter each capture complicated relationships to the French language that involve varying degrees of conscious and unconscious pandering and resistance to linguistic conventions. In a language like French, with its long history of linguistic protectionism, it is not surprising that native languages experience a sense of banishment from the textual space. As we have seen in this chapter, these languages and idioms of origin necessarily find their way back into the migrant text, although their presence is always a mitigated one, as though simultaneously shameful and desired. It is this dynamic that animates the linguistic otherness of the migrant text, manifesting itself in as many ways as there are authors, and yet always returning to the uncomfortable beauty of a poetics that resides in the spaces between monolingual mastery and multilingual versatility, linguistic assimilation and difference.

6

Migrant Feminisms

"Migration and feminism are two of the most dynamic social movements since the nineteenth century," writes Glenda Tibe Bonifacio (2012, 1) in her introduction to a collection of essays on these two bodies of thought. Much as we saw in the introduction to this book, the social sciences have also paved the way of inquiry into the place of women in migration studies, as female migrants are increasingly recognized as actors in today's global landscape.[1] However, while the feminization of migration has become the source of a significant amount of scholarship, feminism and migration has lagged somewhat behind.[2] This chapter delves into the ways in which migration empowers feminism and vice versa when female authors write about immigration. French and Francophone literary studies certainly has never been devoid of a feminist lens, but as the realities of migration complicate global feminist paradigms, our understanding of diversity and intersectional difference also changes.

Following earlier "waves" of feminist thought that critiqued the roles and relationships of women in traditional intellectual discourse, the 1980s and 1990s saw the emergence of a feminist multiculturalism, while the new millennium has brought about its queering, destabilizing the pretences of multiculturalism much as migration itself has. Conceived in the writings of Audre Lorde, Chandra Talpade Mohanty, and others, multicultural (or multiracial) feminism first complicated feminist identity politics with new questions of "difference." These theorists denounced what they saw as the homogenizing and universalizing tendencies of earlier feminist views which, in the name of female solidarity, failed to recognize the markers of age, class, race, culture, and sexual orientation that distinguish women from one another.

Lorde, for example, notes that in the realm of feminist discourse, these differences are often so marked with the seal of alterity that they mutate into even more exclusionary or dehumanizing forms. She takes in particular the case of black women in the United States whose differences are often interpreted as a menace, both in white and black culture. Lorde calls for a recognition of difference and a new consciousness of how language can become abusive, turning difference into aberrance: "It is not our differences that separate women, but our reluctance to recognize those differences and to deal effectively with the distortions which have resulted from the ignoring and misnaming of those differences" (1984, 122). Lorde draws attention to the particular deformations of a language of difference that become obstacles for the possibility of true communication across everything that distinguishes people – for her, a process called "relating across difference."

Mohanty, for her part, asks the question from a more global perspective in order to critique the ways in which Western feminist discourse has obscured the cultural perspectives of the women from developing countries that are so often its objects. She reproaches her colleagues for an ethnocentric universalism evacuated of cultural sensitivity: "The assumption of women as an already constituted, coherent group with identical interests and desires, regardless of class, ethnic, or racial location, or contradictions, implies a notion of gender or sexual difference or even patriarchy that can be applied universally and cross-culturally" (2003, 21). For Mohanty, feminist critique can itself reproduce the hegemonic intellectual model that feminism has so long tried to combat, especially when applied to the Third World. Like Lorde, she views the erasure of difference as the key to establishing norms that allow for power to shift from one side to another. Lorde calls this the "mythical norm" that ensures power will remain in the hands of certain individuals who dictate the destiny of others. Multicultural feminism therefore revolutionized the feminist movement – that had to that point revolved mainly around the axis of sexual difference – and breathed into it a new form of ethical conscience pointed toward the complexities of global politics and anchored in efforts to restore difference in all of its many forms.

Although Lorde placed emphasis on the need to negotiate difference through recognition, Susan Friedman makes the case some ten years afterward that the search for cultural difference has reached another theoretical impasse due mainly to its political intransigence; difference itself has become too restrictive, even paralyzing, for in the struggle to preserve its cultural relevance, it sabotaged the possibility for intercultural affiliation and reconciliation. In the end, then, the same binary distinctions that should be blocked or opposed are reinforced and political possibilities are lost: "the discourse of difference itself has become a place of theoretical and activist 'stuckness'" (1998, 68). Inspired by postcolonial theory and particularly by the writing of Homi Bhabha, Friedman looks to integrate feminist theory into the realities of migration and spatio-cultural displacement that characterize so many aspects of the contemporary moment. She imagines for this purpose a new paradigm of feminist thought called "migratory feminism" that confronts questions of cultural hybridity and makes the negotiation of difference a primary aim. Her theoretical gesture consists of incorporating the Derridean concept of "play" in a performative and dialogical manner that allows for the relationship between identity and difference to emerge. Friedman also appropriates Bhabha's theory of "colonial mimicry," wherein the colonized subject imitates her colonizer and complicates the supposed antagonism between "us" and "them" with an inverse movement: "Dominant groups also act out a ceaseless movement back and forth between separation and imitation of others, often with more power to do so" (1998, 77). In other words, Friedman claims for feminism a utopic route for escaping the post-colonial dynamic via a *translational* hybridity (an adjective that I choose here in order to reiterate an intrinsic sense of all culture, which we saw in chapter 4) that describes both the dominant and the dominated culture. Friedman reengages Bhabha and Derrida along with Judith Butler in order to reconsider difference in light of its migratory permutations. On this view, difference, in order to be reconstituted, must leave a place for hybridity because it captures better – at least for American theorists and researchers – a belief in the possibility of reconciliation and mutual understanding. Hybridity expresses the conjunction between cultures that difference so often erases, Friedman insists, thereby privileging interactions like the "blending" and "clashing" of differences.

All of this might seem to contrast with the critical perspective adopted in this study, which is more often concerned with the clash of cultures and the trauma that so often results from it. Friedman maintains though that feminist discourse has too often favoured the conflicted aspects of difference. This is a problem she remedies by advocating the adoption of hybridity, whereas I have supported literary criticism that questions the utopia implied by that same concept – precisely in order to get back on the path of difference. For my part, I have put trauma at the heart of this "contact zone," as Friedman calls it, in order to nuance the reading of a literature issuing from the phenomenon of migration. Conceived as a mode of writing, the migrant text arises precisely from the traumatic experience that must be narrated in order to get beyond it, to heal. Trauma, as we have seen, can be either the cause or the consequence of immigration, but the contact between cultures becomes exacerbated to the point of needing to be written, quite often in repetitive ways, via another culture and another language altogether. In other words, the trauma of migration brings forth a sort of recoiling, creative movement of alterity and difference.

Although I reject the notion of linguistic hybridity in practical literary terms since it is not realizable in the transnational contexts that most interest me, I do not completely let go of the possibility of a cultural hybridity, especially if it is a nuanced one. What is particularly attractive about this form of hybridity in cultural terms is the political dimension that most interests Friedman about Bhabha's thought. By distancing ourselves from the esoteric propensities of the term that tend toward idealization critiqued in chapter 2, we find that hybridity regains a useful political application that has been much less explored by critics.

For a political approach to the question of hybridity, the work of Chicana feminist Gloria Anzaldúa is especially enlightening. Anzaldúa's notion of a new mestiza consciousness as theorized in *Borderlands/La Frontera: The New Mestiza* (1987) destabilizes gender and culture based definitions of identity considered through the lens of Mexican-American migration. The queering of feminism, enacted so innovatively through the writing of Anzaldúa, brings a much needed dimension to our concept of migrant feminisms. Anzaldúa considers the racial, cultural, and linguistic oppression of the mestizo in the US alongside the sexual subjugation of the mestiza by heteronormative sexual norms within Chicano society. The *mestiza* stands as a border-woman who challenges the intersectional systems of domination all at once:

> As a *mestiza* I have no country, my homeland cast me out; yet all countries are mine because I am every woman's sister or potential lover. (As a lesbian I have no race, my own people disclaim me; but I am all races because there is the queer of me in all races.) I am cultureless because, as a feminist, I challenge the collective cultural/religious male-derived belief of Indo-Hispanics and Anglos; yet I am cultured because I am participating in the creation of yet another culture, a new story to explain the world and our participa-

tion in it, a new value system with images and symbols that connect us to each other and the planet. (Anzaldúa 1987, 80–1)

Rather than a female cosmopolitan consciousness that embraces all, Anzaldúa proposes a dissident queering of multicultural feminism in favour of preserving a sense of strangeness as a source of linguistic, cultural, and socio-political creativity. Ian Barnard points out that Anzaldúa's *mestiza* functions at "all levels of identity ... and shapes the articulation of a queer race" (1997, 50). This radical work of theory and poetry is hence one of the very best examples of migration's queer possibilities.

What we are proposing here is a way to bring the poetics and theory Anzaldúa devises for her new *mestiza* into our study of migrant texts – and to revisit Friedman's notion of "migratory feminism" – now over fifteen years old – through the queer feminist ethic proposed by Anzaldúa.[3] The adjective "migratory" designates for Friedman a dialogical movement between a feminism of difference and one of hybridity, each remedying the other's excesses. Friedman hence deploys migration as metaphor since she uses it to designate an "elsewhere" without giving it a name. In other words, Friedman retraces one of Bhabha's characteristic steps of abstraction as we saw in chapter 2, missing in her own way the opportunity to anchor her formula in the reality that she purportedly seeks: "the metaphor of migrancy may well be the luxury of the housed and relatively stationary" (1998, 102). Without limiting the field of migrant feminisms to writing by immigrants, our goal here is to explore the workings of a feminism that finds in the experience of migration a wellspring of creative possibility – one that allows it to contest all forms of fixity, be they based on national, cultural, sexual, or racial identities. At the same time, migrant feminisms consider the survival tactics of the female subject in global capitalism, refusing to abstract from her material reality in order to argue for a reconciliation of difference and hybridity thinking. Migrant feminisms are often, as we shall see, fuelled by traumatic experiences of displacement that allow for cross-cultural critique. Yet the authors of migrant feminisms are not floating bodies, but those who have chosen to be "housed" – to use Friedman's term – in one country or another from which they construct a feminism couched in the language and politics of migrancy.

RÉGINE ROBIN'S LA QUÉBECOITE: EXCLUSION

La Québecoite is a work that escapes tradition both in its linguistic peregrinations – which we analyzed in chapter 5 – and in its literary genre, which aligns itself only marginally with the customary criteria of autobiography. Proclaimed "bio-fiction" by literary critics, neither biography nor fiction, this inter-generic text mixes poetry and prose, not to mention inventories, lists, catalogues, menus, itineraries, and advertisements, in a plain refusal of simple categorization. In the afterword to the English edition of the novel, which translates the title as *The Wanderer*, Robin explains her choice of intermingling so many genres: "In search of a new meaning in the past, I use false biography, false autobiography: 'autofiction,' the novel in the true sense. Autobiographical elements are inscribed in the narrative and transformed into fiction ... if *The Wanderer* is autobiography, it is intellectual or spiritual, not factual, autobiography" (TW, 179–80). Her text verily explodes the confines of established forms as if to imitate the path of an itinerant subject who refuses to anchor herself in any sort of factual, spatial, or generic specificity. In effect, the English title of the book captures quite well the formal transitivity of such an experimental work. However, it is also through the process of writing outside established categories that Robin calibrates her depiction of just what it means to be a Jewish immigrant in Montreal:

> Fixer cette porosité du probable, cette micromémoire de l'étrangeté. Étaler tous les signes de la différence : bulles de souvenirs, pans de réminiscences mal situées arrivant en masse sans texture, un peu gris ... Fixer cette étrangeté avant qu'elle ne devienne familière, avant que le vent ne tourne brusquement, libérant des giclées d'images évidentes. (LQ, 15)
> [To fix this porousness of the probable, this micro-memory of strangeness. To spread out all the signs of difference: bubbles of memories, pieces of vague reminiscences coming all together without texture, a bit grey ... To fix this strangeness before it became familiar, before the wind suddenly changed, freeing rushes of obvious images. (TW, 5)]

Whereas the narrator is obsessed in her own way with "pinpointing the difference" (of her new country), a refrain that recurs throughout the novel, the narration itself fails to offer an immediate vision of what it is that makes the protagonist so strangely uncomfortable in her own skin. The novel, to borrow the influential formulation of Julia Kristeva, looks to make us "strangers to ourselves" (1988) in imitating the perspectival disorientation of an immigrant in Quebec. The proliferation of words evacuated of context and lists of phrases and names fill the narration with obstacles and demand a form of reading that is particularly laborious. What remains of the plot must be picked out amid piles of extraneous signifiers that seem to block the way to interpretation, but which also hold the key to unlocking meaning. As we saw in chapter 5, there is also a form of multilingual crisscrossing that sometimes leaves the reader at a loss. Robin transforms reading itself into a series of detours, where the text defies convention in favour of performance.

The strange nature of this mirror that Robin holds up to a French or Quebecois reader is hence a way of signaling a form of alterity, one that is also gendered since the protagonist's integration involves amorous heterosexual relationships, if not marriage, although the precise nature of her entanglements are – like so many other elements of the book – left ambiguous. Simply put, it is via a man that she hopes to join the ranks of an imagined community, which is expressed via the division of the novel into three discrete hypothetical stories, each driven by a romantic liaison or a sexual relationship. In order to integrate, she chooses a certain nationality or ethnicity in each of her lovers that can put an end to the feeling of strangeness that haunts her. When she arrives in Montreal from Paris, the narrator chooses to live in Snowdon, "quartier d'immigrants à l'anglais malhabile où subsiste encore l'accent d'Europe central, où l'on entend parler yiddish" (*LQ*, 23) [A neighborhood of immigrants with awkward English, where the accents of central Europe still survive, where you hear Yiddish spoken (*TW*, 13)]. She finds refuge in the Jewish community in Montreal and marries a Jew of Franco-Polish origins. They meet in New York; he is sitting on a bench in Washington Square, reading the poetry of Allen Ginsberg. Bound by a common Jewishness and cosmopolitan outlook, they share an almost identical form of cultural hybridity. As he says, "Je me sens new-yorkais de Paris ou montréalais du Shtetl si vous voulez" (*LQ*, 35) [I feel like a New Yorker from Paris or a Montrealer from the *shtetl*, if you prefer (*TW*, 23)]. Despite this complicity, the marriage is also portrayed as a bit of a social step down for the protagonist, who is offering a course in Jewish Studies at McGill while writing "un roman impossible sur Sabbatai Zevi, le faux messie du XVIIIe siècle" (*LQ*, 37) [an impossible novel on Sabbatai Zevi, the false messiah of the seventeenth century" (*TW*, 24)]. The couple also lives with the narrator's aunt Mimi Yente, as even though the narrator is a teacher, she makes "un salaire de misère" (*LQ*, 31) [starvation wages (*TW*, 19)] and her husband is a professor at Concordia University. She is utterly dependent on him for economic survival in Quebec. Little by little though, an emptiness sets in:

Par moments, quelque chose clocherait. Cela viendrait par surprise,
se faufilant dans les interstices d'un bonheur aux mailles serrées ...
     L'Isolement   La coupure ?
Un vide de quelque chose ?
     Quelque chose d'autre ? (*LQ*, 36)
[Every once in a while, something would grate. It would come by
surprise, slipping between the stitches of a tightly knit happiness ...
     Isolation   Being cut off?
An emptiness of something?
     Something else? (*TW*, 24)].

The ghettoized aspect of Jewish culture in Montreal reveals itself as the
real "trace de Shtetl, à Montréal" she says (*LQ*, 80) [a trace of the *shtetl* in
Montreal (*TW*, 62)]. Integrated into one ethnicity at the expense of all
others, she rebels. She discovers a Jewish culture far too prone to nostalgia, incapable of enjoying the present due to its inability to confront
the unspeakable atrocities of the past:

Et ils auraient ri, heureux d'être ensemble, de pouvoir évoquer tous
ces noms d'Europe centrale, heureux d'être juifs aussi en quelque
sorte. Elle se serait mise à chanter. *Ich bin von Kopf bis Fuss auf Liebe
eingestellt* la chanson de Marlène Dietrich dans le *Blauen Engel*, tous
les trois auraient repris le refrain savourant leur complicité. Elle
aurait rompu ce bien-être :
  – Vous savez à quoi nous ressemblons ... À la fin de *L'Éducation
sentimentale* de Flaubert, Frédéric Moreau retrouve un ami
d'adolescence ... et Frédéric dit à son ami :
  – Je crois que c'est ce que nous avons connu de meilleur. Oui
reprend l'ami, Je crois que c'est ce que nous avons eu de meilleur.
Nous sommes ainsi. Et puis nous déconnons sur l'Europe
centrale. L'entre-deux guerres. Oui. Et tout ça débouche sur
Auschwitz, vous savez bien. (*LQ*, 78–9)
[And they would have laughed, glad to be together, to be able to
call up all these names from central Europe, and somehow glad
also to be Jewish. She would have started to sing. *Ich bin von Kopf
bis Fuss auf Liebe eingestellt*, Marlene Dietrich's song in *Der Blaue
Engel*, and all three would have sung the refrain, enjoying their
closeness. She would have broken the mood of well-being.
"You know what we're like? ... At the end of Flaubert's *Sentimental
Education*, Frédéric Moreau meets an old friend from his adolescence ... and Frédéric says it was 'the happiest time we ever had.'

'Yes,' the friend says, 'it was the happiest time we ever had.' That's what we're like. We go on about central Europe between the wars. Yes. And all that leads to Auschwitz, as you know." (TW, 60–1)]

It is in this part of the novel that the narrative voice often shifts from *je* to *elle*, suddenly adopting the voice of the old Jewish professor. This perspective is that of a man teaching a course on Sabbatai Zevi, reliving the war years in fragments – the German election of 1932, the Nazi camps, the numbers on the arms of prisoners, the round up of Jews in Paris. And then these words – "La grande rafle. Les Français tous collabos, tu disais. Tu ne voulais pas" (LQ, 44, 48) [The big raid. The French all collaborators, you said. You no longer wanted to (TW, 30, 31, 34)] – repeated three times in four pages, with only slight variations, returning like a fugue. We learn that the old professor lost his first wife, called Natacha, and that the narrator lost her mother. The traumatic past awakens in Montreal and renders integration impossible, expressing itself via the experience of abandonment by France, a treacherous collaborator. Suddenly the narrator's marriage, along with the change of name it implies, represents a denial of trauma rather than its confrontation:

Écartèlement des cultures je suis à califourchon ... changer de peau, de langue, de bouffe, d'époque, de sexe, de nom. Le trouble du nom propre lorsqu'il se perd – lorsqu'il change ... Le mien nouveau sonne comme la mer traversée et la mère perdue. Le seul lien, le seul pays, ma mère. Toi perdue, à nouveau l'errance. (LQ, 63)
[Torn between cultures I'm astraddle ... To change one's skin, language, food, time, sex, name. The anguish of the proper name when it's lost, when it changes ... My new one rings like the sea crossed and the mother lost. The only link, the only country, my mother. You lost – again to wander. (TW, 47)]

She refuses all citizenship, all nationalism other than her connection to her mother and the tragedy. She chooses in turn to leave, to dissolve her marriage, in order to find herself once more an immigrant, without identity. Without a husband, she is without nation and language: "La parole immigrante comme un cri, comme la métaphore mauve de la mort, aphone d'avoir trop crié" (LQ, 55) [Immigrant words like a cry, like the mauve metaphor of death, voiceless from shouting too much (TW, 40)].

The two following amorous scenarios of the novel, one in the bourgeois French-speaking neighbourhood Outremont and the other in the immigrant quarter of Jean-Talon, develop along similar lines. The narrator switches lovers from the Jewish professor to a high-ranking Quebecois separatist and then to a factory worker from Paraguay, in each instance unsuccessfully trying to integrate, first into Quebecois middle class and then the multi-ethnic immigrant community of Montreal. At first glance, she might seem to be an object bouncing between men in order to enrich the culture borne by each of them. As if oscillating between the matrimonial economy that Claude Lévi-Strauss analyzes in *La structure élémentaire de la parenté* (1968) and the nationalist economy that Claudia Koonz outlines in her work on the role of women in the Nazi regime (1986), the immigrant woman becomes absorbed in each of these ethnic communities in a way that seems to valorize and restate its utility. Victim of a nationalist patriarchy or patriarchal nationalism, the narrator passes from spouse to spouse in search of an identity that will not be fixed.

Between the narrator and her Quebecois separatist husband, a small crack of difference develops: "Au moment de leurs discussions plus ou moins passionnées, il aurait pris l'habitude de lui dire que n'étant pas d'ici, elle n'y connaissait rien" (*LQ*, 132). [He would have gotten in the habit of telling her during their more heated discussions that, not being from this place, she knew nothing about it (*TW*, 107).] Since it is 1980, it is finally time to vote in the referendum on Quebec's independence from Canada and she hesitates between the *oui* and the *non*, feeling as if she is excluded from the national conversation despite the marriage that ensures her participation:

Comment voterait-elle au référendum ? Par moments, elle serait presque sûre de dire oui. Elle penserait à Maurice Audin, à Henri Alleg, à ceux qui avaient lutté pour l'indépendance de l'Algérie avec les Algériens, à ceux qui avaient porté les valises du FLN. Impossible de dire NON, de voter avec les tenants des multinationales, des Dominants. Par moments, cependant, ces moments qui reviendraient souvent où son mari lui ferait sentir qu'elle n'était pas d'ici, elle hésiterait. La peur. (*LQ*, 133)
[How would she vote in the referendum? At times, she'd be almost sure she would vote yes. She would think of Maurice Audin and Henri Alleg and others who had fought for Algerian independence with the Algerians, who had carried suitcases for the FLN. Impossible to say NO, to vote with the supporters of the multinationals and the ruling class. At other times, however, on those frequent occa-

sions when her husband would make her feel she wasn't from here, she would hesitate. Fear. (TW, 107)]

Throughout this portion of the novel, the narrator explores the national trauma of Quebec in great detail, from the English conquest to the assassinations of the Jesuit priests Lalement and Brébeuf, martyred by the Iroquois, and from the events of October 1970 to Gaétan Montreuil's reading of the FLQ manifesto on Radio-Canada television. Yet the thread of her own trauma, that famous metro route toward Grenelle, intercepts that of the Quebecois around her, pulling her and her husband apart. Explaining her fear of voting in the referendum, she expresses her exclusion from the Quebec nation:

> La peur de l'homogénéité
> de l'unanimité
> du Nous excluant tous les autres
> du pure laine
> elle l'immigrante. (LQ, 133)
> [The fear of homogeneity
> of unanimity
> of the Us that excludes all others
> of the pure
> she the immigrant. (TW, 107)]

Subject to her own trauma but rebelling against France, she refuses a Quebec nationalism that does not allow her to define herself in relationship to "others." Despite her efforts to join her husband, via her own suffering, she is rejected. As the above passage shows, her exclusion, as immigrant, is even expressed typologically on the page, expelled as it were from Quebec's nationalist rhetoric. Each of her two husbands reject the form of hybridity that constitutes the very basis of the narrator's past and her memory thereof. Instead, they are pulled back into the homogenous identities that have defined them for so long.

The third story does not end better than the first two, as the protagonist returns for a last time to France feeling wedded to a migrancy that she now sees as her identity. As she explains to her next lover, "et puis ... j'aime ça, l'errance. J'aime ça être perpétuellement ailleurs" (LQ, 178) [And besides, I like wandering. I like always being elsewhere (TW, 147)]. And despite everything that unites her with the third man, who has been exiled by the fascist regime of Alfredo Stroesner and who refuses Canadian citizenship for national security reasons, she still feels like a stranger within the ghettoized life that is offered to her yet again. The immigrants are set apart from the rest of the city in their own little corner and she lives in Little Italy amid many other populations. But the Paraguayan, like the Franco-Polish Jew and the Quebecois, cannot give her the stability she desires and the narrator admits as much in a meta-narrative gesture about the hopes of her character:

> J'avais essayé pourtant. Impossible de faire le tour de cette ville, de l'assimiler, de se l'incorporer. Impossible simplement de s'arrêter quelque part, de poser son baluchon, de dire ouf ! ...
> Faudrait-il tout recommencer ?
> La changer de quartier, d'espérance ?
> Lui trouver un nouvel amant ou un autre métier ? (*LQ*, 173–4)
> [But I did try. Impossible to fathom this city, to assimilate it, to make it part of you. Impossible simply to stop somewhere, put down your packsack, and say phew! ...
> Would it be necessary to start all over again?
> Give her a new neighborhood, new prospects?
> Find her a new lover, another occupation? (*TW*, 143)]

Through this narrative distanciation, a bifurcation occurs between protagonist and narrator, who up to this point were one and the same. It is thus the narrator who is searching to fix the character, via marriage, into a job and a neighbourhood that matches the social rank of her lover. The man becomes, in the narrator's sense, a way to neutralize the protagonist's trauma and to stabilize her nomadic ways by having her put down roots in Quebec soil. Yet with each hypothetical scenario, the protagonist becomes more resistant to this narrative thrust, and ultimately refuses to marry the last lover by proclaiming herself "déjà errante" (*LQ*, 186) [already wandering (*TW*, 154)] since adolescence. An exasperated narrator interrupts her protagonist at the end of the novel to declare the following: "Le texte m'échappe. Je le sens glisser ... Illusions de l'enracinement. Ce personnage encore une fois m'échappe ... Lui donner des amants de toutes les nationalités et après ? Restera l'exil, l'éternel sentiment d'être ailleurs, déracinée" (*LQ*, 187). [The text is getting away from me. I feel it slipping away ... Illusions of rootedness. This character is eluding me again ... Give her lovers of every nationality – and then? There will still be exile, the eternal feeling of being elsewhere, uprooted (*TW*, 155).] The text doubles back on itself, calling its own literary enterprise of taming the character into question. In so doing, the narrative voice recognizes its own incapacity to contain the protagonist with narration and finally gives her the power to write her own story.

Although the narrator tries to attach the protagonist to the male characters who push her to integrate, the character ends up returning in each of the stories to her beloved Jewish aunt Mimi Yente, herself a Holocaust survivor, who resurfaces in each of the three parts of the novel. While she is with each of her three lovers, the protagonist returns to see her aunt, to eat a meal at her apartment, to observe the Sabbath or a religious celebration or simply to avail herself of the older woman's affection. Mimi Yente, for her part, lodges the first couple, spends time in the country with the second couple, and finds employment for the third couple thanks to which they become co-owners of an antique store. Mimi Yente, along with the memory of her mother, are constants in each of the protagonist's episodes, even as the male characters change. Mimi Yente, a maternal figure, is the one to whom the protagonist returns at the end of each of her relationships and yet the old woman never opposes her decisions: "Mimi Yente n'aurait même pas envisagé de la retenir" (*LQ*, 167) [It wouldn't have occurred to Mime Yente to stop her (*TW*, 137)[4]; "Mimi Yente haussant les épaules n'aurait pas cherché à la retenir" (*LQ*, 206) [Mime Yente would have shrugged her shoulders and made no attempt to stop her (*TW*, 171)]. The resigned narrator cannot manage to get this old aunt out of her text and feels as if the woman has altered the course of the narrative:

Je me sens totalement piégée par elle. Elle finit par me prendre par la main, par me guider. Si je lui compose tel visage, si je lui donne tel destin, elle se rebiffe. C'est elle qui finit par commander. Elle veut sa place, toute sa place. Elle n'accepte pas d'être une ombre, un simple support à l'écriture. Non. Elle sort du papier, elle entraîne son barbudo, Mimi Yente et Bilou [son chat] dans cette émergence. (*LQ*, 187)
[I feel completely trapped by her. She ends up taking me by the hand and guiding me. If I give her some face or some fate, she rebels. She's the one that ends up giving the orders. She wants her place, her whole place. She won't accept being a shadow, a mere prop for writing. No. She leaves the paper, taking her *barbudo* and Mime Yente and Bilou [her cat] with her. (*TW*, 155)]

The character struggles to wrest her identity from an assassinated mother and a traumatized aunt, both victims of the war. For the rest, she chooses migration, refusing the ghetto and its Nazi reminiscences: "À nouveau l'humiliation ? Porter à nouveau l'étoile ? Texte brisé. Extirper la peur, la honte, la solitude" (*LQ*, 19). [Humiliation again? To wear the star again? Broken text. To root out fear, shame, solitude (*TW*, 8).]

The word "migrant" represents for the protagonist a quest for both the universal and the hybrid in a world characterized by cleavages and schizophrenia. At multiple moments the narrator asks, "N'y a-t-il rien d'universel ici ?" [Is there nothing universal here?] caught in the middle of a text which by its own nature refuses both Jewish and Quebecois allegiances. At the end of the novel, the protagonist repositions herself once again, this time away from the immigrant community and toward migrancy. Robin transforms her experience of exclusion into one of empowerment through her own voluntary migration away from domestic situations of oppression that mirror national ones. At a conference in 1985 on literature and minorities entitled "Écrire la différence," Robin made an important distinction between the voices of immigrants and the migrant mode of her work: "I would say that the whole problem for me is how to bring together in writing the immigrant voice and the migrant voice. For me, the real work of the writer –unless he turns himself into a bard, a spokesperson for ethnic groups – consists of a perpetual displacement of stereotypes, a perpetual questioning of clichés, a migration of images" (Moisan and Hildebrand 2001, 164). It is through the female character that she captures at last this migrant vision by reversing sexual norms and embracing a nomadic form of movement opposing the binarism of feminine sedentariness and male wandering. In the national paradigm, it is now the man who insists on fixity and home life, and it is by subverting this oppressive reality that Robin proposes her migrant feminism.

YING CHEN'S *LES LETTRES CHINOISES*: SUBVERSION

The love story of Yuan and Sassa, which comes to a climax in *Les Lettres chinoises*, can be read as a metaphor for the convergence between two forms of nationalism fraught with the problems of migration. Yuan and Sassa, as we know, are separated from each other by Yuan's immigration to Canada. He leaves his lover first for Vancouver then for Montreal, where he waits for her. Even before that story begins, the "poem" referenced in the calligraphic characters on the cover of the book – expressly chosen by Chen to decorate her work – suggests the end of a love affair thwarted by nationalism. The poem evokes the bitter loneli-

ness of someone who, cut off from his or her community, feels abandoned in uncertain time and space. Once more, we remember the
French translation of François Cheng:

Du haut de la terrasse du You-Zhou
[Devant], je ne vois pas l'homme passé
[Derrière], je ne vois pas l'homme futur
Songeant au ciel-terre vaste et sans fin
Solitaire, amer, je fonds en larmes (1977, 130)

The poem gestures at the void felt by those who are estranged from their
national community, and although the poet may not have envisioned
physical migration here, the poem expresses the trauma of separation
that results from a psychological displacement. According to nationalism defined by Benedict Anderson, the call of the imagined community, as we saw in the second chapter, can be extended quite far and, unless
it is explicitly refused, tends to reach all of the diaspora, which continues to evoke its name. At the start of Chen's novel, Yuan observes this dynamic of national imaginary despite the great distance that lies between
him and his lover.

However, as the spatial and temporal distance grows larger between
the couple, Sassa quickly becomes a sort of amalgam of Chinese culture, her feminine body its material incarnation. It is just this sort of
metaphorical gesture of woman that Claudia Koonz calls "national em-
bodiment" in her study of the difference between the roles given to
boys and those given to girls in the national imaginary of the Third
Reich (1986). After he receives the photos Sassa mails him of herself,
Yuan reflects on the ways in which the photo's meaning betrays a sort
of nostalgia wherein woman and nation intermingle:

Chaque fois que je prononce "Sassa", je pense à la chaleur du sable,
à la sonorité de ses soupirs, à la gaieté des pieds nus, à la folie du
vent, à l'éternité du soleil et de la mer. Oh, Sassa, ton prénom seul
suffit à me remplir de tendresse pour toi. Quand tu viendras, je
t'emmènerai à la plage. Nous nous étendrons l'un contre l'autre
sur le tapis de sable, n'ayant devant nos yeux qu'un ciel immense.
(*LC*, 57)
[Each time I pronounce "Sassa," I think of the warmth of the sand,
the sound of sighs, the gaiety of bare feat, the madness of the wind,
the eternity of the sun and the sea. Oh, Sassa, your name alone is

enough to fill me with affection for you. When you come, I will
take you to the beach. We will lay against each other on the carpet
of sand, with only the immense sky before our eyes.]

Thanks to a photo, Yuan calls up memories of Sassa, as well as remarkably sensual ones of the Chinese landscape – the sand, the sun, and the
sea. He promises to one day recreate a scene like this one when they re-
unite in Canada, but seems to forget that the natural surroundings will
be quite different there. He will find it more difficult, obviously, to find
"la chaleur du sable" and "l'éternité du soleil et de la mer" in the North
American country where he now lives. In this letter that idealizes the
past and imagines a future utopia, his words recall those of Ernest
Renan in his definition of the nation.[5]
    As he relates his belief that his nationalist dream will one day come
true, Yuan recalls, as if despite himself, a poem that he hopes confirms
his idealist vision. At the same time, though, the poem seems to con-
tradict that very possibility – resembling much more the poem from
the book's cover – as we saw in our analysis of the novel in chapter 2.
Yuan thus misinterprets the meaning of the poem that returns in his
free associations. Having imagined a love scene on the sand against an
immense sky, he recalls the poem's words without thinking about the
ironic ways in which his own memory betrays him. He follows his romantic reverie with a comparison that turns out to be mostly chimeric:

Comme dit un vieux poème :
Nos larmes coulent dans la solitude
Le ciel est loin et la terre immense
Inutile de chercher ici et là
Nous n'aurons plus d'ancêtres ni d'enfants. (LC, 57–8)
[As the old poem goes:
Our tears flow in solitude
The sky is far and the earth immense
No use in searching here or there
We will have no ancestors or children.]

Then, as if to confirm this hypothesis, Yuan follows this train of thought
in speaking about his arrival in Montreal in the spring, unaware of the
double meaning of the poem, cited here in italics in order to emphasize
the character's distance from this interpretation.
    Chen uses the nationalist pretensions of her character to expose their
fallacious logic. On one hand, the poem suggests that isolation is an in-

herent part of the national project – that imagined communities are effectively impossible outside of fiction. On the other, the text signals the spatio-temporal problem that nationalist ambitions always depend upon, despite Anderson's influential theory. Indeed, most forms of spatial and temporal unity complicate migration. Richard Handler raises this question in his consideration of spatial and temporal delimitation, without which, he claims, there would be no concept of "nation" at all. The poem's lack of ancestors to refer to also invokes Renan's warning about "le culte des ancêtres est de tous [les efforts, les sacrifices et les dévouements du passé d'où aboutit la nation] le plus légitime ; les ancêtres nous ont faits ce que nous sommes" (1882, 26) [Of all cults, that of the ancestors [the long past of endeavours, sacrifice, and devotion which culminate in the nation] is the most legitimate, for the ancestors have made us what we are (1996, 52)]. This dovetails equally with traditions of Chinese thought which, as we learn from the poem by Chen Zi-Ang and the translation of François Cheng, puts ancestry before children. Cheng explains: "L'homme chinois, lui, se place d'instinct dans la grande lignée humaine; ainsi il voit ceux qui l'ont précédé devant soi et il se voit entraîner derrière soi ceux qui vont venir" (1977, 130). [The Chinese man instinctively places himself within the great human lineage; in front of him he sees those who came before him and he sees himself pulling behind him those who are yet to come.] Immigration interrupts this line because it implies a form of cultural hybridity forged in the feelings of emptiness that come with departure: "Mais je pense qu'en quittant une ville où l'on a vécu quelque temps, on sent une partie de sa vie se perdre d'un seul coup dans le nuage que l'avion traverse. Le vide en soi devient sans borne." (LC, 59) [But I think when we leave a city where we have lived for some time, we suddenly feel the loss of a part of ourselves in the cloud that the airplane traverses. The emptiness within knows no bounds.] This reflection by Yuan can be interpreted as a sort of pedagogical transformation, one where he finds himself on the way to a hybrid form of culture, no matter how depressing he might find it.

Sassa, for her part, is more aware of the comparable perils that her love and the idea of a Chinese nation share. Whereas Yuan's letters struggle to relive the nostalgia of their mundane moments together in bad restaurants or the streets of Shanghai, Sassa constantly reminds him about the dangers of excessive imagination: "Ne laisse pas la vie couler dans l'imagination" she warns, "Je pense que l'un de nos pires ennemis est l'imagination" (LC, 85). [Don't let your life sink into imagination. I think one of our worst enemies is the imagination.] Rather

than idealizing the past, Sassa begins to let her love loose and decides
not to join Yuan in Canada. From that moment, her health also begins
to deteriorate and she writes her final letters from a hospital bed. Her
feminine body, so closely aligned in the book with the physicality of
China itself, becomes more and more feeble as Yuan works to integrate
into a new culture. Sassa's letters become shorter and shorter as her illness takes over and her last few letters suggest that she is now in ago-
nizing pain. When Yuan sends her a purple maple leaf that has landed
on his window sill in the Fall, Sassa cites a song that exalts the heroism
of the Chinese soldiers who fought in Vietnam. Rather than think of
the Canadian flag that his gift could evoke, Sassa lets her thoughts drift
to the red flag of the Republic of China and the following song:

> *Si je tombe sans pouvoir me relever,*
> *Si je ferme les yeux sans pouvoir les rouvrir,*
> *Si c'est ainsi, n'insiste pas pour m'attendre,*
> *Si c'est ainsi ne sois pas triste,*
> *Regarde le drapeau de la République*
> *Où est imprégnée la splendeur de notre sang.* (LC, 119)
> [If I fall and am unable to stand,
> If I close my eyes and cannot reopen them,
> If it is hence, do not insist on waiting for me,
> If it is hence, do not be sad,
> Look at the flag of the Republic
> That is stained with the splendour of our blood.]

This song, called *La Splendeur du sang* [The Splendour of Blood], re-
moves the maple leaf from one national framework and recasts it within another. With this shift of meaning, Chen points to the arbitrariness
of the Canadian symbol when it leaves one territory for another, hence
taking on a totally new significance. By colouring the maple leaf with
Chinese blood, Chen creates a poignant moment where a symbolic leaf
must metaphorically adopt a nationality that has renounced its own
meaning. In other words, the allegiance to one nation always involves
the sacrifice of another, a fact all the more powerfully driven home by
Sassa's disappearance at the novel's end.

The character Sassa, however, is far from the type who accepts what
Koonz calls the "burden of cultural representation" that her country demands (1986, 196). Rather, her death, which seems a likely suicide, constitutes an outright refusal of all national allegiance.[6] It is she who begs
her lover not to adhere to an unrealistic vision of China and to resist the
metamorphosis he says he feels after living in Canada. It is by fusing

two national allegories that Sassa declares her anti-nationalist credo: "Bien que je n'aime pas les champs de bataille, que je comprenne mal ce que veut dire la République et que je déteste les drapeaux, j'ai aimé cette chanson. En regardant cette feuille couleur de sang venue du Canada, cette chanson me revient au cœur (LC, 119–20). [Though I do not like battlefields, fail to comprehend what the Republic means and hate flags, I loved this song. As I gaze upon this blood-coloured leaf that came from Canada, this song returns to my heart.] In a letter she writes earlier on to Da Li, Sassa expresses her alienation from her own country – which she calls the cause of her illness. In China, she suffers from a feeling of otherness for which her physical ills are only a symptom:

> Au fond, je me sens aussi déracinée que toi, même si je reste encore sur cette terre où je suis née ... Je suis née étrangère dans mon propre pays. Et cela vaudrait une sentence beaucoup plus sévère. Voilà pourquoi je souffre, Da Li ... J'ai tellement mal au corps que je ne sens plus ma douleur du cœur. (LC, 66)
> [In the end, I am as rootless as you, even though I remain here in this land where I was born ... I am a stranger in my own country. And that deserves a far greater sentence. That is why I suffer, Da Li ... My body hurts so much that I no longer feel my heartache.]

Her body carries this trauma of otherness just as her heart does the wounds of migration. Caught between two nationalities, she refuses both. Sassa claims she is incapable of obtaining a passport to leave China, even though we know that Yuan and Da Li got theirs fairly easily. Passports appear almost like a leitmotif throughout the lovers' letters, and by the end they seem to most obviously represent deception and betrayal. The anxiety that Sassa feels draws on her impressions of being an exile in her own land. She finds herself chained to the place she most desires to leave.

The contradiction inherent to Sassa's character reflects the complex position occupied by woman in the construction of societies, one developed by Julia Kristeva in her essay "Le temps des femmes." According to her analysis, woman is at once drawn and repulsed by the roles she must play in society, in this case a national one. Sassa embodies just this sort of push and pull in her relationships in the novel. She accuses her friend Da Li of not being Chinese due to an illicit affair, even though a few pages later she expresses her own profound alienation from that same national identity. Hers is a character that is both subversive and acquiescent, and this is where she acquires both complexity and force. Near the end of the novel, Yuan proposes that he return to

China to be by her side, but his agonized fiancé rebuffs him. When he begs her, comparing himself to a kite whose string lies in her hands, he also reveals for the first time his own form of immigrant trauma:

> Mais que deviendrai-je sans toi ? ... Ce n'est pas mauvais, mais pas du tout, de vivre comme les Américains. Seulement, je n'ai pas vécu en vain toutes ces années à Shanghai. Je suis marqué pour la vie. Dans ce cas-là, si je ne reste pas fermement moi-même, si je n'essaie pas de rester Chinois, je ne serai rien du tout. Mais comment être moi-même sans toi ? Je suis comme un cerf-volant qui vole très loin ... et dont la corde est entre tes mains. (*LC*, 133–4)
> [But what will I be without you? ... It is not bad, why not at all, to live like Americans. Only, I did not live in Shanghai for all those years in vain. I am marred for life. In that case, if I don't remain firmly myself, if I don't try to remain Chinese, I will be nothing at all. But how can I be myself without you? I am like a kite that has flown far away ... and whose string is in your hands.]

For Yuan, just like Sassa, migration represents a betrayal that is never-theless necessary in order to escape nationalist traps that are sources of oppression. Taking up his kite metaphor, Sassa responds by breaking it apart with a simile of her own: "Un cerf-volant incapable de voler sans sa corde ressemble à cet idiot qui, ayant trouvé un moyen de faire un trou dans un mur pour s'évader de la prison, se croit perdu le jour où ce même mur est enlevé" (*LC*, 136). [A kite that cannot fly without its string resembles that idiot who, having found a way to make a hole in the wall to escape from prison, believes he is lost the day that wall is in fact removed.] Sassa seems therefore to sacrifice herself in order to lib-erate her lover from his nationalist bonds; she knows that as long as he is yoked to her, he will not be able to live without feeling as if he has let down his people and country. Since he is not able to leave behind his links to his country, she does it for him, offering up her own life as a way to ensure the painful success of his migration.

LEÏLA SEBBAR'S
JE NE PARLE PAS LA LANGUE DE MON PÈRE:
RECONCILIATION

In my previous analysis of the linguistic interplay in *Je ne parle pas la langue de mon père*, we saw how Sebbar uses a feminine evocation of Ara-bic to reconcile a traumatic past – punctuated by colonization and the Algerian war – with her mixed origins. In effect, Sebbar is a writer who offers an experience of hybridity in its most vulgar sense, as an experience of cultural clashes that have haunted her since her childhood. Born of a French mother and Algerian father, she spent her formative years in Algeria, moving to France near the end of her adolescence. While it reconsiders her relationship to her father, Sebbar's novel also enacts a return to the country of her childhood, where she pays homage to a generation of women that she remembers but whom she never really knew. In addition to her failed intimacy with her father, she lacks any real relationship to her female relatives in Algeria. The novel reconstructs a fictional account of the relationships, forging an imaginary – yet no less powerful – link to women who are themselves no less marked and alienated by the war. I propose here to consider this novel through the optic of migrant feminisms because Sebbar's text ties the colonized woman to the female colonizer via what can only be called a trauma of "shared exclusion." In doing so, the novel effects a reversal of masculine power by contrasting the separatist logic of war with a feminine, hybrid logic of reconciliation.

The gap that Arabic creates in the novel serves as a sort of base for a story that is much more complicated than the one the narrator relates about her father, since it also entails an intercultural process of discovery. *Je ne parle pas la langue de mon père* announces with its title – as well as the biographical details in the preface – that it is a novel about the relationship between a daughter and her father. But beginning with the second chapter, the first sentence references not him but his mother – "mon père ne m'a pas appris la langue de sa mère" (*JNP*, 33) [my father did not teach me his mother's language] – and follows, one chapter later, with a sentence that cites the names of two maids of the Sebbar family, "Je n'ai pas parlé la langue d'Aïsha et de Fatima" (*JNP*, 49) [I did not speak the language of Aïsha and Fatima]. Two other chapters open with references to women, first to those who are part of her father's people and then to his sisters – that is to say, all of the women that Sebbar's mother tongue has prevented her from knowing intimately. Even so, this arbitrary opposition, created by the force of colonization, also creates a common form of suffering that all of these women share. We saw in chapter 5 how the narrator feels alienated from her father due to hushed discussions that take place behind closed doors between men: "Bientôt, ce serait l'heure des hommes, je les entendrais à peine, des murmures" (*JNP*, 20). [Soon it will be the men's hour, I would barely hear them, whispers.] Although some of these conversations, like the one just mentioned, are about the war and Algerian resistance, others are less serious and take place explicitly to exclude the participation of women:

> Mon père riait, en arabe, avec des hommes inconnus. Ce qu'ils se racontaient les faisait rire, je ne savais pas, je ne saurai pas ce qu'ils se disaient alors ... je restais debout au seuil de la porte, guettant le moment où mon père et ses amis descendraient jusqu'à son bureau, j'entendais les voix s'éloigner vers la pièce magistrale où ils s'enfermeraient pour bavarder encore. (*JNP*, 19)
> [My father was laughing, in Arabic, with unknown men. What they were saying to each other made them laugh, I did not know, I would not know what they were saying then ... I would remain at the threshold of the door, watching for the moment when my father and his friends would go down to his office, I would hear the voices disappear into the great room where they would lock themselves to chat some more.]

In this masculine communication, albeit typical of indigenous culture, the narrator presents a form of sexual injustice since women are excluded and cannot participate in the political decision making process. Describing the preparations for the revolution as they occur in her village, Sebbar emphasizes the sexual division of tasks:

> Dans l'ombre des pauvres cours, où n'entraient que les hommes de la famille après avoir crié leur nom, pour que les femmes sachent ce qu'elles avaient à faire, les unes vers la cuisine, les autres vers les chambres, fermées par un rideau, les enfants petits happés par les sœurs aînées pour laisser le passage aux hommes, à leurs mots politiques qu'il ne fallait pas entendre. (*JNP*, 23)
> [In the shadow of poor courtyards, where only men of the family entered after having shouted out their name, so that the women knew what they had to do, some toward the kitchen, others toward bedrooms, sealed by curtains, little children snapped up by their older sisters to give way to the men, to their political words that we were not to hear.]

The political function of woman here always occurs through her husband, her brother, her son. They are banished from the discussion and the isolation of the narrator from her father becomes just one reflection of a much larger sequestration of feminine culture.

The narrator nonetheless shows us the quite diverse ways in which

Algerian women remain thoroughly implicated in the war for independence even if their contributions are not always recognized at the same level as those of men. Notably, she draws attention to the example of Françoise Josette Audin, the widow of the French mathematician Maurice Audin who was arrested, tortured, and assassinated by the French army for his revolutionary activities in Algeria. After the so-called "disappearance" of her spouse, Josette Audin the "femme au teint clair" (*JNP*, 23) [the woman with fair skin] known for fighting side-by-side with her husband, is treated as a pariah in Algeria where, without a man, she is no longer accepted and encouraged to pack her bags back to France:

Ce pays, la France, n'est pas son pays. Mais sans lui [son mari], dans la ville où il est mort, disparu vraiment, elle n'a pas pu vivre. Elle a cru que ce serait possible, qu'elle ne serait pas étrangère, à deux, peut-être, seule, non. Elle a été une étrangère et personne ne lui a dit le contraire, que ce peuple est son peuple, et qu'elle est fille de ce peuple. Personne. Il n'est pas revenu ... Elle est partie. On ne l'a pas retenue. Elle s'est interdit sa ville, son pays.[7] (*JNP*, 27–8)
[This country, France, is not her country. But without him [her husband], in the city where he died, disappeared really, she could not live. She thought it would be possible, that she would not be a stranger, perhaps, as two, but never alone. She was a stranger and no one suggested the contrary, no one told her these people were her people, and that she was a daughter of the people. No one. He did not come back ... She left. They did not keep her from leaving. She banished herself from the city, from the country.]

The rebellious woman without a husband is thus devoid of political value, and in this case required to leave for a country of origin that is no longer her own. Sebbar follows the example of Josette Audin with the story of a native Algerian from Clos-Salembier who leaves a forced marriage to join the ranks of the FLN: "Mariée de force, un père tyrannique, un mari détesté, elle déserte la maison, le lit du viol, et rejoint la famille des Frères camarades" (*JNP*, 29). [Married by force, a tyrannical father, a hated husband, she deserts her home, the bed where she is raped, and joins the family of the Brothers.] As for Fatima, the maid of whom the narrator has lost all trace, she also takes on a new role, albeit imagined, during armed combat. After having left the Sebbar family, Fatima gets married, but since she is sterile she must raise the sons of her husband, the eldest of whom will become a soldier in the battle against France.

When he is ordered by the head of his regiment to kill the father of the narrator, he refuses to cede to the supplications of his mother, who begs him to spare the life of her old employer: "Si tu le fais, tu n'es plus mon fils, tu entends, tu n'es plus mon fils ... Ne reviens pas dans ma maison, tu trouveras des cailloux à la place du pain" (*JNP*, 53–4). [If you do it, you are no longer my son, you hear, you are no longer my son ... Do not return to my house, you will find stones in the place of bread.] With no reaction from her son, Fatima runs to warn the headmaster and save him from certain death. What is even more significant about this made-up story is that Fatima uses her haik, the large cloth used by muslim women to cover themselves, in order to pass unseen into the school of Clos-Salembier and to secretly alert the narrator's father about the danger that awaits him. The veil, such a contentious symbol in France, is used here as a political arm on the part of a woman as a way to save the life of one of her compatriots.

According to Yuval-Davis, it is misleading to think about women in war only assuming a domestic, pacific function while men leave for combat. "Militaries and warfare have never been just a 'male zone,'" she insists, "Women have always fulfilled certain, often vital, roles within them – but usually not on an equal, undifferentiated basis to that of men" (1997, 93). In the Algerian context, this reality takes on great importance for a writer like Sebbar who, at risk of being associated with the colonizer, wants to give voice to a long and diverse line of resistant women in Algeria. She favours in particular French women like Josette Audin, with whom she identifies herself no doubt since she shares their language, but also because she admires their tenacity and their rebellious spirit. After being alienated from the war because of her father and her French school, Sebbar seeks to rewrite her past by linking it to women with bellicose political sensibilities that resemble her own. To the story of Josette Audin she adds one about the errant stepdaughter of Mohammed Dib. This woman, whose first name we never know, is the daughter of the Algerian writer's French wife, who joined the resistance alongside her husband:

> La fille de sa femme, si jeune encore, seize ans, peut-être dix-sept ans ... cette jeune fille rebelle parmi les rebelles sera arrêtée par des soldats français et l'officier, sidéré, incrédule devant cette combattante en pataugas, exaltée, résolue, parlant la langue de la France métropolitaine, ne croira pas qu'elle s'est engagée dans le maquis pour lutter avec ces jeunes hommes arabes en armes, et libérer ce pays, à peine son pays. (*JNP*, 59–60)

[His wife's daughter, still so young, sixteen years, perhaps seventeen years ... this young rebellious girl among rebels would be stopped by French soldiers. The stunned officer – incredulous before this young fighter in pataugas, exalted, resolved, speaking the language of metropolitan France – would not believe that she has joined the resistance to combat alongside these young Arab men in arms, and liberate this country, barely her own country.]

The text displays great admiration on the part of the narrator, who describes the irony of a French officer's response to a female revolutionary. These are the sorts of characters, often historically based, that complicate the colonial equation on both sides, both French and Algerian. By peppering her text with them, Sebbar stages her own revolt against the misogynist attitudes that so often fail to recognize female contributions to the war and to the resistance movement. She knows, of course, that writing for a French public, she must work to reverse the stereotyped vision of woman in the Western imaginary: "While men have been constructed as naturally linked to warfare, women have been constructed as naturally linked to peace. The image of women resisting war had been in existence in the western imagination at least since *Lysistrata* was first shown in Athens in the fifth century BC" (1997, 94).[8] The argument made by Yuval-Davis nuances my interpretation of Sebbar's text precisely because the writer refuses any sort of reification of the feminine that justifies their political alienation in the name of cultural nativism or pacifist utopia.

We cannot neglect Habiba Deming's argument, however, also considered in chapter 5, in which she criticizes Sebbar for her refusal to question her privileged upbringing in the colonial oasis of French schooling and a French-speaking family – right in the middle of a rural Algerian village. Deming takes particular issue with Sebbar's complaint about the young boys of the village who hurl insults at her and her sisters on their way to school. Comparing the retelling of this incident in several different Sebbarian works, Deming highlights the contradictions between them, and accuses the author of a form of colonial aphasia. It also stands to reason that, in this case, Sebbar may not be ignorant of the reasons for the boys' insults, but rather that she is working through a site of trauma. She narrates on multiple occasions, and via the voice of Fatima's son as well as the point-of-view of Fatima herself, that the Sebbar girls wear French clothes even though they live in Algeria. Dressed by their mother, they all wear short skirts in a land where women habitually cover their legs out of modesty:

Les filles de la Française, il les voyait de loin lorsqu'il allait
travailler au domaine, au-delà de l'école et de la cave vinicole, dans
la plaine. Avec les filles du quartier, elle jouaient à la *galline*, la
marelle ... elles, jambes nues, les sœurs des garçons en saroual, la
culotte longue et bouffante jusqu'aux chevilles. (*JNP*, 60)
[The French woman's daughters, he saw them from afar when he
used to work at the house, beyond the school and the wine cellar,
in the plain. They played *galline*, hopscotch with the girls from the
neighborhood ... they, bare legged, while the sisters of the boys
wore long puffy saroual pants that came down to their ankles.]

Here the young boy accentuates the differences he sees in the girls he
calls French, despite their mixed heritage. Their clothes are markers of
their westernized otherness. The narration takes this up again a page
later with the observations of Fatima, who notes their fateful cultural
mistake: "Fatima s'étonnait des cuisses découvertes, la robe ou la jupe
ne devaient pas couvrir la jambe, elle ne disait rien, elle était la bonne
... Mais jamais elle n'aurait habillé ainsi sa fille ... La honte sur la famille"
(*JNP*, 61). [Fatima was shocked by their visible thighs, the dress or skirt
did not cover their legs, she did not say anything, she was the maid ...
But she never would have dressed her daughter that way ... The family
shame.] The narrator accuses her mother of cultural insensitivity and
her father of neglect and commemorates both with equal outrage. Even
in expressing hate and humiliation, she does not admit any unconscious sexual provocation of the boys:

Ils avaient tous dépassé l'âge du bain avec les femmes, mères, sœurs,
cousines, bain public qui enfermait corps et vapeurs dans l'eau ... Et
là, sous leurs yeux ... ces filles qui ne savaient pas qu'elles étaient
impudiques, étrangères à la langue et à la coutume qui voile depuis
les cheveux jusqu'à la cheville, ces filles ... que leur mère, la
Française, habillait trop court ... et que le père abandonnait à la
voie publique. (*JNP*, 41)
[The boys were all over the age of taking baths with women, mothers, sisters, cousins, public baths that covered bodies and vapors in
the water ... And there, under their eyes ... these girls who did not
realize that they were indecent, strangers to the language and
habits that veil from the hair down to the ankles, these girls ...
whose mother, the French woman, dressed in clothes that were too
short ... and whose father abandoned to the public streets.]

The narrator is well aware of the cultural error committed by the family sheltered in their "citadelle hermétique" (*JNP*, 41) [hermetic fortress] whence they do not integrate into the norms and customs of those around them. Deming does identify this aspect of Sebbar's text, but she seems to overlook the critical pivot of Sebbar's writing which, as we have seen in all the examples here, aims to offer a more three-dimensional portrait of the colonial situation. Yet it is true, as Deming charges, that she does not excuse the violence of the boys in the name of cultural difference, as it does not correspond to the way in which she has experienced her childhood trauma. For her, it is more a question of evaluating the two sides of difference and of revisiting her wounds via a new cultural consciousness that her work strives to put in place through new forms of reconciliation and understanding.

Sebbar's feminist gesture, then, is migrant not only in terms of difference *qua* some possible hybridity, but also in its concrete efforts to move back and forth between France and Algeria. Written in the first instance for her French compatriots, the novel thus takes on an ethico-political function that is all-too important in a country that has historically repressed the details of the Algerian war and that continues to do so to this day. On 25 February 2005, the National Assembly voted on a law mandating that the official teaching of colonial history recognize the "positive role" of France in North Africa.⁹ Although Jacques Chirac removed that article a year later due to the controversy it created, he also declared that the law would simply need to be rewritten. In the months that followed, political discussion in France slipped toward a far less contentious view of slavery. Jane Hiddleston, in her analysis of cultural amnesia during the Algerian war, notes that "facts were distorted, myths were abundant and people in France did not have access to anything approaching a complete or unbiased view" (2003, 61). This cultural amnesia lasted in France well after Algerian independence, and the Algerian war remained excluded from school curricula until the end of the 1980s. It is against this sort of national aphasia that the work of Sebbar is cast, drawing from her experience of immigration to infuse her writing with a political mission in search of a hybrid utopia.

CALIXTHE BEYALA'S *FEMME NUE FEMME NOIRE*: AGGRESSION

In 2003, Franco-Cameroonian author Calixthe Beyala published a novel that sold 1,000 copies in the first week of sales in France. *Femme nue femme noire* was Beyala's twelfth novel and one whose explicitly sexual content sparked a by now familiar but nonetheless controversial response from critics while it met with a warm, if not excited, reception in French bookstores. From her very first novel, Beyala has made waves among her fellow male Cameroonian writers – among whom the most illustrious Mongo Beti – for the way in which her works showcase female African sexuality. In fact, *Femme nue femme noire* was marketed as the first African erotic novel by its publishers at Albin Michel and was launched at a time when female pornography was especially in vogue in France.[10] Amid accusations of plagiarism on the one hand and cheap exoticism and voyeurism on the other, Beyala continues to be the best-selling female African writer in French.[11] So much so, that she has also become a spokesperson for Sub-Saharan immigrants in France and an often sought-after voice of an African and immigrant woman.

Femme nue femme noire, from its very title, is a direct reference to one of Négritude's most famed poems by Léopold Sédar Senghor. With no visible alteration to the title of Senghor's well-known poem, the novel at first glance suggests a tribute that is quickly undone by Beyala's irreverently defiant prose:

> Femme nue, femme noire, vêtue de ta couleur qui est vie, de ta forme qui est beauté...Ces vers ne font pas partie de mon arsenal linguistique. Vous verrez : mes mots à moi tressautent et cliquettent comme des chaînes ... Des mots qui fessent, giflent, cassent et broient ! ... ici, il n'y aura pas de soutiens-gorge en dentelle, de bas résille, de petites culottes en soie à prix excessif. (*FN*, 11)
> [Naked woman, black woman, clothed with your color which is life, with your form which is beauty ... These verses do not belong to my linguistic arsenal. You will see: my words twitch and clang like chains ... Words that spank, slap, break and grind! ... Here, there will be no lace braziers, hairnet stockings, expensive little silk panties.]

It is no longer an Africa – ancestral motherland of Négritude – that is evoked here but an Africa perverted and exploited, sexualized and debauched. With its plotline that combines nymphomania and kleptomania, Beyala took the sexual motifs already present in her earlier works to another level altogether.[12] Yet, it is through extreme forms of literary sensuality that Beyala's own brand of migrant feminism emerges, since it involves overturning sexual prejudice and objectification experienced by female African subjects who, in appropriating their own sexual desire, find emancipation. As each of Beyala's novels push the envelope further, the black female body is unveiled in a brutal nudity that rejects both beauty and mystery. Rather it is frisked, turned over, pierced, and penetrated to the point where violence meets pleasure and physical enjoyment is coupled with obscenity. Beyala's work – and most notably *Femme nue femme noire* – thus walks the fine line between radical feminism and flagrant voyeurism in a gesture that has sown both scandal and critical discord.

This double nature of her work is carried to its climax of sorts in *Femme nue femme noire*, where she sets her brand of feminism apart from that of her fellow African feminists. While African feminist movements have sought to restore women's place in the distribution of work in an industrial and capitalist economy or fight for social emancipation from oppressive societal norms surrounding marriage, celibacy, polygamy, domestic violence, etc., they have strived to distance themselves from an intellectual and elitist Western feminism whose discourse on sexuality is deemed politically inconsequential for women in developing countries.[13] Beyala's narrative technique, on the other hand, privileges a form of feminism that emerges from this missing contact zone between oppressive social forces and the discursive censorship of female sexuality in Africa. *Femme nue femme noire* looks to unearth the politics of feminist discourse in the African context through a narrative blend of violence and sexual commentary that destabilizes male power schemes in the novel:

J'ai un sentiment de puissance sans fin ... Je fais mine de lui prodiguer une caresse palatale. La bouche en cœur, j'envoie sur sa turgescence des souffles chauds qui le mettent en panique. Ses grosses lèvres halètent sur son cou grassouillet. Il s'impatiente, s'exaspère le bangala en l'agitant comme un fouet autour de mes lèvres.
– Prends-le, vite ! râle-t-il. Dépêche-toi !
J'écarte mes dents puis, sans que j'en prenne vraiment conscience, je le mords. Il fait trois bonds en arrière, danse sa douleur sous la lune ahurie. (*FN*, 41–2)
[I have a feeling of infinite power ... I pretend to give him a palatal caress. I blow warm breaths on his hardness through heart-shaped lips, which send him into a panic. His fat lips pant over his plump neck. He becomes impatient, shaking his exasperated *bangala* like a whip around my lips.

– Take it, quickly! He rattles. Hurry up!
I open wide, exposing my teeth and then, almost unconsciously, I
bite him. He bounds back three times, dancing his pain under the
shocked moon.]

Irène Fofo, Beyala's protagonist, is a nymphomaniac who refuses to
pleasure men, verbally and physically demanding her own sexual ful-
fillment instead. Scenes like this one, where Beyala spares no vulgarity
to sexually abase and mock her male character, are rampant throughout
the novel. Her Africanized French vocabulary here marries vulgar terms
from Cameroon – and much of Western Sub-Saharan Africa – to an articulate though alarming French prose which recuses all subtlety. Irène,
whose appropriation of her own sexual prowess will become a source
of social power and healing by the end of *Femme nue femme noire*, distinguishes herself precisely because her sexual acts are always accompanied by the transparency of her sexual discourse.

Beyala's favouring of a feminism that centres on the female body signals a turn away from the earlier feminism of a generation of African
women writers in French who wrote under the spell of Simone de
Beauvoir's *Le Deuxième Sexe*.[14] More akin to the writing of the French
feminists of the 1970s (Hélène Cixous, Julia Kristeva, and Luce Irigaray),
Beyala's work augments the feminist perspective of this second important French feminist wave with that of a third wave inspired by the
African-American queer feminism of Audre Lorde.[15] Lorde's work
points to the empowering function of the erotic: "In touch with the
erotic, I become less willing to accept powerlessness, or those other sup-
plied states of being which are not native to me, such as resignation,
despair, self-effacement, depression, self-denial" (2000, 58). Irène Fofo
takes control of a life otherwise doomed to prostitution, abuse, and violence by reclaiming her own erotic power. "Quel benêt a fait croire
aux femmes qu'à mener une guerre sans merci contre la saleté, on
acquérait le respect des hommes ?" (*FN*, 53) [Who is the idiot who made
women believe that by waging a merciless war against dirtiness, we would
gain the respect of men?] asks Irène Fofo confronting the docility of
her sexual rival, the housewife Fatou, whom she will proceed to seduce
and sleep with not for the pleasure of their mutual male lover, but to
awaken in Fatou an erotic consciousness of her own. Rejecting all the
heteronormative social norms (love, marriage, maternity) that keep female pleasure under male domination, Irène slowly turns the household and then community on its head. Even accused of madness, she
simply appropriates the condemnation thereby transforming it into yet

another source of power and healing, which will take on continental proportions: "J'y déploie des trésors de sophistication sexuelle pour anéantir, à moi seule, tous les maux dont souffre le continent noir – chômage, crises, guerres, misère – et auxquels, malgré leur savoir, les grands spécialistes de l'économie et de la science n'ont pu trouver de solutions" (*FN*, 78). [I deploy treasures of sexual sophistication to wipe out, through me alone, all the ailments that afflict the Black continent – unemployment, crises, wars, poverty – and for which, the great specialists of economics and science, despite their knowledge, could not find solutions.] Inspired by global feminist thought, Beyala thus mobilizes eros in the service of the African continent in *Femme nue femme noire* in what we will call a migrant feminism.

In an earlier work, Beyala defined her own brand of feminism as *féminitude*, a neologism that combines Négritude with feminist thought to precisely rid the Négritude movement of its misogynistic tendencies and reinvent it for twenty-first-century Africa. In *Lettre d'une africaine à ses sœurs occidentales*, Beyala offered the following definition for her newly devised concept: "la différence-égalitaire entre l'homme et la femme" (1995, 20). [The equalizing-difference between man and woman.] Beyala's *féminitude* was also coined in response to African and Third World feminist critiques that accuse the author of selling out to a Western brand of feminism that is out of touch with Africa. *Féminitude* is Beyala's way out of the problem first raised by Chandra Talpade Mohanty's accusations against Western feminism's universalizing tendencies. Geared towards the realities of African life as especially experienced by women in Western Sub-Saharan countries, Beyala's saucy sexualized language is a refusal to abide by a socially imposed silence on all things sex.[16] Critics such as Augustine Asaah – on the heels of others like Mongo Beti and Ambroise Kom – hence reproach Beyala's use of sexual slander as a form of denigration of her native Cameroonian culture.[17] Yet what these critics signal as defamatory in Beyala's novels – as most readily apparent in *Femme nue femme noire* – is nothing less than a provocative overturning of sexual power dynamics in favour of the traditional victim. Her narrative strategy transforms the submissive female prey into a sexual predator herself:

Ils me décrètent folle pour cacher la fureur de leur sang. Je ressens ce qu'ils ressentent à mon égard ... Alors je gueule plus fort...Ils continuent leurs ovations parce que je suis dangereuse. Ils me disent dingue afin de préserver leur suprématie, pour que ne ressuscitent plus jamais les femmes rebelles, mangeuses de sexe. (*FN*, 30)

[They decree that I am mad to hide the furor of their own blood. I sense what they feel towards me ... So I yell even louder ... they continue their ovation because I am dangerous. They call me crazy in order to preserve their supremacy, so that never again will those sex-eating rebellious women be resurrected.]

Beyala's critique of her native culture's sexual reification of woman specifically targets female docility and silence as evidenced in *Femme nue femme noire*, but also in much of the Beyalan literary corpus.

Beyala's migrant feminism is not devoid however of the flagrant voyeurism that her novels are often accused of and *Femme nue femme noire* certainly epitomizes this aspect of the author's work. The sheer number of descriptions of each of Irène's licentious sexual escapades with partners of every age, shape, and gender is inarguably gratuitous. Moreover, the marketing of the novel, with its cover depicting a naked young Black woman covered only by the bouquet of long stemmed white lilies she is holding, plays right along with the novel's description as erotic prose. There cannot be a writer more aware of her market in France and what is needed to get its attention than Beyala. Yet this of course was an image manufactured for her from the dawn of her literary career. As Nicki Hitchkott points out, "from the very beginning of her career, Beyala is contained within the framework of colonial desire, her work deemed 'authentic' because it combines Africa and sex" (2007, 30). Beyala has only exploited this reality to her own advantage, using it to secure a readership for what are ultimately her migrant feminist musings. Though some critics find it difficult to wade through the voyeuristic muck that often muddles this feminism, that is precisely what makes her work such a clear example of a migrant modality.

CONCLUSION: FROM HYBRIDITY TO HOSPITALITY

Migrant feminisms are conceived here as an outgrowth of multicultural and migratory feminism, augmented by work on queer feminism. Drawing from a wealth of feminist insights from the world over, these are immanent subjectivities that refuse to engage in critiques that fall prey to universalism or hegemonic affirmations of power. In this way, perhaps migrant texts are better positioned than other forms of fiction to enter this battle for equality and difference, since they are by definition involved in this same struggle on many fronts. In other words, migrant texts often lend themselves to significant intersectionality because the mode itself confronts so many competing sources of injustice and exclusion at once. As we have seen in the four examples analyzed in this chapter, the migrant text moves woman to a place of profound contestation. Female protagonists in these novels enact their own welcome, drawing on their hybrid experiences of culture and becoming agents of their own hospitality in the exclusionary narrative worlds they inhabit.

Much like Anzaldúa, who creates her own oppositional feminist position within a matrix of domination on multiple fronts, the female authors studied here (Robbin, Chen, Sebbar, Beyala) construct migrant feminisms that force the French-language text to open a space of hospitality for immigrant sensibilities. Though they may be driven by the need to attract an audience as much as they are by the desire to oppose the prejudicial treatment of immigrants, these migrant feminisms also flourish far more in the texts themselves than they do in the persons of their authors, whose struggles for survival may well betray their feminist leanings from one novel or one interview to the next. Instead of conferring the power of the feminist metaphor, as does Anzaldúa, to a figure such as the new *mestiza*, this chapter builds the case that migrant feminisms must be located in the spaces of narrative. These are powerful stories that rethink and reorient culture, language, gender, and sexuality through the poetics and politics of a migrant mode of writing.

A Global French Literature

Texts like those we focus on here signal the dawn of a new literary era for the study of French literature that is decisively new and newly *global*. This is not to obscure the ways that French literature has for centuries entertained connections to the world beyond its borders nor to dismiss the numerous immigrant writers who have inhabited the space of French society in the past. Recognizing this global shift suggests instead that the French language as a medium for artistic creation and individual authorial agency has now decisively cut the umbilical cord with its birth nation and its postcolonial ambitions. The first two chapters of this book survey and analyze the theoretical paradigms that are most often used by critics to study migrant texts, in the process weighing their usefulness, challenging their claims to migrancy, and situating our approach in their midst. The migrant mode, just like the larger field of migration studies outlined in the introduction to this book, is an outgrowth of nationalism, postcolonialism, Francophonie, and World Literature. Yet the suggestion here is that migrant texts escape the grasp of all of these paradigms while being historically indebted to them. If French is today a world language – albeit lagging heavily behind English and Spanish and perhaps soon Chinese and Arabic – it can only enjoy such a status if it relinquishes ties to France and its former colonies, to Francophonie, and to the unrequited dreams of French universalism.

In proposing a "migrant mode" of writing, the intention of this book is to point in this direction by bringing together the study of contemporary French literature with the realities of a world in migration. By elucidating the creative agency of individual authors and the strategies they mobilize to narrativize their experiences of migration (writing techniques, editorial decisions, approaches to marketing), I suggest that these texts are less governed by a formal set of rules than they are by a similar method, mood, or approach to narration and promotion. They are, in many ways, specimens of a technique that falls tactically between nations, cultures, and languages and that accepts the exigencies of global capitalism while resisting the simple reification of otherness, exoticism, and prejudice that the market so often brings.

This complex positioning is fraught with tension, as we have seen in the various literary case studies detailed in this book. By choosing this mode of writing, immigrant authors make a deliberate choice to pitch their complicated identities as a point of entry, as we saw in chapter 3. This move almost always plays out in implicit linguistic, cultural, and political resistance, as the last three chapters show. While the migrant mode is often deployed in the debut work by an immigrant author – as with Naïm Kattan, Azouz Begag, Mehdi Charef, and Dai Sijie – this is not always the case. Moreover, the migrant mode is not exclusively the domain of immigrant writers; though this study has not included any examples, migrant texts by non-immigrant writers abound in the French-speaking world and beyond. Part of the goal in acknowledging the migrant text's function as mode is to eliminate too much concern with the personal itineraries, citizenship, and ethnic identity of authors in order to return to the text itself. I opted to use the word *text* rather than literature because the migrant mode exceeds the grasp of literature alone. It can and should be extended to film and artwork that deliberately muddles national, cultural, and linguistic lines while exploiting the realities of market capitalism and resisting its homogenizing tendencies at the same time. Three of the works studied in this book – Mehdi Charef's *Le Thé au harem d'Archi Ahmed*, Azouz Begag's *Le Gone du Chaâba*, and Dai Sijie's *Balzac et la petite tailleuse chinoise* – were made into films soon after their initial literary success, and certainly qualify as migrant texts in their own right.

This book follows in the footsteps of many others before it that have sought to recognize French literature's global dimensions.[1] It ventures one step further than these, proposing Global French Literature as a way to move forward out of the pitfalls of Francophonie and toward a linguistic inclusiveness that rivals what has taken place in the English-speaking world today. We use "Global" in order to extract this literature not only from the French versus Francophone divide but also from monikers like "allophone" – used in French for works and authors from neither France nor its former colonies – and even from terms like "migrant" when used to qualify writers rather than texts. As suggested in this book, migrant texts remain but *one* of Global French Literature's contemporary forms. Every one of the texts studied here was in some way regarded as peripheral to canonical French literature at the time of its creation, while the authors themselves were labelled as other in France and Quebec. Some were reclaimed by their countries of origin, as in the case of Naïm Kattan and Dai Sijie, while others were not. Either way, national belonging remains a problematic ground for all the writers and texts involved in this study.

In French literary studies today, scholars regularly come up against what German sociologist Ulrich Beck terms "methodological nationalism" – a tendency to privilege the nation-state in our very production of knowledge (2005, 43–50).[2] This may indeed explain our inherent bias as scholars to think in terms of the nation-state, even in the face of rising cosmopolitanism all around us. The Francophone literary venture very much relies on such a division of the world, hoisting as it were the flags of newly independent nation-states by claiming, for each one, a postcolonial literature of its own. The case of Quebec – nation without state – has thus always stood out as an exception, which perhaps accounts for the fact that it is there that the category of "migrant literature" was first devised in an effort to discriminate between native and non-native writing within the nation. Today, however, migrant texts abound everywhere and in every language. They are thus a symptom not of the end of the nation-state nor even its fragility but of its ongoing *cosmopolitanization*.[3] Worldwide nationalisms are as strong today as they ever were, especially in the Global South, and migrant texts, as we have seen in novels by Laferrière, Beyala, Kattan, Chen, and Dai, are constantly reaffirming and rejecting the nation-state at the same time, exploiting the possibilities of global capital and playing upon the unequal exchanges between East and West, North and South. Even while immersed in political critiques of racial, ethnic, and gender stereotypes, they make use of these same discriminatory practices to allure readers, secure sales, and ultimately make literary celebrities of their authors.[4]

Migrant texts are hence a form of Global French Literature rather than French World Literature or *Littérature-monde en français* because, as scholars such as Gayatri Chakravorty Spivak and Emily Apter have argued, World Literature must necessarily encompass writing in all languages not only in one major world language, through translation or otherwise.[5] World Literature cannot thus be modified by one linguistic marker for to do so is to ignore the unequal politics of language whereby some achieve "world" status and others do not. As David Damrosch and Rebecca Walkowitz have pointed out, World Literature is very much about the circulation of the literary work outside the geographic region where it was produced.[6]

The expression Global French Literature tends to be favoured because French has today surpassed the boundaries of the French nation-state and former colonial empire like never before and has made its way through the preponderance of its literary voices to Iraq and China, Russia and Djibouti. In interviews I conducted with authors like Naïm Kattan and Ying Chen about why they chose to write in French after growing up in Baghdad and Shanghai, they never failed to evoke a long-standing literary love affair with French, one that fuelled their own creative work later on. Other authors like Mehdi Charef, Dany Laferrière, and Calixthe Beyala confessed that writing in French was about transforming a language and literature they have always known and loved into something entirely different. As writers like these increasingly cosmopolitanize French literature, scholars are confronted with the need for a new critical vocabulary, as well as a cosmopolitan methodology to understand and analyze their texts. The growing number of migrant texts in French – but also in other languages – calls for a rethinking of literary labels and presents a challenge to students and scholars of literature alike to further reflect, discuss, and assess the future of French literature as it takes on global proportions like never before. This book, I hope, offers one of many such openings that will seek to account for how and why so many authors today choose French as a medium for expressing and creating works that move well beyond national and postcolonial preoccupations.

Notes

INTRODUCTION

1 See for example Christopher L. Miller's point about French being far out-done by English in terms of the global scope of the language: "The Slave Trade, *La Françafrique* and the Globalization of French," in *French Global: A New Approach to Literary History*, eds. Christie McDonald and Susan Suleiman, 2010, 240.

2 This is the case of Mehdi Charef, Azouz Begag, and Leïla Sebbar, who do not master Arabic enough to write in it. Régine Robin, though she is a native French speaker, very deliberately emphasizes her decision to write in French over languages like Hebrew and English which are, respectively, a heritage language and one of the official languages of Canada, her country of adoption.

3 See Gilles Deleuze and Felix Guattari, *Kafka: Pour une littérature mineure*.

4 Kafka, *Lettre à Brod* (June 1921) cited in Deleuze and Guattari, *Kafka: Pour une littérature mineure*.

5 Christopher Prendergast critiques Casanova's reading of Kafka here, arguing that she misreads Kafka's sense of humour as tragedy. See Christopher Prendergast, *Debating World Literature*, 16–17.

6 Gauvin shows that Deleuze and Guattari's conceptualization of minor litera-ture is dependent on the model provided by Kafka himself rather than on Kafka's writing alone. The German word *kleine* means "small" and Gauvin writes: "Lorsque Kafka parle de petite littérature, il a dans l'esprit les littératures en émergence, des littératures qui ont une 'mémoire qui travaille plus à fond le matériel existant,' des littératures 'sans modèles irrésistibles'" (2003, 27).

7 Robin Cohen isolates nine common features of diaspora, some of which are certainly applicable – at least in part – to migration (1–2) more generally

and some less so (3–9): "1. Dispersal from an original homeland, often traumatically, to two or more foreign regions; 2. alternatively or additionally, the expansion from a homeland in search of work, in pursuit of trade or to further colonial ambitions; 3. a collective memory and myth about the homeland, including its location, history, suffering and achievements; 4. an idealization of the real or imagined ancestral home and a collective commitment to its maintenance, restoration, safety and prosperity, even to its creation; 5. the frequent development of a return movement to the homeland that gains collective approbation even if many in the group are satisfied with only a vicarious relationship or intermittent visits to the homeland; 6. a strong ethnic group consciousness sustained over a long time and based on a sense of distinctiveness, a common history, the transmission of a common cultural and religious heritage and the belief in a common fate; 7. a troubled relationship with host societies, suggesting a lack of acceptance or the possibility that another calamity might befall the group; 8. a sense of empathy and co-responsibility with co-ethnic members in other countries of settlement even where home has become more vestigial; and 9. the possibility of a distinctive creative, enriching life in host countries with a tolerance for pluralism."

8   In as early as the 1880s, German cartographer Ernst Georg Ravenstein's work on migration attempted to theorize the movement of people from an individual perspective as explained in Zolberg, 1989. Neoclassical economic theories of international migration followed later in the twentieth century to account for labour migration in the process of economic development on a macro-scale (Lewis 1954; Ranis and Fei 1961; Harris and Todaro 1970; Todaro 1976) and individual choice on a micro-scale (Sjaastad 1962; Todaro 1969, 1976, 1989; Todaro and Maruszko 1987), followed by a "new economics of migration" that extended rational choice to families and households (Stark and Levhari 1982; Stark 1984; Katz and Stark 1986; Lauby and Stark 1988; Taylor 1986; Stark 1991) as opposed to the labour demands of modern industrial societies (Piore 1979). For more on the economic theories of migration see Douglas S. Massey et al. (1993).

9   See Castles, "Understanding Global Migration: A Social Transformation Perspective."

10 See for example J. Dillon Brown's analysis of George Lamming's "immigrant" style, or Allistair Cormack's study of Monica Ali's counter-mimetics in Brick Lane (2003) in Walkowitz 2006, 669–94 and 695–721.

11 See for example Christiane Chaulet-Achour's treatment of Sebbar in "Exils productifs. Quatre parcours méridiens: Jamel Eddien Bencheikh, Leïla Sebbar, Nancy Huston et Chahdorrt Djavann" and Rosa de Diego's study of Chen in "Ying Chen: À la recherché d'une mémoire," in Anissa Talahite-

Moodley 2007, 37–55 and 299–317. See also Paterson's reading of Régine Robin's *La Québécoite* in *Figures de l'autre dans le roman québécois*, 2004, 156–8.

12 See for example Britton, *Édouard Glissant and Postcolonial Theory*, 1999.

13 Postcolonial scholarship like that of Lionnet, *Postcolonial Representations: Women, Literature, Identity* (1995), Bongie, *Islands and Exiles* (1998), Miller, *Nationalists and Nomads* (1999), and Watts, *Packaging Post/Coloniality: The Manufacturing of Literary Identity in the Francophone World* (2005) have brilliantly unearthed the complex workings between the colonial and the postcolonial in Francophone literature, as well as the ways in which each has always been tainted by the former whether in the literary text or paratext. What we are proposing here for the migrant text in its relationship to the nation is very much akin to the theoretical and critical moves made by these scholars of the postcolonial.

14 Writers like Jhumpa Lahiri (*The Namesake*, 2003), Junot Díaz (*The Brief Wondrous Life of Oscar Wao*, 2007), and Vincent Lam (*The Headmaster's Wager*, 2012) in English; Esther Bendahan (*Déjalo, ya volveremos*, 2006) and Lucía Extebarría (*Cosmofobia*, 2008) in Spanish; Najat El-Hachmi *L'últim patriarca*, 2008) in Catalan; Emine Sevgi Özdamarall (*Die Brücke vom Goldenen Horn*, 1998) and Sherko Fatah (*Das dunkle Schiff*, 2008) in German.

CHAPTER ONE

1 My use of the term "French literature" designates literature written in French and not from or about France. In an effort to avoid the awkward phrasing of "French-language literature" and the peripheral implications of "Francophone literature," I will use the term "French literature" despite its national implications, from which I here wish to disassociate the term. Susan Suleiman and Christie McDonald put it best when they write: "While we challenge the notion of a seamless unity between French as language, French as literature, and French as nation (let alone French as 'universal spirit'), we do maintain the idea of literatures in French. The French language exists, performatively and dynamically, as a vehicle for literary and philosophical works produced by individuals with diverse origins, preoccupations, and allegiances both within and outside the geographical and political boundaries of the country known as France" (2010, xix).

2 Franco-Lebanese author Alexandre Najjar (2007) wrote a particularly scathing refutation in *Le Monde* only days after the manifesto was published. Another rebuttal was composed by renowned Senegalese poet Amadou Lamine Sall and one of the very first Francophone Africanists Lilyan Kesteloot (2007). Former president of Senegal and secretary-general of the

Organisation Internationale de la Francophonie Abdou Diouf also authored a strong response against the manifesto (2007).

3 See articles by Françoise Lionnet (2009) and Lydie Moudileno (2010), for example, who defend the idea of Francophonie(s) as a literary category that was fought for long and hard against the hegemony of a French-only literary canon and that already implies an opening to the world beyond France's national borders.

4 Apter cites Barbara Cassin's *Vocabulaire européen des philosophies: Dictionnaire des intraduisibles* (Paris: Le Seuil/Le Robert, 2004) and Franco Moretti's *The Novel* (Princeton, NJ: Princeton University Press, 2006) as examples of monumental projects (especially in the case of the latter) that seek to provide a global non-totalizing account of their respective genres. See also Apter, *Against World Literature*.

5 Unless otherwise indicated, all English translations are my own.

6 In Gilles Dupuis's article historicizing "Écritures migrantes," he points to the advent of "littérature migrante" in Quebec as the failed referendum for independence in 1980 that sealed the divide between native Quebec authors and immigrant ones, while the turn toward "écritures migrantes" coincided with a short period between the late eighties and the early nineties during which authors of various origins sought to either integrate their work into the Quebec literary canon or to reject any and all national monikers whatsoever. Finally, Dupuis signals the dawn of "écritures transmigrantes" with the narrow defeat of Quebec's bid for sovereignty association within Canada in 1995, in what he terms "a transmigration of identities from one literary 'corpus' to the other, from the 'migrant' text to the 'national canon'" (2008, 508).

7 Susan Ireland and Patrice J. Proulx's *Textualizing the Immigrant Experience in Contemporary Quebec* (2004) is the first English language study of the phenomenon. Monique Lebrun and Luc Collès's *La Littérature Migrante dans l'Espace Francophone* (2007) extends the term to France, Belgium, and Switzerland, while Danielle Dumontel and Frank Zipfel's edited volume *Écriture Migrante* (2008) rejoins with further applications from Quebec to Germany.

CHAPTER TWO

1 This neologism is a translation of Berrouët-Oriol's French neologism "migrance" to define the migrant condition. See Berrouët-Oriel.

2 A recently published work of political theory by Thomas Nail seeks to create an exception to this general rule by redefining the figure of the migrant through an analysis of "the kinopolitics of migration" (2015). Nail argues for a mobility-centred approach to the study of the migrant rather than one that relies on *stasis* and the prevalence of the state.

3 Benedict Anderson confirms Acton's prediction by citing the current example of the UN, which with its various member states replaced the League of Nations that was only composed of seven members. See "Long-distance Nationalism: World Capitalism and the Rise of Identity Politics" (Centre for Asian Studies Amsterdam, 1992), 1.

4 Renner, Austrian Chancellor from 1918 to 1920, opposed the claims for independence by Austria's national movements in the name of the Habsbourg Empire. Bauer's book promotes the Austrian state, but only temporarily because he had by then predicted the end of the state apparatus in favour of a standardization of all material life at the level of culture (i.e. the nation) rather than at the state level.

5 Ernest Lavisse cited by Hobsbawm, *Nations and Nationalism since 1780*, 87–90.

6 Historian and pioneer of French immigration history studies, Gérard Noiriel, also refers to these two traditions which he terms "contractual" (*contractuelle*) and "ethnic" (*ethnique*). See *État, nation, et immigration*, 222.

7 Edmond Michelet, a fervent promoter of social Catholicism, led the Resistance movement in Limousin during Nazi occupation. He spent two years in the Nazi concentration camp of Dachau before becoming de Gaulle's minister of army in 1946 and serving as minister of justice from 1959 to 1961. Charles Péguy, poet, writer, and French playwright, was a fierce political critic of the Third Republic's anti-Semitism and abusive political powers while defending a nationalism borne out of Christian universalism and Catholic conservatism.

8 See Ella Shohat's discussion of Alavi in "Notes on the Postcolonial," 322.

9 See Bhabha, "Signs Taken for Wonders: Questions of Ambivalence and Authority under a Tree Outside Delhi, May 1817."

10 See Bhabha, "Sly Civility."

11 Alec Hargreaves and Mike McKinney make just the opposite case in their introduction to *Post-Colonial Cultures in France* (1997), insisting that a postcolonial framework still very much applies to the study of migration in France because the "cultural practices [of formerly colonized people] continue to display the marks of this experience [of colonization]" (18). While I certainly do not disagree with this assessment wholesale, the aim of this book is to consider the migrant works of those who do and do not come from formerly colonized countries in order to look for other ways of reading and interpreting texts about immigration than always linking back to the scars of a colonial past.

12 For Huggan, postcolonialism "concerns largely localized agencies of resistance" while postcoloniality "refers to a global condition of cross-cultural symbolic exchange" (2001, ix).

13 Achac was formed in 1989 by a group of young historians in France to inves-
tigate the clash between memory and history in light of France's colonial
past. Today it has broadened its mission to include immigration from the
Global South, colonial ideology, and post-colonial legacies. Jean-Marc
Moura's *Littérature francophones et théorie postcoloniale* first published in 1999
is an introduction in French to postcolonial theory. The 2013 revised edition
signals important translations of postcolonial theory's master texts in 2006
(Niel Lazarus, *Penser le postcolonial*, Paris, Amsterdam), 2007 (Homi K.
Bhabha, *Les Lieux de la culture*, Paris, Payot), and 2009 (Gayatri Spivak, *Les
subalternes peuvent-ils prendre la parole*, Paris, Amsterdam and *En d'autres
mondes, en d'autres mots : essai de politique culturelle*, Paris, Payot).

14 These are the three thinkers that Mbembe mentions in his piece, although
others such as Elizabeth Boyi, Mireille Rosello, and Françoise Lionnet can
also be included here.

15 Lewis Gordon's *What Fanon Said* actually not only argues for the relevance of
Fanon's writing for the postcolonial, but also for planetary thinking in the
global age.

16 As we saw in Chapter 1, the migrant was very much the subject of significant
work in French-speaking Quebec, albeit in its relation to questions of the nation rather than postcolony.

17 See Eric Prieto, "Edouard Glissant, Littérature-monde, and Tout-monde,"
2010 and Typhaine Leservot, "Maryse Condé: Post-Postcolonial?" in Charles
Forsdick and David Murphy ed., *Postcolonial Thought in the French-Speaking
World*, 2009.

18 Edouard Glissant himself stated of *Le Soleil de la conscience* that "everything is
already there," quoted in Christina Kullberg, *The Poetics of Ethnography in
Martiniquan Narratives: Exploring the Self and the Environment*, University of
Virginia Press, 2013.

19 This being said, Condé also seeks to set herself apart from Glissant's earlier
writing which celebrates "the collective expression of the West Indian soul."
See Maryse Condé, "Order, Disorder, Freedom and the West Indian Writer,"
Yale French Studies 83.2 (1993), 128.

20 See Dawn Fulton's introduction in *Signs of Dissent: Maryse Condé and Postcolonial Criticism*, 2008.

CHAPTER THREE

1 See Roger Chartier and Henri-Jean Martin's discussion of the commercializa-
tion of books beginning with the invention of the Gutenberg press in *Histoire de l'édition française*, tome 3 (1985).

2 In *Literature, Money and the Market: From Trollope to Amis* (2002), Delaney

traces the entwined story of writers and their earnings in England as far back as the 16th century. Lee Erickson's *The Economy of Literary Form: English Literature and the Industrialization of Publishing, 1800–1850* (1996) zeroes in on the birth of the publishing industry in nineteenth-century England, just as French critics Roger Chartier and Henri-Jean Martin do in *Histoire de l'Édition française* (1985), pointing to the unprecedented explosion of literary production due to new-found distribution channels and the growing preponderance of newspapers and advertisements. Lise Quéffelec's analysis of the French serial novel (*Le roman-feuilleton français au XIXe siècle*, 1989) and Anne-Marie Thiesse's study of popular fiction during the Belle Epoque (*Le roman du quotidien. Lecteurs et lectures populaires à la Belle Epoque*, 2000) signal the ways in which a literary marketplace was created to foster the consumption of novels among a growing urban population. Thiesse traces the rise of the novel as the select beneficiary of a cultural revolution that popularized literature from about the time of the French Restoration (or the July Monarchy beginning in 1830). Saint-Beuve's admonition of such mass access to literary objects – in what was known as the "Querelle du roman-feuilleton" – unsuccessfully attempted to dissociate literature from serial-novels, accusing the latter of killing the first in a pamphlet entitled *De la littérature industrielle* (*La Revue des Deux mondes*, 1839). The choice of wording here is significant as popular fiction was made to be synonymous with industrial production and print capitalism, while "literature" remained the vanguard of an earlier era of pure art and values unadulterated by market conditions, an ostensibly pre-commercial rendering of social life. This prejudice is explained by Chartier and Martin as French history's nostalgia for the *livre ancien*, a cultural vestige of the Old Regime – a three-hundred-year-old book-crafting tradition – that was abolished by the Revolution and left nineteenth-century mass literary production rather lackluster in comparison (1985, 8). The growing publishing industry was short on cultural capital during the Belle Époque, owing to a deliberate effort to strip its contributing authors of any social prestige (Thiesse 469).

3 The move towards formalism that arose in response to burgeoning Marxism and the Communist Revolution in Russia – between 1910 and 1930 – was propagated by critics in search of an apolitical approach to the literary object. A Romanticism-inspired idealization of art as entirely autonomous rather than socially constructed was hence what the early writings of Roman Jakobson, Viktor Shklovski, and Martin Eichenbaum privileged in the face of prevailing historical materialist readings. As Victor Erlich points out in his work on Russian Formalism, the movement at first completely rejected any ideologically informed account of literature. According to Eichenbaum "no cultural phenomenon can be reduced to, or derived from, social facts of a dif-

ferent order," while Shklovski "suggested that the question of applying Marxist doctrine to literature was a matter of critical expediency rather than of
methodological principle" (Erlich 109). Their hardnosed approach to literary
criticism was fuelled not only by the overtly biased ideological readings of
their Marxist contemporaries, but also by the Symbolist and Realist schools'
overemphasis on poetic content and meaning rather than form. Though
over time, the Russian Formalists and later Prague Structuralists would make
their way back towards sociology, anthropology, and even history – inform-
ing the work of French theorists like Claude Lévi-Strauss and Roland
Barthes – the commercial reality undergirding a work of literature would be
held at bay by criticism that favoured style and even politics over economics.
Part of the reason for excluding discussions of commercial loss and gain
where literature is concerned was the difficulty in realizing such a pursuit in
literary criticism. Some early Formalist efforts to do so culminated, for example, in a limited study of commercial output by one specific Russian publishing house. Marxist critics were quick to point to the inability of such studies
to account for the larger workings of the industry, opting instead to impose
overarching structural inequalities onto specific readings of literature. Victor
Erlich's history of Russian Formalism extols the early Formalist inclination
to consider the sociology and economics of literature, even while critiquing
their results as "pedestrian" and "narrow empiricism" (Erlich 129). Erlich recognizes the dangers of occluding discussions of economics in literature, arguing against a Marxist abstraction that would take over much of literary
studies in the decades that ensued.

4 Bourdieu compares Gallimard's "Le Chemin" collection, directed by George
   Lambrich and oriented toward a more popular literature, to the revered "La
   Pléiade" or trusty "Folio" collections that include more illustrious canonical
   works (1992, 207). An earlier version of this essay by Bourdieu makes reference to an interview conducted with Svan Nielson CEO of Presses de la Cité
   who explains how Gallimard's use of branding inspired similar marketing
   strategies by other publishers in order to produce reader-specific material for
   every literary genre and social demographic (Bourdieu 1977, 25–6).

5 Others among this first generation of immigrant writers in the province included Polish born Alice Parizeau and Monique Bosco, Haitian born Gérard
   Étienne and Émile Ollivier, Lebanese born Greek writer Pan Bouyoucas,
   French born Belgian author Michel Van Schendel, French born Jewish
   writer Régine Robin, and Egyptian born Anne-Marie Alonzo.

6 The novel has been selling over 1,000 copies a year in France and Quebec respectively, according to figures from marketing firm GFK in France (data
   available as of 2003) and Editions VLB in Quebec (data available as of 2000).

7 David Homel translates "perdu" as "past," while its meaning may be better
   rendered here as "lost."

8 The first Beur novels to be published were *Le Thé au Harem d'Archi Ahmed* (Mehdi Charef 1983), *Les ANI du "Tassili"* (Akli Tadjer 1984), and *Le Sourire de Brahim* (Nacer Kettane 1985). These were followed in 1986 by six novels other than Begag's one, namely *Georgette!* (Farida Belghoul), *Les Beurs de Seine* (Mehdi Lallaoui), *Le Jardin de l'intrus* (Kamal Zemouri), *L'Escargot* (Jean-Luc Yacine), *Palpitations intra-muros* (Mustapha Raïth), and *Point kilométrique 190* (Ahmed Kalouaz). The term "Beur" is no longer in usage today partly due to its origins in derogative racial language. Sylvie Durmelat's history of the word points to its origins in the vernacular of the Parisian Cités and explains its limited meaning beyond this context (1998). Most of the authors who were relegated to this category in the eighties and early nineties have since rejected the designation. This has not been the case however for Mehdi Charef, whose work we discuss later in this chapter, as he continues to use Beur as a form of identity empowerment even today.

9 Seuil's "Cadre rouge" collection is reserved for works classified as French literature and comes with the red-framed seal of prestige, just as Gallimard has a recognizable off-white cover page that demarcates a work of high literature from genres such as fantasy, science-fiction, romance, and children's literature. This collection also comes with a higher price tag.

10 These figures are based on data available as of 2003.

11 Among others, these included Dounia Bouzar (one of two women on the French Council of the Muslim Faith (CFCM) in 2001), Malek Boutih (national secretary of Socialist Party in 2003), and Tokia Saïfi (French UMP politician in 2004).

12 When the novel was placed on school curricula in its first year of publication by two teachers in Lyon, however, it was met with fierce opposition by parents who asked for its removal because it contained explicitly sexual material that was not appropriate for children. See Pascale Robert-Diard, "Azouz contre Racine," 1988.

13 See for example Ma Xiaonan's Chinese interview with Dai Sijie (2003).

14 See also Illeana Chirila's reading of this exchange in "La République réiventée : Littérature transculturelle dans la France contemporaine" (2012).

15 I conducted several interviews with Mehdi Charef in June 2006 and again in June 2008. Other excerpts from the interview can be found in Subha Xavier, "Mehdi Charef and the Politics of French Immigration."

CHAPTER FOUR

1 Such is the case of Dany Laferrière's *Comment faire l'amour avec un nègre sans se fatiguer* or Dai Sijie's *Balzac et la petite tailleuse chinoise*. See chapter 3 for more detailed analyses of these two examples.

2 Richard Watts makes a similar argument in his analysis of the paratext in

postcolonial Francophone literature, highlighting the tension between the inevitable colonial exotica to which postcolonial literature falls prey and the need to integrate the post/colonial centre by accepting just that. For more on this see *Packaging Post/Coloniality: The Manufacture of Literary Identity in the Francophone World*, 2005.

3 *Farewell, Babylon*, Toronto: McClelland and Stewart, 1976.

4 This last sentence is left untranslated in the American version of the novel. I have added it in quotes.

5 This first sentence is left untranslated in the American version (David R. Godine 2007) of the novel although it is translated in the Canadian version (Raincoast 2005, 118).

6 "À cet âge-là, je ne connaissais pas le Canada, ni sa culture, ni sa littérature. La littérature arabe m'était trop connue et manquait d'exotisme, la France par contre ... Et puis me voilà qui écrivait en français." [At that age, I didn't know Canada, its culture nor its literature. I knew Arabic literature all too well and it lacked all exoticism for me, France on the other hand ... And then there I was writing in French.] In Subha Xavier, 2006e.

7 "C'est ainsi qu'il s'est fait aimé par ses professeurs de français ... et puis plus tard par ses lecteurs." [That is how he became liked by his French professors ... and then later by his readers.] In Subha Xavier, 2006b.

8 "J'aurais pu écrire en arabe, mais c'est à l'Occident que je voulais parler" [I could have written in Arabic, but it was to the West that I wanted to speak] (Xavier 2006e).

9 See reviews by Andrew Kett (*Quill and Quire*), Samantha Ellis (*Jewish Quarterly*), and Jeremy Seal (*Sunday Telegraph*).

10 For a comparative analysis of the film and novel in terms of immigration see Subha Xavier, "Mehdi Charef and the Politics of Immigration," 2010.

11 The real Cité des Fleurs is a pedestrian area in the Epinettes neighbourhood of the 17th district of Paris and known for its picturesque architecture and surrounding greenery. Two of its founding conventions launched conservation efforts in order to preserve its historical authenticity and beauty.

12 In its English translation this passage loses some of its meaning: "Even when Balou translated Archimedes' theorem as Archi Ahmed's Tea Room" writes Charef's translator Ed Emery, striving to preserve the word play in English (*Tea in the Harem*, 85).

13 This is also the case of the earlier generation of men in the novel, many of whom have left their wives and children for other women in desperate search of a way out. See *THA*.

14 The term "cultural jet lag" was coined by psychologist Marc Perraud as a way to account for the partial socialization of children who grow up amid two or more cultures or nationalities when physical displacement is involved.

15 See for example the *Site du groupe lecture*
http://www.voixauchapitre.com/archives/2002/balzac_tailleuse.htm or *Mondalire* http://perso.orange.fr/mondalire/Balzac.htm.

16 See for example articles by Yvonne Hsieh and Bradley Winterton and a book review by Natalie Cornelius.

17 The English translation omits the word "content" here, even though it is emphasized in the original French.

18 "Les autorités chinoises auraient-elles eu raison d'interdire les livres d'Occident désignés comme sources de 'pollution spirituelle' ? La 'rééducation balzacienne' constitue-t-elle un lavage de cerveau encore plus dangereux que la rééducation maoïste ?" (Hsieh, 102–3). [Were Chinese authorities right in banning books from the West that were qualified as "spiritual pollution?" Could a "Balzacian re-education" have constituted a more dangerous form of brainwashing than a Maoist re-education?]

19 Grief's analysis is based on an earlier usage of the term within its initial conception in Quebec literary studies to discuss the works of Ying Chen and Sergio Kokis, for example. See Hans-Jürgen Grief, "Quelle littérature migrante ?" 2007.

CHAPTER FIVE

1 Though the first set of these terms are directly attributed to Mikhail Bakhtin, the second are also often conflated with his thought. The distinction I draw serves only to signal the difference between two sets of prefixes (hetero versus multi/pluri/poly), which suggest two very different theoretical moves. Another more recent study of multilingualism in cities proposes "metrolingual," a term that evades the distinctions implied by the previous prefixes. See Pennycook and Otsuji, *Metrolingualism: Language in the City*, 2015.

2 Quebec's Ministry of Immigration, created in 1968, launched the first provincial government efforts to regulate language use among its immigrant populations with the establishment of their Centres d'orientation et de formation pour les immigrants (COFI). Other measures would follow, culminating in Bill 101 which made French the official language of the province and ensured that all immigrant children would attend school in French.

3 Translated in part in the annex entitled "Guide de la phraséologie bouzidienne" (GC, 199).

4 See *Béni ou le paradis privé* (1989) and *Les voleurs d'écritures* (1990).

5 This obsession resurfaces in many other works by Sebbar: *Si je parle la langue de ma mère* (1978), *La langue de l'exil* (1985), *Lettres parisiennes, Autopsie de l'exil* (1986), *Femme entre terre et langue* (1987), *Si je ne parle pas la langue de*

mon père, Voies de pères, voix de filles (1988), *Le corps de mon père dans la langue de ma mère* (1991), *Les mères du peuple de mon père, dans la langue de ma mère* (1998), *Le silence de la langue de mon père, l'arabe, l'Algérie à plus d'une langue* (2001), *L'ombre de la langue* (2005), and *L'étrangère aimée, ma langue vivante* (2006).

6 Today the station is called Bir Hakeim on Line 6 of the Paris metro, not to be confused with La Motte-Piquet-Grenelle station also on the same line.

7 Indeed, the English translation of the novel has it aptly titled *The Wanderer* since the French title's wordplay is inaccessible outside of the French language and thus untranslatable.

8 Pierre L'Hérault is also citing Régine Robin, *L'amour du Yiddish*, 1982.

9 The virgule (/) in the English translation signals a break that is absent from the original French.

10 Frédéric's analysis draws on Jean Chesneaux's concept of *modernité-monde* to illuminate Robin's frantic, fast-paced, disjointed representation of Montreal. See Jean Chesneaux, *Modernité-monde*, 1989.

11 Some of the most important critical work on this novel has been done by eminent scholars of Canadian Studies such as Émile Talbot, Betty McLane-Iles, Roseanna Dufault, Irène Oore, Yvon Lebras, Christian Dubois, and Christian Hommel.

12 In an interview, Ying Chen told me that after *Les Lettres chinoises* became a bestseller, she was asked by many book critics to confirm her Chinese identity with a photograph of herself. Subha Xavier, Interview with Ying Chen, 2006c.

13 François Cheng, *L'écriture poétique chinoise*, 130. *Devant* and *derrière* are used by Cheng in keeping with the Western understanding of the future as lying ahead, while the past lies behind. The Chinese philosophical tradition reverses the spatial nature of the temporal relationship of past to future.

14 Jerome Seaton's translation of Cheng states: "The translations of the poems in this anthology were made from the original Chinese with reference to the word-for-word and interpretive translations by François Cheng which appeared in the French edition of the work" (Cheng 1982, 95). Maclane-Isles's translation, titled *Ballad on Climbing Youzhou Tower*, reads as follows: I see no ancient faces ahead, / and behind me no coming ages. / Thinking of the vast eternity of time and space / I am sad and shed tears (Mclane-Isles 1997, 228).

CHAPTER SIX

1 See Katherine Donato and Donna Gabaccia, *Gender and International Migration: From the Slavery Era to the Global Age*, 2015.

2 See Bonifacio's introduction for an overview of this theoretical discrepancy.

Her point especially concerns the practice of feminism among migrants and the study thereof, which she claims is not as yet established.

3 Friedman draws on Anzaldúa's *Borderlands / La Frontera* just as we are doing here, although, as was mentioned before, her intervention treats migration as a theoretical tool for metaphoric abstraction. Though Anzaldúa's work is now almost thirty years old, it has remained a constant reference point of queer theory over the last three decades. See Judith Butler, *Bodies that Matter: On the Discursive Powers of Sex*, 1993, Robert McRuer, *The Queer Renaissance: Contemporary American Literature and the Reinvention of Lesbian and Gay Identities*, 1997, and E.L. McCallum and Mikko Tuhkanen, *Queer Times, Queer Becomings*, 2011.

4 The name of the character Mimi Yente in the original French version of the novel undergoes a slight change in spelling in the English version to become Mime Yente.

5 "Avoir des gloires communes dans le passé, une volonté commune dans le présent; avoir fait de grandes choses ensemble, vouloir en faire encore, voilà la condition essentielle pour être un peuple" (1882, 26). [To have common glories in the past and to have a common will in the present; to have performed great deeds together, to wish to perform still more – these are the essential conditions for being a people (1996, 52).]

6 The theme of suicide returns in Chen's next novel that is also about national allegiances and metaphors invoking Chinese nationalism. See Ying Chen's *L'Ingratitude* (1995).

7 In 2007, fifty years after the disappearance of this professor of mathematics at the Université d'Algers, his widow Josette Audin marked the anniversary of her husband's death on June 11 with an open letter addressed to then French president Nicolas Sarkozy asking him to shed light on the mystery of Maurice Audin's disappearance and to take responsibility for his murder in the name of France. (See Josette Audin, "La Vérité pour Maurice Audin. Lettre Ouverte À Nicolas Sarkozy"). This was not the first time that Josette Audin had complained to the French government seeking justice for her spouse's untimely death, but each one of her efforts was met with resistance due to the 1962 and 1968 Laws of Amnesty which decreed: "Sont amnistiés de plein droit toutes infractions commises en relation avec les événements d'Algérie." Josette Audin wrote to President François Hollande in February 2014 and in March 2014 the Human Rights League launched an appeal titled "Appel des 171 pour la vérité sur l'assassinat de Maurice Audin" (see http://images.math.cnrs.fr/Appel-des-171-pour-la-verite-sur-l.html).

8 *Lysistrata* is a comedy by Aristophanes in which Athenian, Spartan, and Corinthian women get together to declare a strike against their husbands until the men cease waging war against each other.

9 Article 4 of bill 158 stipulates: "Les programmes scolaires reconnaissent en particulier le rôle positif de la présence française outre-mer, notamment en Afrique du Nord et accordent à l'histoire et aux sacrifices des combattants de l'armée française issus de ces territoires la place éminente à laquelle ils ont droit."

10 See Hitchcott, *Calixthe Beyala: Performances of Migration*, 29.

11 Only Marie N'Diaye comes close to competing with Beyala in the literary marketplace among a handful of female Sub-Saharan writers today.

12 Earlier works by Beyala that involve sexual motifs such as prostitution and rape are *Tu t'appelleras Tanga* (1988), *Lettre d'une Africaine à ses sœurs occidentales* (1995), *Amours sauvages* (1999), *Comment cuisiner son mari à l'Africaine* (2000), and *Les arbres en parlent encore* (2002).

13 See articles by Allison Drew and Marie-Louise Eteki-Otabela for examples of feminist battles waged by Africans in their home countries as well as the way in which they seek to demarcate themselves from Western feminist discourse.

14 See Femi Ojo-Ade, "Still a Victim? Mariama Bâ's *Une si longue lettre*," 1982, 71–87 and Molara Ogundipe-Leslie, "Stiwanism: Feminism in an African Context," 1994.

15 Among these perhaps most notable is Sharon Patricia Holland (2012) who analyzes the role of desire in racism. She argues for a revalorization of Simone de Beauvoir's *Second Sex* through the writings of Judith Butler, Sara Heinämaa, and Sonia Kruks. Lorde's essay "Uses of the Erotic: The Erotic as Power" continues to be a founding text for Afro-American Queer feminism as well.

16 Dominique Zahan argues that in Bambara society sexual mockery is tantamount to religious blasphemy (1963, 78).

17 See Augustine Asaah, "Veneration and Desecration in Calixthe Beyala's *La petite fille du réverbère*," 166.

CONCLUSION

1 See Christophe Pradeau and Tiphaine Samoyault (ed.), *Où est la littérature mondiale?* (2005); Michel Le Bris and Jean Rouaud (ed.), *Pour une Littérature-Monde* (2007); Pascale Casanova, *République mondiale des lettres* (2008); Christie McDonald and Susan Suleiman (ed.), *French Global* (2010); François Provenzano, *Historiographies périphériques* (2011); Dominique Viart and Laurent Demanze (ed.), *Fins de la littérature. Historicité de la littérature contemporaine* (2012); Emmanuel Fraisse, *Littérature et mondialisation* (2012); Oana Panaïté, *Des Littératures-mondes en français* (2012); Adlai Murdoch, *Creolizing the Metropole. Migrant Caribbean Identities in Literature and Film* (2012); Joël Des Rosiers, *Métaspora* (2013).

2 Ulrich Beck posits this as a problem for the social sciences rather than the humanities per se, although it is certainly applicable to the study of literature.

3 I owe this use of the term to Ulrich Beck who adapts Roland Robertson's concept to account for the "interrelation between de and re-nationalization, de and re-ethnicization, and de and re-localization in society and politics" (2006, 94).

4 Certainly one must distinguish here between literary celebrity in the English-speaking world – where rights to film adaptations quickly follow the success of a literary text and writers become in-demand speakers in both academic and non-academic settings – and the French-speaking context where celebrity is rarely accompanied by such fame or wealth for that matter. French literature nonetheless carries a certain literary prestige that is quite unrivalled by other linguistic traditions and the immediacy of translations today launch writers onto the global scene in ways which allow them to live off and profit from their careers in unprecedented fashion.

5 See Gayatri Chakravorty Spivak's admonition of comparative literature's eurocentrism and the need for a better marriage of the discipline with area studies in *Death of a Discipline* (2003) and Emily Apter's *Against World Literature: On the Politics of Untranslatability* (2013).

6 See David Damrosch, *What is World Literature* (2003) and Rebecca L. Walkowitz, "Unimaginable Largeness: Kazuo Ishiguro, Translation and the New World Literature," *Novel* 40. 3 (Summer 2007): 217.

Bibliography

Abella, Irving M. 1988. "Foreword." In *Whence They Came: Deportations from Canada 1900–1935*, edited by B. Roberts. Ottawa: University of Ottawa Press.

Acton, Lord. 1967. *Essays in the Liberal Interpretation of History*. Chicago: University of Chicago Press.

– 2000. "Nationality." In *Mapping the Nation*, edited by Gopal Balakrishnan. London: Verso. 17–38.

Ahmad, Aijaz. 1995. "Postcolonialism: What's in a Name?" In *Late Imperial Culture*, edited by Roman De La Campa, Michael Sprinker, and E. Ann Kaplan. London: Verso. 11–32.

Al-Ali, Nadje, and Khalid Koser. 2002. *New Approaches to Migration? Transnational Communities and the Transformation of Home*. New York: Routledge.

Alavi, Hamza. 1972. "The State in Postcolonial Societies: Pakistan and Bangladesh." *New Left Review* 74: 59–80.

Allard, Jacques. 1985a. "Entrevue avec Naïm Kattan." *Voix et images* 11.1: 10–32.

– 1985b. "Naïm Kattan ou la fortune du migrant." *Voix et images* 11.1: 7–9.

Albert, Christiane. 2005. *L'immigration dans le roman francophone contemporain*. Paris: Karthala.

Anderson, Benedict. 1983. *Imagined Communities: Reflections on the Origin and Spread of Nationalism*. London: Verso.

– 1992. *Long-distance Nationalism: World Capitalism and the Rise of Identity Politics*. Amsterdam: Centre for Asian Studies.

Anonymous. "*Balzac et la Petite Tailleuse chinoise*," *Perso Orange Monde à lire*. http://perso.orange.fr/mondalire/Balzac.htm. Last accessed 3 May 2007.

Anzaldúa Gloria. 1987. *Borderlands/La frontera: the New Mestiza*. 1st ed. San Francisco: Spinsters/Aunt Lut.

Appadurai, Arjun. 1990. "Disjuncture and Difference in the Global Economy." *Theory Culture Society* 7.2: 295–310.

Appadurai, Arjun, and Carol Breckenridge. 1988. "Why Public Culture?" *Public Culture* 1.1: 5–9.

Appiah, Kwame Anthony. 1996. "Is the Post- in Postmodernism the Post- in postcolonial?" In *Contemporary Postcolonial Theory: A Reader*, edited by Padmini Mongia. New York: Arnold. 55–71.

Apter, Emily. 2004. "Global Translatio: The 'Invention' of Comparative Literature, Istanbul, 1933." In *Debating World Literature*, edited by Christopher Prendergast. New York: Verso. 76–109.

– 2008. "Untranslatable: A World System." *New Literary History* 39.3 (Summer): 581–98.

– 2013. *Against World Literature: On the Politics of Untranslatability*. New York: Verso.

Asaah, Augustine H. 2005. "Veneration and Desecration in Calixthe Beyala's *La petite fille du réverbère*." *Research in African Literatures* 36.4 (Winter): 155–71.

– 2007. "Entre 'Femme noire' de Senghor et *Femme nue, femme noire* de Beyala : réseau intertextuel de subversion et d'échos." *French Forum* 32.3 (Fall): 107–22.

Audin, Josette. 2007. "La vérité pour Maurice Audin. Lettre ouverte à Nicolas Sarkozy." *L'Humanité* June 21.

Auerbach, Erich. 1969. "Philology and *Weltliteratur*." Translated by Marie and Edward Said. *The Centennial Review* XIII. 1 (Winter): 1–17.

Bakhtine, Mikhaïl. 1978. *Esthétique et théorie du roman*. Paris: Gallimard.

Barme, Geremie. 1979. "Chaotou Wenxue – China's New Literature." *The Australian Journal of Chinese Affairs* 2: 137–48.

Barnard, Ian. 1997. "Gloria Anzaldúa's Queer Mestizaje." *Ethnicities Sexualities* 22.1 (Spring): 35–53.

Barreiro, Carmen Mata. 1999. "Écriture migrante et langue française : déconstruction et reconstruction de l'identité dans *Les Lettres chinoises* de Y. Chen, *Les raison de la galère* de T. Ben Jelloun et *la Trilogia* de M. Micone." In *Voix de la francophonie : Belgique, Canada, Maghreb*, edited by Lidia Anoll and Marta Segarra. Barcelone: Universitat de Barcelona. 225–34.

Basch, Linda, Nina Glick Schiller, and Cristina Szanton Blanc. 1993. *Nations Unbound: Transnational Projects, Postcolonial Predicaments and Deterritorialized Nation-States*. London: Routledge.

Bauer, Otto. 1987. *La question des nationalités et la social-démocratie*. Collection Histoires et émancipations. Montreal: Arcantère Éditions.

– 2000. *The Question of Nationalities and Social Democracy*. Translated by Joseph O'Donnell and edited by Ephraim Nimni. Minneapolis: University of Minnesota Press.

Beck, Ulrich. 2006. *Cosmopolitan Vision*. Cambridge: Polity Press.

Begag, Azouz. 1986. *Le Gone du Chaâba*. [GC] Paris: Éditions du Seuil.
– 1989. *Béni ou le paradis privé*. Paris: Seuil.
– 2007. *Shantytown Kid*. [SK] Translated by Naïma Wolf and Alec G. Hargreaves. University of Nebraska Press.
Begag, Azouz, and Catherine Louis. 1990. *Les Voleurs d'écritures*. Paris: Seuil.
Benhabib, Seyla. 2006. *Another Cosmopolitanism*. London: Oxford University Press.
Benjamin, Walter. 1979. *Illuminations*. Translated by Hannah Arendt. London: Fontana, 1982.
– *One-way Street, and Other Writings*. 1979. Translated by Edmund Jephcott and Kingsley Shorter. London: NLB.
Berger, James, ed. 2003. *There's No Backhand to This*. Lincoln, NE: University of Nebraska Press.
Bernier, Sylvie. 1999. "S'exiler de soi." *Francophonia* 37: 115–31.
Berrouët-Oriol, Robert. 1986/1987. "L'effet d'exil." *Vice Versa* 17: 20–1.
– and Robert Fournier. 1992. "L'émergence des écritures migrantes des métisses au Québec." *Études québécoises* 14: 7–22.
Berry, Ellen E., and Mikhail Epshte. 1999. *Transcultural Experiments: Russian and American Models of Creative Communication*. Basingstoke: Macmillan.
Beyala, Calixthe. 1987. *C'est le soleil qui m'a brûlée*. Paris: Stock.
– 1995. *Lettre d'une Africaine à ses sœurs occidentales*. Paris: Spengler.
– 1998. *Tu t'appelleras Tanga*. Paris: Stock.
– 2003. *Femme nue femme noire*. [FN] Paris: Albin Michel.
Bhabha, Homi K. 1984. "Of Mimicry and Man: The Ambivalence of Colonial Discourse." *October* 28: 125–33.
– 1990a. "Difference, Discrimination and Discourse of Colonialism." *Nation and Narration*. New York: Routledge. 194–211.
– 1990b. "The Third Space: Interview with Homi Bhabha." In *Identity: Community, Culture, Difference*, edited by John Rutherford. London: Lawrence & Wishart. 207–21.
– 1994. *The Location of Culture*. London: New York: Routledge.
Blankenagel, John C. 1925. "Madame de Staël, Goethe and Weltliteratur." *Modern Language Notes* 40. 3 (March): 143–8.
Bongie, Chris. 1998. *Islands and Exiles: The Creole Identities of Post/Colonial Literature*. Stanford: Stanford University Press.
Bonifacio, Glenda Tibe, ed. 2012. *Feminism and Migration: Cross-Cultural Engagements*. New York: Springer.
Bourdieu, Pierre. 1977. "La Production de la croyance. Contribution à une économie des biens symboliques." *Actes de la recherche en sciences sociales* 13 (February): 3–43.
– 1980. *Le Sens pratique. Le Sens commun*. Paris: Éditions de Minuit.

– 1981. "Mais qui a créé les créateurs?" *Questions de sociologie*. Paris: Minuit. 207.

– 1992. *Les Règles de l'art*. Paris: Seuil.

– 1993. "But who created the creators?" *Sociology in Question*. London: Sage: 139–48.

– 1993. "The Production of Belief: Contribution to an Economy of Symbolic Goods." Translated by Richard Nice. In *The Field of Cultural Production: Essays on Art and Literature*, edited by Randall Johnson. London: Polity. 74–111.

Braziel, Jana Evans. 2003. "Trans-American Constructions of Black Masculinity, Dany Laferrière, le Nègre, and the Late-Capitalist American Racial machine-désirante." *Callaloo* 26.3: 867–900.

Britton, Celia M. 1999. *Édouard Glissant and Postcolonial Theory: Strategies of Language and Resistance*. Charlotteville: University of Virginia Press.

Brouillette, Sara. 2007. *Postcolonial Writers and the Global Literary Marketplace*. New York: Palgrave McMillan.

Butler, Judith. 1990. *Gender Trouble: Feminism and the Subversion of Identity*. New York: Routledge.

– 1993. *Bodies that Matter: On the Discursive Powers of Sex*. New York: Routledge.

Caccia, Fulvio. 1992. "Le Roman francophone d'immigration en Amérique du Nord et en Europe : Une perspective transculturelle." In *Métamorphoses d'une utopie*, edited by Jean-Michel Lacroix and Fulvio Caccia. Paris: Presses de la Sorbonne Nouvelle. 91–103.

Cantor, Paul, and Stephen Cox. 2010 *Literature and the Economics of Liberty*. Auburn, AL: Ludwig von Mises Institute.

Caruth, Cathy. 1995. *Trauma: Explorations in Memory*. Baltimore: Johns Hopkins University Press.

– 1996. *Unclaimed Experience: Trauma, Narrative, and History*. Baltimore: Johns Hopkins University Press.

Casanova, Pascale. 1997. "Nouvelles considérations sur les littératures mineures." *Littératures classiques*, 31.

– 1999. *La République Mondiale des Lettres*. Paris: Seuil.

Castells, Manuel. 1996. *The Rise of the Network Society*. Oxford: Blackwell.

– 1997. *The Power of Identity*. Oxford: Blackwell.

– 1998. *End of Millennium*. Oxford: Blackwell.

Castells, Manuel, Ramon Flecha, Paulo Freire, Henry A. Giroux, Donaldo Macedo, and Paul Willis. 1999. *Critical Education in the New Information Age*. Lanham: Rowman and Littlefield.

Castles, Stephen. 2010. "Understanding Global Migration: A Social Transformation Perspective." *Journal of Ethnic and Migration Studies* 36.10 (2010): 1647–63.

Césaire, Aimé. 1956, 2000. *Cahier d'un retour au pays natal*. Paris: Présence Africaine.

Charef, Mehdi. *Tea in the Harem*. [TH] Translated by Ed Emery. 1989. London: Serpent's Tail.

– *Le Thé au harem d'Archi Ahmed*. [THA] 1983. Paris: Mercure de France.

Chartier, Daniel. 2003. *Dictionnaire des écrivains émigrés au Québec 1800–1999*. Québec: Nota Bene.

– 2002. "Les Origines de l'écriture migrante. L'immigration littéraire au Québec au cours des deux derniers siècles." *Voix et images* 27. 2 (Winter): 303–16.

Chartier, Roger, and Henri Martin. 1983–1987. *Histoire de l'édition française* Tome I–IV. Paris: Promodi.

Cheah, Pheng, and Bruce Robbins. 1998. *Cosmopolitics*. Minneapolis: University of Minnesota Press.

Cheah, Pheng. 2008. "What is a World? On World Literature as World Making Activity." *Daedelus* (Summer): 26–38.

Chen, Ying. 1992. *La mémoire de l'eau*. Québec: Leméac.

– 1993. *Les lettres chinoises*. Québec: Leméac.

– 1995. *L'ingratitude*. Montréal: Leméac.

Cheng, François. 1977. *L'écriture poétique chinoise*. Paris: Seuil.

Cheng, François. 1982. *Chinese Poetic Writing*. Translated by Jerome P. Seaton. Bloomington: Indiana University Press.

Chesneaux, Jean. 1989. *Modernité-monde*. Paris: Éditions de la Découverte.

Chirila, Ileana Daniela. 2012. "La République réinventée: Littératures transculturelles dans la France contemporaine." PhD dissertation, Duke University.

Christian, Barbara. 1996. "The Race for Theory." In *Contemporary Postcolonial Theory: A Reader*, edited by Padmini Mongia. New York: Arnold. 148–57.

Clifford, James. 1988. *The Predicament of Culture: Twentieth-Century Ethnography, Literature and Art*. Cambridge: Harvard University Press.

Cohen, Robin. 2008. *Global Diasporas*. New York: Routledge.

Collès, Luc, and Monique Lebrun. 2007. *La Littérature migrante dans l'espace francophone*. Fernelmont, Belgique: EME.

Condé, Maryse. 1993. "Order, Disorder, Freedom and the West Indian Writer." *Yale French Studies* 83.2: 121–35.

Cornelius, Nathalie. 2001. "Compte-rendu de *Balzac et la Petite Tailleuse chinoise* de Dai Sijie." *French Review* 74.6: 1285–86.

D'Orves, Nicolas d'Estienne. 2000. "Un Chinois sauvé par Balzac." *Le Figaro Littéraire* 20 (January): 8.

Dai, Sijie. 2000. *Balzac et la Petite Tailleuse chinoise*. [BPT] Paris: Gallimard.

– *Balzac and the Little Chinese Seamstress*. [BLC] 2001. Translated by Ina Rilke. New York: Knopf.

Damrosch, David. 2003. *What is World Literature?* Princeton: Princeton University Press.

Dash, Michael J. 1995. *Edouard Glissant*. New York: University of Cambridge Press.

De Souza, Pascale. 1999. "Comment écrire un roman sans se fatiguer : stratégies perlocutoires d'un best-seller chez Dany Laferrière." *Études québécoises* 27: 62–69.

– 2001. "De l'errance à la dé(sap)ppartenance : Journal 'Nationalité : immigrée' de S. Boukhedenna." *The French Review* 75.1: 94–109.

Deleuze, Gilles, and Felix Guattari. 1980. *Capitalisme et Schizophrénie : Milles Plateaux*. Paris: Minuit.

– 1975. *Kafka: Pour une littérature mineure*. Paris: Minuit.

– 1986. *Kafka: Towards a Minor Literature*. Translated by Dana Polan. Minneapolis: University of Minnesota Press.

Deniau, Xavier. 1983. *La Francophonie*. Paris: Presses Universitaires de France.

Delvaux, Martine. 1995. "L'ironie du sort : Le tierce espace de la littérature beure." *The French Review* 68.4: 681–93.

Deming, Habiba. 2005. "Espaces coloniaux et identités linguistiques au Maghreb." In *Discursive Geographies: Writing Space and Place in French*, edited by Jeanne Garane. Amsterdam: Rodopi. 175–92.

Derrida, Jacques. 1967. "La structure, le signe et le jeu dans le discours des sciences humaines," *L'écriture et la différance*. Paris: Seuil. 409–28.

– 1996. *Le Monolinguisme de l'autre ou la Prothèse d'origine*. Paris: Galilée.

– 1998. *Monolingualism of the Other or the Prosthesis of Origin*. Translated by Patrick Mensah. Stanford: Stanford University Press.

Des Rosiers, Joël. 2013. *Métaspora: Les Patries intimes*. Montréal: Tryptique.

Dharwadker, Vinay. 2007. "The Cosmopolitan Condition: From Multilingualism and Sociability to Democracy and Peace." *Cosmopolitan Histories, Cosmopolitan Cultures*. University of Wisconsin, Madison.

Diouf, Abdou. 2007. "La francophonie, une réalité oubliée." *Le Monde* 20 March.

Dirlik, Arif. 1996. "The Postcolonial Aura: Third World Criticism in the Age of Global Capitalism." In *Postcolonial Theory: A Reader*, edited by Padmini Mongia. London and New York: Arnold. 294–321.

Documentation française. 2005 *La politique d'immigration (1974–2005) – Chronologie*.

Donato, Katherine, and Donna Gabaccia. 2015. *Gender and International Migration: From the Slavery Era to the Global Age*. New York: Russell Sage Foundation.

Dupuis, Gilles. 2005. "Littérature migrante." In *Vocabulaire des études francophones. Les concepts de base*, edited by Michel Beniamino and Lise Gauvin. Limoges: Presses Universitaires de Limoges. 117–20.

– 2006. "Les écritures transmigrantes. Les exemples d'Abla Farhoud et de Guy Parent." In *Littérature, immigration et imaginaire au Québec et en Amérique du Nord*, edited by Daniel Chariter, Véronique Pepin, and Chantal Ringuet. Paris: Harmattan. 259–73.

– 2008. "Transculturalism and Écritures Migrantes." In *History of Literature in Canada*, edited by Reingard M. Nischik. Rochester, NY: Camden House. 497–508.

Durmelat, Sylvie. 1998. "Petite histoire du mot beur : ou comment prendre la parole quand on vous la prête." *French Cultural Studies* 9.ii (26): 191–208.

Drew, Allison. 1995. "Female Consciousness and Feminism in Africa." *Theory and Society* 24.1 (February): 1–33.

Eagleton, Terry. 1999. "In the Gaudy Supermarket." *London Review of Books* 21.10: 3–6.

Eley, Geoff, and Ronald Grigor Suny, eds. 1996. *Becoming National: A Reader*. New York and Oxford: Oxford University Press. 41–55.

Ellis, Samantha. 2007. "Regina's Lost World." *Jewish Quarterly* 205 (Spring).

Epstein, Mikhail. 2005. "Transculture: A Broad Way between Globalism and Multiculturalism." *The Green Cross Optimist* 5.

Eteki-Otabela, Marie-Louise. 1992. "Dix ans de luttes du Collectif des femmes pour le renouveau (CFR) : quelques réflexions sur le mouvement féministe camerounais." *Recherches féministes* 5.1: 125–34.

Étoké, Natalie. 2009. "Mariama Barry, Ken Bugul, Calixthe Beyala, and the Politics of Female Homoeroticism in Sub-Saharan Francophone African Literature." *Research in African Literatures* 40. 2 (Summer): 173–89.

Fanon, Frantz. 1965. *Peau noire, masques blancs*. Paris: Seuil.

– 2008. *Black Skin White Masks*. Translated by Charles Lam Markmann. London: Pluto Press.

Felman, Shoshana, and Dori Laub. 1992. *Testimony: Crises of Witnessing in Literature, Psychoanalysis, and History*. New York: Routledge.

Ferry, Vincent, and Hervé Lhotel. 2005. "Chronique partielle d'un récente histoire sombre. Immigration et la politique : glossements sémantique et violences (1978–1984)." In *20 ans de discous sur l'intégration*, edited by Piero-D. Gallero, Vincent Ferry, and Gérard Noiriel. Paris: L'Harmattan. 19–29.

Fetzer, Glenn W. 1995. "The Novels of Mehdi Charef." CLA 38.3: 331–41.

Fonkoua, Romuald. 1995. "Édouard Glissant : Naissance d'une anthropologie antillaise au siècle de l'assimilation." *Cahier d'études africaines* 35.140: 797–818.

Forsdick, Charles, and David Murphy, eds. 2009. *Postcolonial Thought in the French-Speaking World*. Liverpool: Liverpool University Press.

Fraisse, Emmanuel. 2012. *Littérature et mondialisation*. Paris: Honoré Champion.

Frédéric, Madeleine. 1991. "L'écriture mutante dans *La Québécoite* de Régine Robin." *Voix et Images* 48: 493–502.

Friedman, Susan Stanford. 1998. *Mappings: Feminism and the Cultural Geographies of Encounter*. Princeton, NJ: Princeton University Press.

Fulton, Dawn. 2008. *Signs of Dissent: Maryse Condé and Postcolonial Criticism*. Charlotteville: University of Virginia Press.

Garland, Caroline. 1998. *Understanding Trauma: A Psychoanalytic Approach*. Tavistock Clinic Series. New York: Routledge.

Gauvin, Lise. 1993. "Une surconscience opérante: les stratégies textuelles des années 80." *Discours social* 5.3–4: 139–57.

– 1999. "L'imaginaire des langues: Entretien avec Édouard Glissant." (1993) *Les Langues du roman*. Montréal: Presses de l'Université de Montréal.

– 2003. "Littératures mineures en langue majeure." In *Littératures mineures en langue majeure : Québec, Wallonie-Bruxelles*, edited by Jean Pierre Bertrand and Lise Gauvin. Montreal: Presses de l'Université de Montréal. 17–40.

Gellner, Ernest. 1983. *Nations and Nationalism. New Perspectives on the Past*. Ithaca: Cornell University Press.

Giddens, Anthony. 1990. *The Consequences of Modernity*. Oxford: Polity.

Giddings, Paula. 1995. "The Last Taboo." In *Words of Fire: An Anthology of African-American Feminist Thought*, edited by Beverly Guy-Sheftall. New York: New Press. 413–28.

Goethe, Johann Wolfgang von. 1901. *Sämtliche Werke*, Leipzig: M. Hesser.

Goethe, Johann Wolfgang von, and Johann Peter Eckermann. 1930. *Conversations of Goethe with Eckermann*. New York: E.P. Dutton & Co.

Gordon, Lewis. 2015. *What Fanon Said*. New York: Fordham University Press.

Glissant, Edouard. 1956. *Le Soleil de la conscience*. Paris: Falaize.

– 1990. *Poétique de la Relation*. Paris: Gallimard.

– 1996. *Introduction à une poétique du divers*. Paris: Gallimard.

Gramsci, Antonio. 1996. *Cahiers de prison*. Paris: Gallimard.

Grief, Hans-Jürgen. 2007. "Quelle littérature migrante ?" *Québec français* 145 (Spring): 43–7.

Guha, Ranajit. 1988a. "On Some Aspects of the Historiography of Colonial India." In *Selected Subaltern Studies*, edited by Ranajit Guha and Gayatri Chakravorty Spivak. New York: Oxford University Press. 37–44.

– 1988b. "The Prose of Counter-Insurgency." In *Selected Subaltern Studies*, edited by Ranajit Guha and Gayatri Chakravorty Spivak. New York: Oxford University Press. 45–86.

Hall, Stuart. 1992. "The Question of Cultural Identity." In *Modernity and its Futures*, edited by S. Hall, D. Held, and T. McGrew. Oxford: Polity.

Handler, Richard. 1988. *Nationalism and the Politics of Culture in Quebec. New Directions in Anthropological Writing*. Madison: University of Wisconsin Press.

Harel, Simon. 1989. *Le Voleur de parcours : Identité et cosmopolitisme dans la littérature québécoise contemporaine*. Montréal: XYZ.

– 2005. *Les Passages obligés de l'écriture migrante. Théorie et littérature*. Montréal: XYZ.

Hargreaves, Alec G. 1992. *Immigration and Identity in Beur Fiction: Voices from the North African Community in France*. New York: Berg.

– 1995. "Beur Fiction: Voices from the Immigrant Community in France." *The French Review* 62.4: 661–8.

Hargreaves, Alec G., Charles Forsdick, and David Murphy, eds. 2010. *Transnational French Studies*. Liverpool: Liverpool University Press. 296–300.

Harris, J.R., and Michael P. Todaro. 1970. "Migration, unemployment, and development: A two-sector analysis." *American Economic Review* 60: 126–42.

Hiddleston, Jane. 2003. "Cultural Memory and Amnesia: The Algerian War and 'Second Generation' Immigrant Literature in France." *Journal of Romance Studies* 3.1: 59–71.

Hitchcott, Nikki. 2006. "Calixthe Beyala: Prizes, Plagiarism, and 'Authenticity.'" *Research in African Literatures* 37.1 (Spring): 100–9.

– 2007. *Calixthe Beyala: Performances of Migration*. Liverpool University Press.

Hobsbawm, E.J., and American Council of Learned Societies. 1992. *Nations and Nationalism since 1780. Programme, Myth, Reality*. Cambridge University Press.

Holland, Sharon Patricia. 2012. *The Erotic Life of Racism*. Durham: Duke University Press.

Hroch, Miroslav. 1985. *Social Preconditions of National Revival in Europe: A Comparative Analysis of the Social Composition of Patriotic Groups among the Smaller European Nations*. New York: Cambridge University Press.

Hsieh, Yvonne Y. 2002. "Splendeurs et misères des mots : *Balzac et la Petite Tailleuse chinoise* de Dai Sijie." *Études Francophones* 17.1: 93–105.

Huggan, Graham. 2001. *The Postcolonial Exotic: Marketing the Margins*. London: Routledge.

Hull, Katie Lee. 2009. "Publishing in China. Growth, Opportunity, Piracy, Censorship." *Publishing Trends* 16.9 (July).

Ireland, Susan, and Patrice J. Proulx, eds. 2004. *Textualizing the Immigrant Experience in Contemporary Quebec*. Westport: Praeger.

Jama, Sophie. 2005. Entretiens avec Naïm Kattan. *Le temps du nomade. Itinéraire d'un écrivain*. Montréal: Liber de vive voix.

Jazouli, Adil. 1982. *La Nouvelle génération issue de l'immigration maghrébine : essai d'analyse sociologique*. Paris: L'Harmattan.

Journal Officiel de la République Française. 2005. *LOI n° 2005–158 du 23 février 2005 portant reconnaissance de la Nation et contribution nationale en faveur des Français rapatriés*.

Jules-Rosette, Benetta. 1998. *Black Paris: The African Writer's Landscape*. Urbana: University of Illinois Press.

Kafka, Franz, and Max Brod. 1989. "June 1921." In *Eine Freundschaft: Briefwechsel*, edited by Malcolm Pasley. Frankfurt: Fisher.

Kafka, Franz. 1977. *Letters to Friends, Family and Editors*. Translated by Richard and Clara Winston. New York: Schocken.

Kaganoff, Penny. 1990. "Paperbacks: Fictions Originals Tea in the Harem." *Publishers Weekly* 237.49: 76.

Katz, E., and Oded Stark. 1986. "Labor Migration and Risk Aversion in Less Developed Countries." *Journal of Labor Economics* 4: 131–49.

Kattan, Naïm. 1975. *Adieu, Babylone*. [AB] Paris: Éditions Julliard.

– 2005. *Farewell Babylon*. Translated by Sheila Fischman. Vancouver: Raincoast Books.

– 2007. *Farewell Babylon: Coming of Age in Jewish Baghdad*. [FB] Translated by Sheila Fischman. Boston: David R. Godine.

Kattan, Naïm, and Jacques Allard. 2002. *Naïm Kattan : L'écrivain du passage*. Montréal: Hurtubise HMH.

Kett, Andrew. 2005. "*Farewell Babylone: Coming of Age in Jewish Baghdad*." *Quill and Quire*.

Kleppinger, Kathryn. 2015. *Branding the "Beur" Author: Minority Writing and the Media in France 1983–2013*. Liverpool: Liverpool University Press.

Koonz, Claudia. 1986. *Mothers in the Fatherland: Woman, the Family and Nazi Politics*. London: Cape.

Kristeva, Julia. 1979. "Le Temps des Femmes." *34/44: Cahiers de recherche de sciences des textes et documents* 5: 5–19.

– 1988. *Étrangers à nous-mêmes*. Paris: Fayard.

L'Hérault, Pierre. 1991. "Pour une cartographie de l'hétérogène : dérives identitaires des années 1980." In *Fictions de l'identitaire au Québec*, edited by Pierre L'Hérault, Robert Shwartzwald, Sherry Simon, and Alexis Nouss. Montréal: XYZ. 53–114.

Lacan, Jacques. 1966. *Écrits*. Paris: Seuil.

Laferrière, Dany. 1985. *Comment faire l'amour avec un nègre sans se fatiguer*. [CFA] Paris: Le Serpent à Plumes.

– 1994. *Why Must a Black Writer Write About Sex?* [WMB] Translated by David Homel. Toronto: Coach House.

– 2000. "Why Must a Negro Writer Always Be Political?" [WMN] In *Fiery*

Spirits and Voices: Canadian Writers of African Descent, edited by Ayanna Black. Toronto: Harper Collins.

– 2002. *Cette grenade dans la main du jeune nègre est-elle une arme ou un fruit?* [CGM] Paris: Le Serpent à Plumes.

– 2010. *How to Make Love to a Negro without Getting Tired*. [HML] Translated by David Homel. Vancouver: Douglas & McIntyre.

Laplanche, Jean, and J.B. Pontalis. 1973. *Vocabulaire de la psychanalyse*. [4. éd. revue] Paris: Presses universitaires de France.

Laronde, Michel. 1996. *L'Écriture décentrée : la langue de l'autre dans le roman contemporain*. Paris, France: L'Harmattan.

– 2002. "Voleur d'écriture: Ironie textuelle, ironie culturelle chez Azouz Begag." *Expressions maghrébines* 1.2: 49–63.

Lauby, Jennifer, and Oded Stark. 1988. "Individual Migration as a Family Strategy: Young Women in the Philippines." *Population Studies* 42: 473–86.

Le Bris, Michel, et al. 2007. "Manifeste pour 'une littérature-monde en français." *Le Monde*, March 16.

Le Bris, Michel, and Jean Rouard. 2007. *Pour une littérature-monde*. Paris: Gallimard.

Léger, Jean-Marc. 1987. *La Francophonie, grand dessein, grande ambiguïté*. Montréal: Hurtubise.

Leveau, Rémy, and Catherine Withol de Wenden. 2001. *La Beurgeoisie : Les trois âges de la vie associative issue de l'immigration*. Paris: Editions CNRS.

Lévi-Strauss, Claude. 1968. *Les Structures élémentaires de la parenté*. 2e Edition. Paris: Mouton et Co.

Levy, Lital. 2006. "Self and the City: Literary Representations of Baghdad." *Prooftexts* 26.1–2:163–211.

Lewis, W. Arthur. 1954. "Economic development with unlimited supplies of labor." *The Manchester School of Economic and Social Studies* 22: 139–91.

Leys, Ruth. 2000. *Trauma: A Genealogy*. Chicago: University of Chicago Press.

Lionnet, Françoise. 1995. *Postcolonial Representations: Women, Literature, Identity*. Ithaca: Cornell University Press.

– 2009. "Universalisms and francophonies." *International Journal of Francophone Studies* 12: 2/3 (December). 203–21.

Loichot, Valérie. 2013. *The Tropics Bite Back: Culinary Coups in Caribbean Literature*. Minneapolis: University of Minnesota Press.

Lorde, Audre. 1984. *Sister Outsider: Essays and Speeches*. Trumansburg: Crossing Press.

– 2007. *Sister Outsider: Essays and Speeches*. Berkeley: Crossing Press.

Ma, Xiaonan. 2003. "戴思杰：小裁缝变了，我也变了" [Dai Sijie: The Little Seamstress Changed, I Changed]. *Enorth.com*. 9 September.

Mabanckou, Alain. 2007. "Le chant de l'oiseau migrateur." In *Pour une littérature-monde*, edited by Michel Le Bris and Jean Rouaud. Paris: Gallimard: 55–75.

– 2009. "'The Song of the Migrating Bird': For a World Literature in French." Translated by Dominic Thomas. *Forum for Modern Language Studies* 45.2 (April): 144–50.

Mardorossian, Carine M. 2002. "From Literature of Exile to Migrant Literature." *Modern Language Studies* 32.2 (Autumn): 15–33.

Marx, Karl, and Friedrich Engels. 1954. *Manifesto of the Communist Party.* Translated by Samuel Moore. *"Marx" Great Books of the Western World* 50: 415–34. Chicago: Encyclopaedia Britannica.

Massey, Douglas S. 1990. "Social Structure, Household Strategies and the Cumulative Causation of Migration." *Population Index* 56: 3–26.

Massey, Douglas S., Joaquin Arango, Graeme Hugo, Ali Kouaouci, Adela Pellegrino, and J. Edward Taylor. 1993. "Theories of International Migration." *Population and Development Review* 19.3 (September): 431–66.

– 1998. *Worlds in Motion: Understanding International Migration at The End of the Millennium.* Oxford: Oxford University Press.

Matateyou, Emanuelle. 1996. "Calixthe Beyala : entre le teroir et l'exil." *The French Review* 69.4 : 605–15.

Mathis-Moser, Ursula. 2003. *Dany Laferrière. La dérive américain.* Montreal: VLB Éditeur.

Matic, Ljiljana. 2007. "Naïm Kattan, écrivain de passage et passeur de cultures." In *Parcours québécois*, edited by Pierre Morel. Chisinau: Cartier. 228–38.

Mbembe, Achille. 2011. "Provincializing France?" Translated by Janet Roitman. *Public Culture* 23.1: 85–119.

McCall, Ian. 2006. "French Literature and Film in the USSR and Mao's China: Intertexts in Makine's *Au temps du fleuve d'amour* and Dai Sijie's *Balzac et la Petite Tailleuse chinoise.*" *Romance Studies* 24.2: 157–70.

McCallum, E.L., and Mikko Tuhkanen. 2011. *Queer Times, Queer Becomings.* Buffalo: SUNY Press.

McLane-Iles, Betty. 1997. "Memory and Exile in the Writing of Ying Chen." In *Women by Women*, edited by Rosanna Dufault. London: Associated University Press. 221–30.

McRuer, Robert. 1997. *The Queer Renaissance: Contemporary American Literature and the Reinvention of Lesbian and Gay Identities.* New York: New York University Press.

Meyers, Eytan. 2000. "Theories of International Immigration Policy: A Comparative Analysis." *International Migration Review* 34.4 (Winter): 1245–82.

Miller, Christopher. 1999. *Nationalists and Nomads: Essays on Francophone African Literature and Culture.* Chicago: University of Chicago Press.

Michaud, Ginette. 1999. "À voix basse et tremblante : phonographies de l'accent de Derrida à Joyce." In *Les Langues du roman*, edited by Lise Gauvin. Montréal: Presses de l'Université de Montréal. 15–35.

Ministère de l'Immigration. 2010. *Plan d'immigration du Québec.* http://www.midi.gouv.qc.ca/publications/fr/planification/Plan-immigration-2010.pdf. Last accessed 18 January 2016.

Mohanty, Chandra Talpade. 2003. "Under Western Eyes: Feminist Scholarship and Colonial Discourses." In *Feminism without Borders: Decolonizing Theory, Practicing Solidarity*. Durham: Duke University Press. 17–42.

Moisan, Clément, and Renate Hildebrand. 2001. *Ces Étrangers du dedans.* Montréal: Nota Bena.

Moretti, Franco. 2004. "Conjectures on World Literature." In *Debating World Literature*, edited by Christopher Prendergast. New York: Verso.

Moudileno, Lydie. 2006. "Femme nue, femme noire : tribulations d'une Vénus." *Présence Francophone* 66: 147–61.

– 2010. "*Francophonie*: Trash or Recycle?" In *Transnational French Studies: Postcolonialism and Littérature-Monde*, edited by Alec Hargreaves, Charles Forsdick, and David Murphy. Liverpool: Liverpool University Press. 109–24.

Moura, Jean-Marc. 2010. "French Language Writing and the Francophone Literary System." *Contemporary French and Francophone Studies* 14.1 (January): 14–28.

Murdoch, Adlai H. 2012. *Creolizing the Metropole. Migrant Caribbean Identities in Literature and Film*. Bloomington: Indiana University Press.

Nail, Thomas. 2015. *The Figure of the Migrant*. Stanford: Stanford University Press.

Najjar, Alexandre. 2007. "Contre la manifeste 'Pour une littérature-monde en français.'" *Le Monde*, March 26. http://www.lemonde.fr/livres/article/2007/03/29/expliquer-l-eau-par-l-eau_889166_3260.html?xtmc=alexandre_najjar&xtcr=19#meter_toaster. Last accessed 18 January 2016.

Nfah-Abbenyi, Juliana Makuchi. 1997. *Gender and African Women's Writing: Identity, Sexuality and Difference*. Indiana University Press.

Nepveu, Pierre. 1988. *L'Écologie du réel : Mort et naissance d'une littérature québécoise contemporaine*. Montréal: Boréal.

Noiriel, Gérard. 2001. *État, nation, et immigration*. Paris: Belin.

Ogundipe-Leslie, Molara. 1994. "Stiwanism: Feminism in an African Context." *Recreating Ourselves: African Women and Critical Transformation*. Trenton, NJ: Africa World Press.

Ojo-Ade, Femi. 1982. "Still a Victim? Mariama Bâ's *Une si longue lettre*." *African Literature Today* 12: 71–87.

Ouellet, Pierre. 2003. *L'Esprit migrateur : Essai sur le non-sens commun.* Montreal: Trait d'union.

Ouellet, Pierre, ed. 2003. *Le Soi et l'autre : L'énonciation de l'identité dans les contexts interculturels*. Quebec: CELAT.

Panaïté, Oana. 2012. *Des Littératures-mondes en français. Écritures singulières, poétiques transfrontalières dans la prose contemporaine*. Amsterdam: Rodopi, 2012.

Paré, François. 1994. *Les Littératures de l'exiguité*. Hearst: Le Nordir.

Parry, Benita. 1994. "Resistance Theory/Theorising Resistance or Two Cheers for Nativism." In *Colonial Discourse/Postcolonial Theory*, edited by Peter Hulme, Francis Barker, and Margaret Iverson. Manchester: Manchester University Press. 172–93.

Paterson, Janet. 2004. *Figures de l'autre dans le roman québécois*. Quebec: Nota Bene.

Payot, Marianne. 2003. "Freud et le petit psy chinois." *L'Express*, 12 December.

Pennycook, Alastair, and Emi Otsuji. 2015. *Metrolingualism: Language and the City*. New York: Routledge.

Pieterse, Jan Nederveen. 2004. *Globalization and Culture: Global Mélange*. New York: Rowman and Littlefield.

Piore, Michael J. 1979. *Birds of Passage: Migrant Labor in Industrial Societies*. Cambridge: Cambridge University Press.

Point of No Return. 2007. "Minority Reports: Babylon Book Reviews. *Jewish Refugees Blogspot*. http://jewishrefugees.blogspot.com/2007/03/minority-reports-babylon-book-reviews.html. Last accessed 18 January 2016.

Potvin, Claudine. 1996. "La (dé)construction de la mémoire: *La Québécoite* de Régine Robin." In *Multi-culture, multi-écriture : la voix migrante au féminin en France et au Québec*, edited by Lucie Lequin and Maïr Verthuy. Montréal: L'Harmattan. 261–74.

Pradeau, Christophe, and Tiphaine Samoyault, eds. 2005. *Où est la littérature mondiale?* Paris: Presses Universitaires Vincennes.

Prendergast, Christopher, ed. 2004. *Debating World Literature*. New York: Verso.

Provenzano, François. 2011. *Historiographies périphériques, Enjeux et rhétoriques de l'histoire littéraire en francophonie du Nord (Belgique, Suisse romande, Québec)*. Bruxelles: Académie royale de Belgique.

Radstone, Susannah. 2007. "Trauma Theory: Contexts, Politics, Ethics." *Paragraph* 30.1: 9–29.

Rahimieh, Nasrin. 1990. "Naïm Kattan, 'le discours arabe' and His Place in Canadian Literary Discourse." *Canadian Literature* 127: 32–8.

Rangina, Béatrice Gallimore. 2001. "Écriture féministe ? Écriture féminine ? : les écrivaines francophones de l'Afrique subsaharienne face au regard du lecteur/critique." *Études françaises* 37.2: 79–98.

Ranis, Gustav, and J.C.H. Fei. 1961. "A theory of economic development." *American Economic Review* 51: 533–65.

Raucy, Catherine. 2007. *Balzac et la petite tailleuse chinoise de Dai Sijie*. Écrits-vains.com. 27 February.

Reeck, Laura. 2011. *Writerly Identities in Beur Fiction and Beyond*. Lanham: Lexington Books.

Renan, Ernest. 1882. *Qu'est-ce qu'une nation? : conférence faite en Sorbonne*, 11 March. Paris: Calmann Lévy.

Robert-Diard, Pascale. 1988. "Azouz contre Racine." *Le Monde*. 25 February.

Robertson, Roland. 1992. *Globalization*. London: Sage.

Robertson, Roland. 1997. "Values and Globalization: Communitarianism and Globality." In Luiz E. Scares, ed., *Cultural Pluralism, Identity, and Globalization*. Rio de Janiero: UNESCO and Candido Mendes University. 73–97.

Robin, Régine. 1982. *L'amour du Yiddish*. Paris: Le Sorbier.

– 1989. *Le Roman mémoriel*. Montréal: Préambule.

– 1993a. "Langue-délire et langue-délit." *Discours social/Social Discourse* 5.3–4: 3–30.

– 1993b. *La Québecoite*. [LQ] Montréal: XYZ.

– 1997. *The Wanderer*. [TW] Montreal: Vehicule Press.

Robin, Régine. 1997. "The writing of an Allophone from France: Afterward to *The Wanderer* fifteen years later." In *The Wanderer (La Québécoite)*, translated by Phillis Aronoff. Montreal: Alter Ego.

Rosello, Mireille. 1993. "The 'Beur Nation': Toward a Theory of 'Départenance.'" *Research in African Literatures* 24.3: 13–24.

– 1998. *Declining the Stereotype: Ethnicity and Representation in French Cultures. Contemporary French culture and society*. Hanover, NH: University Press of New England.

– 2001. *Postcolonial Hospitality: The Immigrant as Guest*. Stanford: Stanford University Press.

Rushdie, Salman. 1992. "Commonwealth Literature does not exist." *Imaginary Homelands*. London: Granata. 61–70.

Said, Edward W. 1979. *Orientalism*. New York: Vintage Books.

– 1994. "Reflections on Exile," in *Altogether Elsewhere: Writers on Exile*. Edited by Marc Robinson. Boston: Faber & Faber. 137–49.

– 2000. *Reflections on Exile and Other Essays*. Cambridge: Harvard University Press.

Sall, Amadou Lamine, and Lilyan Kesteloot. 2007. "Un peu de mémoire, s'il vous plaît." *Le Monde*, 6 April.

Sandrine. "Dai Sijie, *Balzac et la Petite Tailleuse chinoise*." *Voix aux chapitres*. http://www.voixauchapitre.com/archives/2002/balzac_tailleuse.htm. Last accessed 3 May 2007.

Seal, Jeremy. 2007. "Nothing new about religious troubles in Baghdad." *Sunday Telegraph* 24. London.

Sebbar, Leïla. 1986. *Lettres parisiennes, Autopsie de l'exil*. Paris: Bernard Barrault.

– 2003. *Je ne parle pas la langue de mon père*. [JNP] Paris: Éditions Julliard.

Sénat de la République Française. *Loi Relative à l'Immigration et à l'Intégration*. http://www.senat.fr/dossier-legislatif/pjl05-362.html. Last accessed 18 January 2016.

Senghor, Lépold Sédar. 1962. "Le français langue de culture." *Esprit*, November.

– 1977. *Liberté* Tome 3 (Négritude et civilisation de l'universel). Paris: Seuil.

Sharpe, Jenny. 1989. "Figures of Colonial Resistance." *Modern Fiction Studies* 35.1:139.

Siskind, Mariano. 2010. "The Globalization of the Novel and the Novelization of the Global." *Comparative Literature* 62.4 (Winter): 336–60.

Shohat, Ella. 1996. "Notes on the Postcolonial." In *Postcolonial Theory: A Reader*, edited by Padmini Mongia. London: Arnold. 322–34.

Simard, Sylvain. 1985. "Naïm Kattan romancier : La promesse du temps retrouvé." *Voix et images* 11.1: 32–44.

Simon, Sherry. 1991. *Fictions de l'identitaire au Québec*. Montréal: XYZ.

– 1994. *Le Trafic des langues : traduction et culture dans la littérature québécoise*. Montréal: Boréal.

Simpson, Leo. 1976. "A Conversation with Naïm Kattan." *Quill and Quire* 42.17: 9–36.

Slemon, Stephen. 1996. "Unsettling the Empire: Resistance Theory for the Second World." In *Contemporary Postcolonial Theory: A Reader*, edited by Padmini Mongia. New York: Arnold. 72–83.

Smith, Joan. 2007. "Minority Report." *Times Online* 3 March.

Sourdot, Marc. 1996. "Un héros récentré : Le Gone du Chaâba d'Azouz Begag." In *L'écriture décentrée*, edited by Michel Laronde. 109–21.

Spettigue, D.O. 1977. "Farewell Babylone." *Queen's Quarterly* 84.3: 510–11.

Spivak, Gayatri Chakravorty. 1981. "French Feminism in an International Frame." *Yale French Studies* 62 Feminist Readings: French Texts/American Contexts: 154–84.

– 1988. "Can the Subaltern Speak?" In *Marxism and the Interpretation of Culture*, edited by Larry Grossberg and Cary Nelson. Urbana: University of Illinois Press. 271–313.

– 1990. "Poststructuralism, Marginality, Postcoloniality and Value." In *Literary Theory Today*, edited by Peter Collier and Helga Geyer-Ryan. Ithaca, NY: Cornell University Press: 219–44.

– 1999. *A Critique of Postcolonial Reason: Towards a History of the Vanishing Present*. Cambridge: Harvard University Press.

– 2003. *Death of a Discipline*. New York: Columbia University Press.

Sassen, Saskia. 1991. *The Global City*. Princeton: Princeton University Press.

– 1988. *The Mobility of Labor and Capital. A Study in International Investment and Labor Flow*. Cambridge: Cambridge University Press.

Sjaastad, Larry A. 1962. "The costs and returns of human migration." *Journal of Political Economy* 70S: 80–93.

Staël, (Anne-Louise-Germaine) Madame de. 1906. *De l'Allemagne*. Edited by Henry Weston Eve. Oxford: Clarendon Press.

Staël-Holstein, Madame the Baroness de. 1850. *Germany* 1. Translated by Murray. Boston: Houghton, Mifflin and Co.

Stark, Oded. 1984. "Migration Decision Making: A Review Article." *Journal of Development Economics* 14: 251–9.

– 1991. *The Migration of Labor*. Cambridge: Basil Blackwell.

Stark, Oded, and D. Levhari. 1982. "On Migration and Risk in LDCs." *Economic Development and Cultural Change* 31: 191–6.

Strich, Fritz. 1949. *Goethe and World Literature*. London: Routledge.

Talahite-Moodley, Anissa, ed. 2007. *Problématiques identitaires et discours de l'exil dans les littératures francophones*. Ottawa: University of Ottawa Press.

Talbot, Émile. 2004a. "Rewriting *Les Lettres chinoises*: The Poetics of Erasure." *Études québécoises* 36: 83–91.

– 2004b. "Ying Chen's Evolving Lettres Chinoises: An Addendum," *Études québécoises* 37: 125–6.

Taylor, J. Edward. 1986. "Differential migration, networks, information and risk." In Oded Stark, ed. *Research in Human Capital and Development*, vol. 4 *Migration, Human Capital, and Development*. Greenwich, Conn.: JAI Press. 147–71.

Tchakam, Stéphane. 2004. "Calixthe Beyala en toute franchise." *Cameroon Tribune* 8 (January).

Têko-Agbo, Ambroise. 1997. "Werewere Liking et Calixthe Beyala. Le discours féministe et la fiction." *Cahier d'études africaines* 37.145: 39–58.

Thränhardt, Dietrich. 1995. "The Political Uses of Xenophobia in England, France and Germany." *Party Politics* 1.3: 323–45.

Todorov, Tzvetan. 1981. *Mikhaïl Bakhtine : Le principe dialogique*. Paris: Seuil.

Todaro, Michael P. 1969. "A Model of Labor Migration and Urban Unemployment in Less Developed Countries." *The American Economic Review* 59: 138–48.

– 1976. *Internal Migration in Developing Countries*. Geneva: International Labor Office.

– 1980. "Internal Migration in Developing Countries: A Survey." In *Population and Economic Change in Developing Countries*, edited by Richard A. Easterlin. Chicago: University of Chicago Press. 361–401.

– 1989. *Economic Development in the Third World*. New York: Longman.

Todaro, Michael P., and Lydia Maruszko. 1987. "Illegal Migration and US Immigration Reform: A Conceptual Framework." *Population and Development Review* 13: 101–114.

Tomlinson, John. 1999. *Globalization and Culture*. University of Chicago Press.

Vallières, Pierre. 1968. *Nègres blancs d'Amérique : autobiographie précoce d'un "terroriste" québécois*. Montréal: Parti Pris.

Vassal, Anne. 1989. "Lecture savante ou populaire : *Comment faire l'amour avec un Nègre sans se fatiguer*." *Discours social : Analyse du discours et sociocritiques des textes* II. 4: 185–202.

Viart, Dominique, and Laurent Demanze, eds. 2012. *Fins de la littérature. Historicité de la littérature contemporaine*. Paris: Armand Colin.

Walkowitz, Rebecca. 2006. *Immigrant Fictions: Contemporary Literature in an Age of Globalization*. Madison: University of Wisconsin Press.

– 2007. "Unimaginable Largeness: Kazuo Ishiguro, Translation and the New World Literature." *Novel* 40. 3 (Summer): 216–39.

Wallerstein, Immanuel. 1974. *The Modern World System: Capitalist Agriculture and the Origins of the European World-Economy in the 16th Century*. New York: Academic Press.

Watts, Richard. 2005. *Packaging Postcoloniality: The Manufacture of Literary Identity in the Francophone World*. New York: Lexington Books.

De Wenden, Catherine Wihtol. 1994. "Immigrants as Political Actors in France." In *The Politics of Immigration in Western Europe*, edited by M. Baldwin-Edwards and M.A. Schain. London: Frank Cass. 91–109.

Whitaker, Reg. 1987. *Double Standard: The Secret History of Canadian Immigration*. Toronto: Lester and Orpen Dennys.

Winock, Michel. 1990. *Nationalisme, anti-sémitisme et fascisme en France*. Paris: Seuil.

Winock, Michel, and Pierre Birnbaum. 1993. *Histoire des haines nationalistes*. Paris: Seuil.

Winterton, Bradley. 2001. "A Picturesque Look at China's Cultural Revolution." *Taipai Times* 21 October.

Xavier, Subha. 2005. "Exiled Metaphors: Women and Nation in Three Novels by Ying Chen." *International Journal of Canadian Studies* 31: 37–56.

– 2006a. "Interview with Isabelle Gallimard." Paris. 18 June.

– 2006b. "Interview with Jacques Allard. 22 March.

– 2006c. "Interview with Ying Chen." Vancouver. 18 April.

– 2006d, 2008a. "Interview with Mehdi Charef." Paris. 6 June.

– 2006e, 2012a. "Interview with Naïm Kattan." Montreal. 22 March and 7 July.

– 2008b. "Interview with Calixthe Belaya." Paris. 20 June.

– 2008c. "China and Its Other: The Economy of Writing in Dai Sijie's *Le Complexe de Di.*" *Concentric: Literary and Cultural Studies* 34.2 (September): 63–85.

– 2010. "Mehdi Charef and the Politics of French Immigration." *The French Review* 84.2 (December): 328–41.

– 2012b. "Entre féminisme et voyeurisme : L'éros migrant chez Calixthe Beyala." *Zizanie* 1.1.

Young, Robert C. 1995. *Colonial Desire: Hybridity in Theory, Culture, and Race.* New York: Routledge.

Young, Robert C. 2004. *White Mythologies: Writing History and the West.* New York: Routledge.

Young, Suzie Sau Fong. 1998. "Encountering (China, My) Sorrow." *Asian Cinema*: 107–11.

Yuval-Davis, Nira. 1997. *Gender & Nation.* London: Sage Publications.

Zahan, Dominique. 1963. *La dialectique du verbe chez les Bambara.* Paris: Mouton.

Zolberg, A.R. 1978. "International Migration Policies in a Changing World System." In *Human Migration Patterns and Policies*, edited by W.H. McNeil and R.H. Adams. Bloomington: Indiana University: 241–86.

– 1989. "The Next Waves: Migration Theory for a Changing World." *International Migration Review*, 23.3. 403–30.

Zolner, Mette. 2000. *Re-imagining the Nation: Debates on Immigrants, Identities and Memories.* Brussels: Peter Lang.

Index